Reassessing the Responsibility to Protect

This book explores conceptual and operational questions regarding the development and implementation of the Responsibility to Protect.

The mass atrocity norm known as the Responsibility to Protect (R2P) has enjoyed meteoric success since the concept was introduced in 2001. But perhaps precisely because of how quickly the concept secured its privileged place in the pantheon of ideas and concerns in international affairs, many fundamental questions remain concerning its origins, its conceptual contents and its relevance to actual cases of mass atrocity. This book seeks to explore that terrain by drawing together a group of scholars diverse enough to engage with the complex array of political, legal and ethical questions raised by R2P. Critical questions raised here include: What are the limits of the authority that R2P confers on international actors? What does the evolution of R2P mean for North–South relations? Just how significant is R2P in the context of the broader human rights landscape? In addition to those conceptual and theoretical matters, special attention is given to the operational context in which the meaning of R2P is ultimately rendered. As events in Africa have figured so significantly into the norm's development, the contributors pay special attention to the problems and prospects of mass atrocity prevention in that context.

This volume will be of much interest to students of the Responsibility to Protect, war and conflict studies, peacebuilding, international law and IR/Security Studies.

Brett R. O'Bannon is Leonard E. and Mary B. Howell Professor of Political Science and Director of Conflict Studies at DePauw University, USA, and Senior Fellow, Canadian Centre for the Responsibility to Protect.

Global Politics and the Responsibility to Protect

Series Editors:
Alex J. Bellamy
Griffith University

Sara E. Davies
Griffith University
and
Monica Serrano
The City University of New York

The aim of this book series is to gather the best new thinking about the Responsibility to Protect into a core set of volumes that provides a definitive account of the principle, its implementation and its role in crises, that reflects a plurality of views and regional perspectives.

Global Politics and the Responsibility to Protect
From words to deeds
Alex J. Bellamy

The Responsibility to Protect
Norms, laws and international politics
Ramesh Thakur

Humanitarian Intervention and the Responsibility to Protect
Security and human rights
Cristina G. Badescu

Sri Lanka and the Responsibility to Protect
Politics, ethnicity, genocide
Damien Kingsbury

International Responsibility and Grave Humanitarian Crises
Collective provision for human security
Hannes Peltonen

Global Justice, Kant and the Responsibility to Protect
A provisional duty
Heather M. Roff

UN Emergency Peace Service and the Responsibility to Protect
Annie Herro

International Organizations and the Implementation of the Responsibility to Protect
The humanitarian crisis in Syria
Edited by Daniel Silander and Don Wallace

Moral Responsibility, Statecraft, and Humanitarian Intervention
The US response to Rwanda, Darfur, and Libya
Cathinka Vik

Reassessing the Responsibility to Protect
Conceptual and operational challenges
Edited by Brett R. O'Bannon

Reassessing the Responsibility to Protect

Conceptual and operational challenges

Edited by Brett R. O'Bannon

Routledge
Taylor & Francis Group

LONDON AND NEW YORK

First published 2016
by Routledge
2 Park Square, Milton Park, Abingdon, Oxon OX14 4RN

and by Routledge
711 Third Avenue, New York, NY 10017

Routledge is an imprint of the Taylor & Francis Group, an informa business

© 2016 selection and editorial material, Brett R. O'Bannon; individual chapters, the contributors

British Library Cataloguing in Publication Data
A catalogue record for this book is available from the British Library

Library of Congress Cataloging-in-Publication Data
Reassessing the responsibility to protect : conceptual and operational
  challenges / edited by Brett R. O'Bannon.
    pages cm. — (Global politics and the responsibility to protect)
  Includes bibliographical references and index.
  1. Responsibility to protect (International law)   I. O'Bannon, Brett R.
  KZ4082.R43 2016
  341.4′8—dc23
  2015018880

ISBN: 978-0-415-66757-9 (hbk)
ISBN: 978-1-315-88251-2 (ebk)

Typeset in Times New Roman
by Apex CoVantage, LLC

For Valerie and Rowan

Contents

Contributors

Séverine Autesserre is Associate Professor of Political Science, Barnard College, Columbia University, New York, United States.

Alex J. Bellamy is Professor of Peace and Conflict Studies and Director of the Asia Pacific Centre for the Responsibility to Protect at The University of Queensland, Brisbane, Australia.

Carol Berger is an anthropologist who specializes in South Sudan. She is a former foreign correspondent, reporting for the BBC, *The Guardian* and *The Economist* from the Middle East and the Horn of Africa. She lives in Cairo, Egypt.

David Chandler is Professor of International Relations at the University of Westminster, London, United Kingdom.

Brett R. O'Bannon is Associate Professor of Political Science and Director of Conflict Studies, and Leonard and Mary B. Howell Professor at DePauw University, Indiana, United States.

Anne Orford is Michael D. Kirby Professor of International Law at The University of Melbourne, Australia.

Jeremy Sarkin is Professor of Law at The University of South Africa, Pretoria, South Africa.

John K. Roth is Professor Emeritus of the Philosophy of Religion at Claremont McKenna College, Los Angeles, California, United States.

Acknowledgements

The origins of this book lie in the symposium *Imperfect Duties? Humanitarian Intervention in Africa and the Responsibility to Protect in the Post-Iraq Era*, held at the Janet Prindle Institute for Ethics at DePauw University, in Greencastle, Indiana and co-sponsored by the West Africa Bureau of the UN Office for the Coordination of Humanitarian Affairs. A number of debts were accrued in the course of organizing the symposium and in producing this volume. I would first like to thank my friend and colleague John Roth for his extraordinary collegiality and for his keen insights into the problem of mass atrocity, both of which proved essential to our endeavor. I'm grateful to Sharon Crary, who brought her singular perspective and abiding commitment to service and global civic engagement. Hervè deLys, then head of office at UN OCHA West Africa, first proposed this collaborative venture and remained committed to it throughout. His continuing dedication to self-reflective humanitarian action in Africa is inspiring. The financial support of DePauw University and the Prindle Institute was greatly appreciated. President Brian Casey, Prindle Institute Director Robert Bottoms, and Executive Vice President Neal Abraham were steadfast in their support of our enterprise.

In addition to the participants included in this volume, I would like to thank Karen Koning AbuZayd, Jeremy Anderson, Marion Arnaud, Assefaw Bariagaber, Rich Cameron, B. Welling Hall, Catherine Dumait-Harper, Gareth Evans, Jerry Fowler, Amos Sawyer, Rebecca Upton and Gordan Vurusic for their excellent contributions to the symposium. Thanks to Beth Buggenhagen and Amy Patterson for their helpful reviews of an earlier version of chapter four.

A special thank-you to Linda Clute and Sarah Hughes is in order for their tireless efforts in support of the project. My colleague Deepa Prakash continues to help me refine my thinking about R2P and a great many other issues. Finally, I wish to offer my special thanks for Alex Bellamy's warm collegiality and significant efforts in ushering this book to completion.

B.R.O.

Introduction

Ontological insecurity and the origins of R2P

Brett R. O'Bannon

There is, according to proverb, *always something new out of Africa*. If the recent crises of human protection in Côte d'Ivoire and Libya are instructive, and Alex Bellamy and Paul Williams think they are, then the latest thing out of Africa is a new international "politics of protection" (2011). And as they and others, such as Ed Luck, former Secretary-General's Special Advisor on R2P, have suggested, this new politics is indeed rooted in Africa. In the words of the Secretary General, "the responsibility to protect [(R2P)] has emerged from the soil, spirit, experience and institutions of Africa" (Ban 2009).

It is in light of these two claims – that R2P is said to constitute a significant development in, indeed the basis of an established norm of, human protection and that this norm is of particular relevance to Africa – that we offer this contribution. Both propositions remain fully contestable empirical as well as theoretical claims. And it is to that end that the contributors to this volume have offered their voices. We seek to problematize, first, claims about the status of R2P an operative principle – the degrees to which and/or the ways in which it might be said that R2P is a significant and determinative element of the legal/normative architecture of international society. Second, we interrogate the degrees to which and/or the ways in which R2P is or might be relevant to crises of human protection in Africa.

Contributors to this volume speak with one voice on one central matter: the significance of the human suffering witnessed on a massive scale in the late twentieth and early twenty-first centuries. Beyond that, however, there is a great deal of difference with respect to how or if R2P might constitute a legitimate and functional instrument for alleviating, and hopefully preventing, human misery. In order to begin that inquiry, we place the R2P norm in historical, theoretical and discursive context. We do that by first exploring the concept of norms and how they articulate with problems of mass human suffering.

Norms and the new world disorder

Norms, of course, matter. Those widely shared "collective expectations about proper behavior for a given identity" are critical elements in the explanatory matrix of contemporary world politics (Jepperson, Wendt and Katzenstein 1996, 54). It was not always thus, but even the staunchest structural realist now recognizes the myriad ways in which the sovereignty norm, for example, influences the behavior of states. More frequently recognized in the breach perhaps, but even the most powerful states in international society, as a matter of course, publicly legitimate their actions in terms of sovereignty principles (Krasner 1999, Finnemore 2009). It is this apparent capacity of norms to obtain behavioral compliance from otherwise autonomous sovereign states that has, at least since the "ideational turn" in International Relations, made them of such great interest. It was undoubtedly a faith in this capacity of norms to influence state action that brought together twelve notables from around the world in the form of the International Commission on Intervention and State Sovereignty (ICISS) in search of "some new common ground." For it was this commission, relatively obscure according to a co-chair, that delivered the report *The Responsibility to Protect*, and set in train some of the most remarkable normative developments of the last half century.

Wendt surmised that states "obey" norms – as opposed to having their behavior merely coerced – for one of two reasons: self-interest and legitimacy (Wendt 1999). On the one-hand, Rationalists (e.g., liberals, Marxists, some critical theorists perhaps) find in norm compliance various forms of self-interest at work. Often understood in materialist terms, norms themselves are less compelling and less determining of state behavior than the interests they reflect (or mask). On this view, developing countries might adopt R2P in order to obtain development assistance associated with its prescribed capacity-building work, or great powers might invoke it as a justification for action – as with the recent NATO intervention in Libya – when doing so is consistent with *raison d'état*. For the rationalist, then, norms are better understood as complementary (to interest) explanations.

Constructivists, on the other hand, find in norms – in the constitutive values shared by norm compliers – quite significant explanatory power. Norms have both behavioral and constitutive effects (Risse, Ropp and Sikkink 1999; Finnemore and Sikkink 1998; Katzenstein 1996). States and/or their decision-makers comply with normative pre- and proscriptions because they subscribe to and identify with the values on which the norm is predicated. On this view, action by NATO members in Libya can be understood as, at least, having been *made possible* by R2P, if not *compelled* by belief in the legitimacy of the values of human protection. As Fearon puts it, actors do not simply "do X to get Y" as the rationalist would have it, but it is rather a case of "good people do X" (cited in Risse and Sikkink 1999, 8). These scholars admit to the possibility that actors might well be moved by motives other than, or in addition to, human protection. The instrumental adoption of norms is, in fact, especially common at early stages of internalization (Risse, Ropp and Sikkink 1999). They call attention, however, to the fact that even in such cases states still appear compelled to justify their actions in terms established by the collective understanding (Wheeler 2000). Thus, even if R2P is used instrumentally, as critics charge in the case of Libya, its very use indicates the need to seek legitimacy, a remarkable gesture for a hegemonic actor like NATO. For the constructivist, the normative landscape matters a good deal in the social life of states.

The question with respect to R2P is not merely why states might comply but rather why states appear to have actively sought to construct such a norm in the first place, especially with the knowledge that doing so could subsequently delimit their behavior. Exploring the question of why states might seek out and adopt the "Friends of R2P" identity when doing so could commit them to actions that might counter their material or normative interests, responds to a persistent need in the literature.[1] That is, while there is a great deal of interest in the ways in which norms develop and change over time – indeed, we share that interest – the emergence on the scene of new ideas, new formulations of would-be norms, remains an under-theorized problem. For a start, we find the mutual exclusion among competing explanations unhelpful and envision a position that includes both legitimacy and interest.

From its inception, it should be noted, R2P has appeared to offer clear material incentives to developing countries. In particular, the "prevention" element indicates potential rewards for membership with its call for root cause or structural prevention, which "might involve development assistance and cooperation . . . promotion of economic growth and opportunity; better terms of trade and permitting greater access to external markets for developing countries" (ICISS 2001, 3.22). Co-chair of the commission, Gareth Evans articulated this position further, even after the 2005 World Summit, whose Outcome Document greatly reduced the scope of the concept: "[T]here is every reason," he holds, "from a conflict and mass atrocity perspective, to make a major effort to dramatically close the income and opportunity gap between rich and poor countries, and to dramatically reduce levels of both absolute and relative deprivation within countries that are suffering" (2008, 91). And more recently, Secretary-General Ban Ki-moon forcefully reiterated this position, arguing that

> donor agencies should be encouraged to support countries and programmes that seek to enhance the prevention and protection of populations from crimes and violations relating to the responsibility to protect," because "[o]n balance, substantial increments in levels of general development assistance could well reduce the aggregate incidence of crimes and violations relating to the responsibility to protect.
>
> (2009, paras. 32 and 43)

These benefits, as compelling as they may be, cannot explain why wealthier countries would adopt the norm. Nor do they account for how governments of developing countries weigh the costs of the conditions associated with structural prevention assistance, which lie at the heart of sovereignty and the potential for maintaining power. And though one might be tempted to explain Africa's early and important support for R2P from this self-interest perspective, there is too much variation in support across Africa to sustain such a position.

As we discuss below, the R2P norm has been, from its inception, a social affair. Its emergence lies in a collective crisis of identity, of ontological insecurity (Giddens 1979, 1984). On that insight, we suggest that states and decision-makers, for reasons both self-interested *and* value-laden, might well seek to establish new norms, indeed to create something of a normative community. By normative community we mean states and non-state actors who forge a common commitment to the "institutionalization of dependable expectations" regarding international society's posture, in this instance, toward crises of human protection.[2] In forging a new normative community around the many questions raised by complex humanitarian emergencies, we have in mind that "Deutschian perspective [that] relies on shared knowledge, ideational forces, and a dense normative environment" (Adler and Barnett 1998, 8). Just why such a normative project would have emerged, and how, merits some explanation. For the ontological nature of R2P can't fully be mapped without some sense of what conditions brought it into existence.

Norms, as is often noted, are both *regulative* – they enable and constrain the behavior of actors – as well as *constitutive* – they create new actors, new identities and new ways of thinking and acting (Jepperson, Wendt and Katzenstein 1996). Through the construction of identities, norms greatly influence the ways actors perceive their interests. In turn, they have important consequences for the ways that actors pursue objectives. State identities, such as "sovereign," "civilized," "liberal" or "developing" influence the ways in which actors come to recognize the means at their disposal and delimit the ways they might connect those means to the ends they seek (Kowert and Legro 1996). As a result, norms – via identities and interests – can be expected to stabilize and narrow responses to similar circumstances encountered by actors with a shared identity.

Identities are inherently social, of course. Thus, standards of appropriate conduct, around which collective understandings can be forged, provide the means for *intersubjective* identity formation, or community building. As Risse and Sikkink note, "the very idea of 'proper' behavior presupposes a community able to pass judgments on appropriateness (1999, 7). States and other actors (disaggregated below) signing on as friends of R2P articulate a common set of principled ideas and values, a collective normative commitment, regarding the moral status of individuals in international affairs and responses to violations or threatened violations to individuals' integrity. We suggest that doing so reconstitutes those actors into a *normative community*, a society of states and non-state actors dedicated to the diffusion of R2P principles. The formation of this sort of community reinforces more than just the referent normative commitment but, in recursive fashion, the actors' identities which determined the interests in the first place. Thus interest and legitimacy, to return to the categories of explanation for norm compliance, need not exclude each other when standards of legitimate conduct are seen to provide the necessary basis for articulating one's interest and for facilitating the requisite agency for its pursuit.

The latter point implies that actors need a certain level of normative certainty – an adequately established and familiar normative context – in order to be effective agents. This idea has considerable significance in the forthcoming analysis. Assuming interests – which we do not – without norms it is hard for actors to know what means are appropriately put to the pursuit of those ends. As Kowert and Legro note,

> Norms affect not only actor interests but also the ways actors connect their preferences to policy choices. More precisely, norms shape the instruments or

means that states find available and appropriate. In other words, norms shape actors' awareness and acceptance of the methods and technologies on which they might rely to accomplish their objectives.

(1996, 463)

It is in this fashion that normative discourses inherently "entail identity-related arguments. What I find morally appropriate depends to some degree on who I am and how I see myself" (Risse and Sikkink 1999, 13). Consider the tactics and strategies actors with varying identities employ in war. The laws/norms of war are now said by some to be irrelevant to many of the actors who wage "new war" such as child soldiers, *sobels* and non-state combatants (Kaldor 2012). The use of terror tactics and the wide-scale commission of atrocities is said to be the strategy of actors who lack the military capacity to seize and maintain control of territory (Kaldor 2012, Gberie 2005, Richards 1996). Without *collective* understandings it is impossible, or at least much more difficult, to know what means others may "have at their disposal." Without a requisite level of certainty about the normative context, it is impossible to determine proper behavior or to calculate the costs associated with violating norms that may be operative, or the potential benefits of compliance.

The relationship between identity and normative behavior is complex, of course. It not only runs in the direction stipulated by Kowert and Legro (1996) but in reverse as well. Well-patterned behavior is essential to the forging of identity. As Campbell (following Judith Butler) sees it, an actor has

no ontological status apart from the various acts which constitute its reality . . . and the identity of any particular state should be understood as "tenuously constituted in time . . . through a stylized repetition of acts," and achieved, "not [through] a founding act, but rather a regulated process of repetition."

(Campbell 1998, 10)

It follows, then, that when no such pattern is evident or achievable, the ontological status of an actor necessarily falls into question.

It is in this light that we suggest that state and non-state actors pursued, or at least entertained, a human protection norm as a means of navigating a crisis of ontological insecurity that resulted from the dramatic material and social transformation of international society in the wake of the Soviet Union's abrupt disappearance. The unexpected end of the Cold War, a dramatic upsurge of massively violent – and some say new forms of – civil war, the emergence of a newly functioning UN Security Council, a string of unprecedented, but highly selective, international interventions into crises of human protection and a global clash of narratives about these interventions gave rise to a profound uncertainty about the legal and normative architecture of international society. Though woefully inadequate to capture the complex structure of this material and social crisis, the "humanitarian intervention dilemma" of which ICISS speaks, nevertheless indicates a "damned if they do and damned if they don't" mentality operating at state level decision-making throughout the 1990s.

The political origins of R2P

In the domain of human protection, the first decade of the post–Cold War era was an epoch of iconic moments. It opened with a ferocious civil war in Liberia, in which president Samuel Doe's gruesome execution was captured on videotape and disseminated widely through the region. The civil war(s) in Liberia eventually engulfed the entire sub-region and led to the deeply troubled involvement of West African regional actors. In some respects, however, the new era truly dawned with the UN-authorized, but ultimately ill-fated, *Black Hawk Down* intervention in Somalia. And it was in the shadow of that disaster that the world marveled at a Hotel in Rwanda left defenseless by the international community only to be revulsed the following year by a brazen act of genocide in Srebrenica.

As this increasingly chaotic decade progressed, the initial post–Cold War harmony on the Security Council dissipated. As a result, the decade's penultimate intervention was the "unlawful but legitimate" intervention in Kosovo, the approach which gave us the expression *humanitarian bombing*. The seventy-eight-day NATO campaign stopped ethnic cleansing, but with pilots required to fly at altitude, it also claimed the lives of hundreds of non-combatants – as well as the Chinese embassy – and created a refugee crisis as significant as the one the intervention aimed to alleviate. The decade closed with a coerced invitation for a UN peacekeeping mission to East Timor.

For the most part, as the decade unfolded, these crises of human protection arose, raged and receded. But war and its very worst atrocities raged almost unceasingly across many parts of Africa. The state in Liberia and Sierra Leone collapsed and became infamous for conflict minerals and warlord poster children. The same became true in the Democratic Republic of the Congo, whose first war (1996–1997) gave way to "Africa's First World War," which eventually became the world's deadliest conflict since World War II. As the decade came to a close, the world's rate of internal conflict mercifully began to fall from its spike of the early 1990s, except, again, in Africa. Between 1989–2000, more than half the countries in Africa experienced some form of violent armed conflict, ending the decade with nearly twice as many conflicts as at the outset.[3]

It was at the end of such a tumultuous decade that Secretary-General Kofi Annan issued his now famous charge "to forge unity behind the principle that massive and systematic violations of human rights – wherever they take place – should not be allowed to stand" (1999, par.14). Much has been made of this call, but as a source for the emergence of R2P, there are limitations to an explanation that relies simply on a call by the Secretary-General. For one, Kofi Annan made more than a few such calls to action around a great many important questions. He may have referred to this project as the "core challenge to the Security Council and the United Nations as a whole," but *We the Peoples*, Kofi Annan's report to the Millennium Summit, was as much, if not more, about tackling poverty and the looming environmental crisis as about the specific problem of humanitarian intervention (Annan 2000, par. 15). If we consider the oft-cited claim that R2P is the most successful initiative in the normative arena since the genocide convention

(Weiss 2006), the ask-and-receive explanation indeed seems inadequate. If the impetus for the most extraordinary normative innovation in fifty years were but the voice of the Secretary General, then international society would suffer constant and dramatic cultural upheaval. Kofi Annan's charge must have been but the tip of an iceberg of demand.

Additionally, if Kofi Annan's call to forge unity were the explanation for R2P's dramatic entrance into the normative arena, then how might we account for the failure of all the other potential norms that have similarly enjoyed the Secretary General's attention? Why was a human protection norm, centered on sites of acute mass atrocity, apparently international society's "most favored norm" and not some other set of principles whose advocates aim to alleviate other forms of mass human suffering, such as extreme poverty or infectious disease? As Valentino has noted, the international community could obtain a much greater humanitarian return on its investment if it simply chose to pursue, for example, a global measles vaccination program rather than militarized humanitarian interventions (2011).

Last, and perhaps most challenging, is if the Secretary General's call represents even but the tip of an iceberg of *demand* for new rules to resolve the humanitarian intervention dilemma, Bates and Ostrom have both demonstrated the need to ask "Why are they supplied?" (Ostrom 1990, 42). That is, the *problem of institutional supply* requires us to consider how "incentives to free ride undermine the incentives to organize a solution to the collective dilemma" or how, or why, these disincentives appear to have been overcome (Bates 1988, 394–395, quoted in Ostrom 1990.). In short, on the question of R2P's emergence and meteoric rise, a number of important questions have been left to assumption.

Beyond the call from the UN Secretary General, we suggest that the decade of the 1990s wore progressively heavy on states and their decision-makers as the seemingly endless stream of human protection crises overwhelmed the normative and material capacity of international society to make sense of events. The ways in which the society of states responded to these complex humanitarian emergencies differed dramatically – in number and in kind – from the ways in which they were handled under the Cold War order (Wheeler 2000). So-called new war gave rise to new humanitarianism; that is, as the goals, methods and financing of war changed (Snow 1996, Kaldor 2012) so did "the scale, scope and significance of humanitarian action" (Barnett 2005, 723). In short, an ontological shift in world affairs was taking place. The inability to cope with it effectively gave states and non-state actors alike something approaching common purpose, even if not, ultimately, common interests. That common ground was enough normative certainty to facilitate collective or even unilateral action in the face of the new era's threats. What international society lost in the wake of these profound disruptions was a normative basis for the agency needed to effectively respond to the many challenges before it. Consider the view from the unsettled hegemon.

At the dawn of this new era, only a few months after making a New World Order address to the United Nations, President George H. W. Bush led the Unified Task Force into Somalia, where more than 300,000 people faced conflict-induced starvation. This was the UN's first Chapter VII intervention without the target state's permission. Widely remarked upon at the time, the concept of international peace and security was being rewritten (Campbell 1998); in the 1990s poverty, famine, starvation, environmental degradation and infectious disease were being securitized (Buzan, Waever and deWilde 1998). Personifying this ontological break, it was none other than then US Ambassador George H. W. Bush who, almost twenty years to the day before launching Operation Restore Hope, blasted India for its "clear cut aggression" when it intervened in East Pakistan to halt a massacre that had taken over *one million* lives and sparked the exodus of nearly *ten million* refugees (Wheeler 2000, 65). The times were indeed changing.

But what President Bush launched with seemingly good intentions,[4] and with high levels of domestic and international support, quickly devolved into President Clinton's first foreign policy fiasco. That it later became the subject of a Hollywood blockbuster film attests to the growing salience of the "intervention dilemma." Having been excoriated by the right wing for Somalia, Clinton was thus understandably uncertain about his promised effort to "stop the horrible atrocities" in Haiti. Predictably, when a Port-au-Prince mob shouting "Somalia, Somalia!" appeared to force the retreat of the *USS Harlan County*, arriving with hundreds of armed soldiers and engineers, Clinton again suffered in the media (Siegel 1996).

Apparently still unsettled by Somalia at the decade's critical midpoint, Clinton – like much of the rest of the world – remained effectively silent on Rwanda. His initial reaction to the war in Bosnia was equally low key. Srebrenica, however, appeared to change the calculus. "I'm getting creamed" the president is said to have barked at aids as the first-term president found himself under intense pressure to get involved. This time the pressure came from sources "both domestic and foreign," and from the left as well as the right (Power 2002, 422). By the time Kosovo took center stage, the Clinton administration – like much of the rest of the world – was deeply divided about the morality and political wisdom of military intervention for human protection purposes.[5] As a result, when the intervention was ordered – without the UN approval that Somalia enjoyed – uncertainty about potential political costs and rewards was so great that NATO's force protection posture seemingly contradicted the ethical imperative that presumably drove the alliance to embark on the intervention.[6]

Thus it was that, at Cold War's end, the normative fabric of international society began to fray. At its center was enormous human suffering and loss of life. The complex and often contradictory reactions to some crises, the failures to react to others, sea changes in opinion about them and subsequent reversals of that opinion – all this constituted the great uncertainty of the first decade of the post–Cold War era, an era which itself, it is worth noting, came wholly unexpectedly. This state of affairs represents quintessentially what Giddens refers to as a "critical situation." By that he means "circumstances of radical disjuncture of an unpredictable kind which affect substantial numbers of individuals, situations that threaten or destroy the certitudes of institutionalized routines (Giddens 1984, 61). Following as it did almost fifty years of an institutionalized pluralist world order (Wheeler 2000), this period was, for international society, an "extreme disruption of accustomed forms of daily life" (Giddens 1984, 61). And, we suggest, the result of this critical situation, for states and non-state actors alike, was the loss of the ontological security that comes from the known routines of "normal times" (Giddens 1984, 61; Zaretsky 2002; Mitzen 2006; Steele 2008).

The loss of certainty in one's knowledge of how the world works, of what and of whom it is composed, undermines one's self as well as one's collective identities – and with them their associated interests. After the decade concluded, Kofi Annan would indeed suggest that there was "a yearning in many quarters for a new consensus on which to base collective action" (Annan 2005, 1). So unsettling was this "critical situation" that even at the outset of the post–Cold War era, voices could be heard pining for the certitude of simpler times (Mearsheimer 1990).

Such a condition is untenable. States, like individuals, are ontological security-seekers (Mitzen 2006, Steele 2008). Consistent with our view, Steele argues "When . . . self-identity is dislocated an actor will seek to re-establish routines that can, once again, consistently maintain self-identity" (2008, 3). Steele sees in this effort an actor's concern with shame, which is one of the many reasons we can envision such an effort. Hafner-Burton (2008) notes, for example, the increasing popularity of the "naming and shaming" strategy for human rights norms enforcement. For us, however, the fundamental motive derives from the larger implication of ontological insecurity – a loss of agency. The loss of ontological security dramatically undermines the agentic capacity of state and non-state actors. As Mitzen notes, "Where an actor has no idea what to expect, she cannot systematically relate ends to means, and it becomes unclear how to pursue her ends" (Mitzen 2006, 342). This results, in her view, in a "deep, incapacitating state of not knowing which dangers to confront and which to ignore, i.e., how to get by in the world" (Mitzen 2006, 345).

Such a profound unmooring renders threat assessment and the most basic cost–benefit calculations seemingly impossible. And seeing the era in these terms helps make sense of the more curious choices made by some of international society's principal actors and the contradictory qualities of their actions. For a start, the decade began with a collective determination – and the apparent will to act forcefully on that determination – that starvation *in* Somalia was, famously, a threat to *international* peace and security. As Whitworth has so well explored, however, peacekeeping responses like Somalia proved to be, at their very core, a contradiction; sending soldiers to do a job that negates much of what they have been taught constitutes good soldering often led to grave injuries among the population meant to be protected (Whitworth 2004). As the torture and murder of Somali teen Shidane Arone attests, the forces of even a country like Canada, a state whose identity is "a peacekeeping country *par excellence,*" were among the perpetrators of heinous crimes against protected populations (Whitworth 2004, 85). It is Canada, of course, that will convene the ICISS.

While the international community responded assertively, though perhaps perversely, to *prevent* massive starvation in the Horn of Africa, the international community responded to massive ethnic cleansing actually unfolding in the Balkans – where the assassination of one person in 1914 sparked the First World War – with but the creation of so-called safe havens, which proved to be anything but.

Similarly, three hundred thousand *potential* victims of starvation moved the international community to act with dispatch in Somalia, yet only a year later, as the killing in Rwanda surpassed *eight hundred* thousand, the international community remained largely silent.[7] This new era was said to have been presaged with the massive international coalition mobilized to "protect" Kuwaitis from Iraq's aggression. Yet only a few years later, existing security forces already on the ground in Srebrenica – a UN Security Council declared "safe haven" – could not be mobilized to prevent the mass execution of some 7,000 men and boys.

In terms of tragic choices, however, Rwanda occupies a singular place in the historical landscape. Ends and means indeed appear to suffer a disconnect when one compares the enormous costs incurred with the full-scale interventions in Kuwait, Somalia, Haiti, Kosovo and East Timor with the (unexpended) costs of, for one notable example, merely flying radio jamming aircraft above Rwanda to interdict genocidal instructions broadcast on Rwanda's *Radio Télévision Libre des Mille Collines* (Power 2002, 371).[8] Though he would later make the call himself for us to expand greatly our moral imagination, while head of the UN Department of Peacekeeping Operations prior to the Rwandan genocide, then Under-Secretary-General Kofi Annan made assiduously conservative interpretations of the mandate of the UN mission in Rwanda. Annan himself received the infamous Dallaire telegram indicating proof of an arms cache and of the Interahamwe's plans and preparation for the genocide. He apparently failed to make the Security Council aware of its presence and denied repeated requests for authorization to seize the weapons before they were distributed to *génocidaires* (Barnett 2003, Gourevitch 1999).

How should we make sense of all this, these extraordinary inconsistencies? Brown sees in a string of contradictory decisions and actions by the international community a functional calculus and "practically-minded judgment taken in the round based on all the circumstances of a particular case" (2003, 45). Actors, in this view, assess the implications of intervention in specific contexts and – using their best moral judgment – act accordingly. We are more inclined to see this scattered array of "choices" as a reflection of the deep and widely shared confusion about what might be morally and politically appropriate. It reflects the loss of "collective understandings" and standard operating procedures on which the peace operations community relies (Autesserre 2010).

We suggest that this assault on international society's normative architecture by the nearly ceaseless stream of human protection crises that arose in the early post–Cold War era generated the very conditions of the "critical situation" Giddens has explored. In the 1990s, the legal/moral/normative order of world affairs appeared to move some way from an ordered, Lockean anarchy (Wendt 1999), or a pluralist order of international society (Wheeler 2000), to something approaching normative chaos.

This condition matters because states are ontological security-seekers (Mitzen 2006). Because an actor's identity is intersubjectively constructed, that is in relationships with others, actors seek to maintain their sense of self "by routinizing relationships with significant others" (Mitzen 2006, 341). Doing so brings uncertainty within acceptable limits and with it the obstacles to effective agency. By re-establishing standards of legitimate conduct for actors with known identities these actors obtain the conditions in which means can be identified and connected to ends sought.

For us, this means that the chaotic conditions of the 1990s constituted precisely the assault on state identity necessary for effective agency. Hurrell notes that under normal conditions

> [h]ow we calculate consequences is often far from obvious and not easily separable from our understanding of legal and moral norms. Think, for example, of how states sought to calculate the consequences of alternative courses of action in the Kosovo campaign and how those actions were deeply shaped by the existing legal and moral normative framework.
>
> (2002, 144)

In our view, however, there was effectively little of the Cold War normative framework left by the time decisions about Kosovo were rendered. NATO failed to gain UN Security Council approval for its mission. For that reason, the Independent International Commission on Kosovo determined the intervention to be unlawful. Yet, it also found it to be legitimate (The Independent International Commission on Kosovo 2000). But since the UN is the principal legitimating body in international society, this finding of legitimacy seems to indicate considerable disarray in the international normative arena.

To wit, NATO's decision to intervene to stop ethnic cleansing indicates one normative standard (human protection). The decision to publically foreswear from the outset the use of ground troops, and to bomb from such high altitudes that greater levels of collateral damage is assured, seem to indicate a separate contradictory standard (domestic politics). President Clinton's decision to intervene without UN approval indicates he was not as risk averse as critics of his strategy have argued, and that the NATO countries could, in fact, act on principle (human protection). Yet, to announce publically the decision to prosecute the war without ground troops certainly emboldened Slobodan Milosevic in a way that countered NATO interests. Such a blunder would seem to indicate a force protection standard with such power that it undermined both the humanitarian and the military strategic dimensions of the mission. For it is one thing to deploy forces in ways that minimize casualties; it is quite another to announce one's plans in ways that embolden the target of your intervention and ensures the loss of the very ones the mission is meant to protect. The effect of these contradictory normative impulses or behavioral standards was to undermine the agency of presumed hegemonic actors in world politics.

To summarize, it is only under these conditions that a mere call to resolve the humanitarian intervention dilemma, or "to forge unity" around new collective understandings, would constitute the source of not just a new norm, but one that "has moved farther and faster in the normative arena" than anything else since the genocide convention (Weiss 2006, 741). The chaos of the 1990s constituted a critical situation, one of radical disjuncture from known patterns of behaviors. This represented a threat to core identities – self and collective – of state and non-state actors across international society. The threats to these identities undermined the agentic capacity of even the most powerful actors in world politics, a phenomenon which explains better than rational calculation and moral judgment the kinds of contradictory and irrational decisions these actors made with respect to the string of human protection crises they confronted.

Assuming that actors are ontological security-seeking, the importance of routinization helps explain the effort to establish new standards of appropriate conduct. For it is only with identity-constituting norms that these actors can articulate their emergent post–Cold War selves, identify their interests and know the means with which they might pursue them. In short, it is only via the constitution of a normative community, referred to by some as the "Friends of R2P," that actors could establish intersubjectively new standards with which to structure international society's efforts to tackle crises of human protection.

Our explanation helps resolve the puzzle of why actors would seek to create a new norm when doing so would bind them in future courses of action. Our view is that a shared interest in renewed normative clarity does not, in fact, bind agents to *a priori* specified courses of action within narrowly defined issue areas. In fact, the constitution of a new norm, with its solution to the problem of ontological insecurity, creates the conditions *for* agency, not its restriction. As Ken Booth reminds us, it is *in*security that is determining, not security, "security offers choices" (2007, 101–108). "What," he notes, "the achievement of a level of security brings to people and groups is some time, energy, and scope to choose to do other things than simply survive" (Booth 2007, 110). We think this is particularly true when the security in question is of the ontological sort.

As the divergent interpretations of R2P offered by our contributors indicate, international actors were postured to create the conditions of a post–Cold War international society – a new normative community – in which both individual and collective identities might be affirmed, individual and collective interests re-associated and thus some basis for agency obtained. But norms, it has long been argued, are not determinative. Within an R2P-constituted capacity to effectively respond to crises of human protection, to associate ends and means, the costs and benefits of norm compliance and norm *violation* become knowable. Thus, what Kofi Annan tapped into, and ICISS gave structure to, was far more fundamental than a desire to resolve a Clash-like "do we stay or do we go" dilemma. It was interest in a new normative order altogether. In this view, the sources of the R2P's emergence and meteoric rise are neither purely interest-based nor legitimacy-based. The interest of international society *is in* legitimacy, or its restoration (Kaldor 2012).

Chapter summaries

In her contribution, Anne Orford agrees with other observers that much of the significance of R2P lies in its justification of the expansion of international authority in situations where states have failed to protect their populations from gross human rights abuses. She raises important questions, however, about the unavoidably political nature of R2P's "prevention, reaction and rebuilding" toolbox and about the proper limits on this expanded executive, or police, authority. The R2P, she suggests, is at the center of a dilemma confronting the United Nations as it wrestles with the possibly irreconcilable imperatives of being the guarantor of human protection while also holding itself up as the apolitical representative of humanity's collective conscience.

Many critics of R2P have argued that the principle constitutes an "intervener's charter" that will pave the way toward ever more frequent violations of sovereignty in the global south. For his part, however, David Chandler argues that, instead, R2P represents an element of a broader politics of disengagement from the global south by Western states reflecting their post–Cold War lack of strategic concern with large areas of the world, particularly sub–Saharan Africa. It is in this lack of concern on the part of Western states that Chandler locates a significant gap between R2P's promise of an international society more committed to human protection and the harsh realities of the contemporary policy environment.

In the fifteen years since ICISS introduced the concept, R2P has been said by many to have enjoyed meteoric success, while others have announced its effective demise. Jeremy Sarkin weighs into this debate and offers a nuanced assessment of R2P's significance in the contemporary human rights landscape. He demonstrates through consideration of what he sees as failed tests such as Burma and Zimbabwe, as well as qualified successes such as Libya, that R2P's significance will, for any given human protection crisis, continue to be contingent on largely unpredictable constellations of interests at international, regional and national levels.

Brett O'Bannon explores a question long ago posed by renowned Africanist scholar Crawford Young in relation to what was then known as Zaire: *Is there a State?* For O'Bannon, however, this question needs to be asked about Africa more generally because many of the vectors of state decay Young found in Zaire can be found across Africa. This is problematic because R2P is a decidedly state-centric human protection norm; that is, R2P presupposes a universe of Westphalian states. Such an assumption may not be sound in Africa for numerous historical and contemporary reasons. Though R2P has been said to have been born in the soil and blood of the African experience, its implementation there may be troubled by a state centrism that does not match the experience of statehood in contemporary Africa.

Turning to the application of R2P to critical cases, Séverine Autesserre explores the meaning of the principle for the human protection project in the Democratic Republic of Congo. In a word, it has been a failure. But a failure of what, exactly? As Autesserre explains, the experience of the DRC makes clear that the real issue for advocates of R2P ought to be the apparent loss of emphasis on *prevention*. The ICISS report was emphatic that among the concept's three responsibilities (prevention, reaction and rebuilding) prevention was the most important. But preventing the atrocities committed in the Congo on such a wide scale is precisely what UN forces failed to do. The explanation for this abject failure lies in the dominant culture of the international peacebuilding community. This culture shaped the intervention in ways that effectively precluded preventative action at the grassroots level, which, she notes, doomed international efforts to bring peace to the Congo.

Alex Bellamy's chapter uses the case of the 2008–2009 Sri Lankan crisis and a highly critical internal report on UN action there to think about implementing the R2P principle in ways that confront cultural, structural and systemic dimensions of the UN system held responsible for its failure to better protect civilians. According to Bellamy, there are critical lessons to be learned from the Sri Lankan case that can strengthen the UN's capacity to respond to human protection crises in the future. Improving the UN's protective capacity turns on the degree to which it can more deeply institutionalize mechanisms such as early warning and assessment and the convening authority of the Office on Genocide Prevention and the Responsibility to Protect, as well as how well it can mainstream an atrocity prevention lens across the UN system.

In her reflection, Carol Berger examines the militarization of post-war South Sudan and identifies factors reinforcing the use of uniforms and regimental hierarchy. She argues that the UN and other international agencies have, paradoxically, strengthened the position of militaristic elements within the government of South Sudan. The international community's failure to recognize prevailing hierarchies within the region has led to deteriorating security conditions and the subordination of non-military actors to military prerogatives in virtually all spheres of South Sudanese life.

In the final chapter, John Roth offers a moving call to heed the voices of the dead – the voices of those whose lives have been cut short in crimes of mass atrocity, such as the Holocaust. Doing so, he argues, might well help today to get the moral motives to bite at what ICISS understood was the more crucial but difficult phase of prevention. Roth argues powerfully that more than any other, "those unjustly robbed of life by human decisions and human actions are the ones we need especially to see and to heed . . .". Roth concludes that improving our preventive capacity "depends significantly on respecting and heeding the "conscience shocking" calls for action crying out, as they alone can, from 'voices that can be heard only in silence.'

Notes

1 The expression "Friends of R2P" has been used more or less informally by states and civil society to refer to those actors agreed on the need "to engage in a more concentrated and coordinated effort to defend and promote the norm" (Global Center for the Responsibility to Protect 2008, 8).
2 We chose not to employ the familiar and relevant concept of "transnational advocacy network" (Keck and Sikkink 1998, Risse-Kappen 1995, Risse, Ropp and Sikkink 1999) because not all actors in the community we have in mind are activists. Many states benefit from the community's constitution, for reasons we explore, but cannot be said to have played a critical role in the norm's diffusion. The United States, for example, until the Obama administration perhaps, has stayed far from the front lines in the war for R2P.
3 Uppsala Conflict Data Program (Date of retrieval: 11/06/17) UCDP Database: www.ucdp.uu.se/database, Uppsala University.

4 Contra interest-based arguments about airfields and communication arrays, Rutherford (2008, 66–89) makes a convincing case that human protection, rather than geopolitics, explains the lame duck president's decision to lead the intervention.
5 See Mueller (2005) and Gelpi and Mueller (2006) for a debate that reveals the complex task that is estimating political costs of intervention.
6 ICISS advises, "force protection of the intervening force is important, but should never be allowed to become the principle objective" (2001a 7.34). Fear of Serbia's anti-air-craft weaponry, however, meant that NATO sorties were initially restricted to 15,000 and subsequently 10,000, feet. Bombing from such a height increases the probability of collateral damage. Were the human protection imperative determinative, the options to deploy ground troops and more rotary-wing aircraft would have at least been on the table.
7 The major exception, of course, was France's Operation Turquoise, which largely had the effect of aiding the *génocidaires*.
8 Power cites a US Department of Defense memo that "testifies to the unwillingness of the U.S. government to make even financial sacrifices to diminish the killing" (2002, 371).

References

Adler, E. and Barnett, M. (1998), "Security Communities in Theoretical Perspective," in their (eds.) *Security Communities*, Cambridge: Cambridge University Press.
Annan, K. (1999), Address to the 54th Session of the General Assembly, 20 September 1999, Press Release SG/SM/7136 GA/9596.
Annan, K. (2000), *We the Peoples: The Role of the United Nations in the Twenty-First Century,* Millennial Report of the Secretary General, New York: UN Department of Public Information.
Annan, K. (2005), "In Larger Freedom: Towards Development, Security and Human Rights for All," A/59/2005, 21 March 2005.
Autesserre, S. (2010), *The Trouble with the Congo: Local Violence and the Failure of International Peacebuilding*, Cambridge: Cambridge University Press.
Ban K. (2009), *Implementing the Responsibility to Protect*, A/63/677, 12 January 2009.
Barnett, M. (2003), *Eyewitness to Genocide: The United Nations and Rwanda*, Ithaca: Cornell University Press.
Barnett, M. (2005), "Humanitarianism Transformed," *Perspectives on Politics* 3(4): 723–740.
Bates, R. (1988), "Contra-Contractarianism: Some Reflections on the New Institutional-ism," *Politics and Society* 16: 387–401.
Bellamy, A. and Williams, P. (2011), "The New Politics of Protection? Côte d'Ivoire, Libya and the responsibility to protect," *International Affairs* 87(4): 825–850.
Booth, K. (2007), *Theory of World Security*, Cambridge: Cambridge University Press.
Brown, C. (2003), "Selective Humanitarianism: in Defense of Inconsistency," in Chatterjee, D. and Scheid, D. (eds.) *Ethics and Foreign Intervention*, Cambridge: Cambridge University Press.
Buzan, B., Wæver, O., and de Wilde, J. (1998), *Security: A New Framework for Analysis,* Boulder: Lynne Rienner Press.
Campbell, D. (1998), *Writing Security: United States Foreign Policy and the Politics of Identity*, Minneapolis: University of Minnesota Press.
Evans, G. (2008), *The Responsibility to Protect: Ending Mass Atrocities Once and For All,* Washington: Brookings Institution Press.
Finnemore, M. (2009), "Legitimacy, Hypocrisy, and the Social Structure of Unipolarity," *World Politics* 61(1): 58–85.

Finnemore, M. and Sikkink, K. (1998), "International Norm Dynamics and Political Change," *International Organization* 52(4): 887–917.

Gberie, L. (2005), *A Dirty War in West Africa: The RUF and the Destruction of Sierra Leone*, Bloomington: Indiana University Press.

Gelpi, C. and Mueller, J. (2006), "The Cost of War," *Foreign Affairs* 85(1): 139–144.

Giddens, A. (1979), *Central Problems in Social Theory: Action, Structure, and Contradiction in Social Analysis*, Berkeley and Los Angeles: University of California Press.

Giddens, A. (1984), *The Constitution of Society: Outline of the Theory of Structuration*. Cambridge: Polity Press.

Global Centre for the Responsibility to Protect. (2008), "Uniting to Support the Responsibility to Protect: Preserving the Spirit of the 2005 Agreement," Meeting Summary, 25 September 2008, Millennium UN Plaza Hotel, One United Nations Plaza.

Gourevitch, P. (1999), *We Wish to Inform You that Tomorrow We Will be Killed with Our Families: Stories from Rwanda,* New York: Picador Press.

Hafner-Burton, E. (2008), "Sticks and Stones: Naming and Shaming the Human Rights Enforcement Problem," *International Organization* 62(4): 689–716.

Hurrell, A. (2002), "Norms and Ethics in International Relations," in Carlsnaes, W., Risse, T. and Simmons, B. (eds.) *Handbook of International Relations*, London: Sage.

Independent International Commission on Kosovo. (2000), *The Kosovo Report: Conflict, International Response, Lessons Learned*, Oxford: Oxford University Press.

International Commission on Intervention and State Sovereignty. (2001), *The Responsibility to Protect*, Ottawa: IDRC.

Jepperson, R., Wendt, A., and Katzenstein, P. (1996), "Norms, Identity and Culture in National Security," in Katzenstein (ed.) *The Culture of National Security: Norms and Identity in World Politics*, New York: Columbia University Press.

Kaldor, M. (2012), *New and Old Wars: Organized Violence in a Global Era*, Stanford: Stanford University Press.

Katzenstein, P. (ed.) (1996), *The Culture of National Security: Norms and Identity in World Politics*, New York: Columbia University Press.

Keck, M.E. and K. Sikkink (1998), *Activists Without Borders: Advocacy Networks in International Relations,* Ithaca: Cornell University Press

Kowert, P and J. Legro. (1996), "Norms, Identity and Their Limits: A Theoretical Reprise," in Katzenstein (ed.) *The Culture of National Security: Norms and Identity in World Politics*, New York: Columbia University Press.

Krasner, S. (1999), *Sovereignty: Organized Hypocrisy*, Princeton: Princeton University Press.

Mearsheimer, J. (1990), "Back to the Future: Instability in Europe after the Cold War," *International Security*, 15(1): 5–56.

Mitzen, J. (2006), "Ontological Security in World Politics: State Identity and the Security Dilemma," *European Journal of International Relations* 12(3): 341–370.

Mueller, J. (2005), "The Iraq Syndrome," *Foreign Affairs* 84(6): 44–54.

Ostrom, Elinor (1990), *Governing the Commons: The Evolution of Institutions for Collective Action*, Cambridge: Cambridge University Press.

Power, S. (2002), *"A Problem from Hell," America and the Age of Genocide,* New York: Basic Books.

Richards. P. (1996), *Fighting for the Rainforest: War, Youth and Resources in Sierra Leone*, The International African Institute, James Currey & Heinemann.

Risse, T. and Sikkink, K. (1999), "The Socialization of International Human Rights Norms into Domestic Practices: Introduction," in Risse, T., Ropp, S., and Sikkink, K. (eds.) *The*

Power of Human Rights: International Norms and Domestic Change, Cambridge: Cambridge University Press.

Risse, T., Ropp, S., and Sikkink, K. (eds.) (1999), *The Power of Human Rights: International Norms and Domestic Change*, Cambridge: Cambridge University Press.

Risse-Kappen (1995), *Bringing Transnatoinal Relations Back In: Non-State Actors, Deomestic Structures and International Intuitions.* Cambridge: Cambridge University Press.

Rutherford, K. (2008), *Humanitarianism Under Fire: The US and UN Intervention in Somalia,* Sterling: Kumarian Press.

Siegel, A. (1996), "The Intervasion of Somalia," Professional Paper 539, Alexandria, VA: Center for Naval Analyses.

Snow, D. (1996), Uncivil *Wars: International Security and the New Internal Conflicts.* Boulder: Lynne Rienner Publishers.

Steele, B. (2008), *Ontological Security in International Relations: Self Identity and the IR State*, New York: Routledge.

Valentino, B. (2011), "The True Costs of Humanitarian Intervention: The Hard Truth about a Noble Notion," *Foreign Affairs* 90(6): 60–73.

Weiss, T. (2006), "R2P after 9/11 and the World Summit," *Wisconsin International Law Journal* 24: 741–759.

Wendt, A. (1999), *Social Theory of International Politics*, Cambridge: Cambridge University Press.

Wheeler, N. (2000), *Saving Strangers: Humanitarian Intervention in International Society*, Oxford: Oxford University Press.

Whitworth, S. (2004), *Men, Militarism, & UN Peacekeeping: A Gendered Analysis*, Boulder: Lynne Rienner Press.

Zaretsky, E. (2002), "Trauma and Dereification: September 11 and the Problem of Ontological Security," *Constellations* 9(1): 98–105.

1   The responsibility to protect and the limits of international authority

Anne Orford

In 1999, then UN Secretary-General Kofi Annan described the United Nations as the champion of 'the collective conscience of humanity'.[1] In so doing, he drew on an idea of international actors as somehow transcending the politics of any given state that had gained ground in the decade since the ending of the Cold War. As the representatives of conscience, the UN and nongovernmental organisations were understood to exist outside the sometimes unsavoury world of political calculation and statecraft. The emergence and embrace of the responsibility-to-protect concept since 2001 has expressed a shift in that allocation of roles between states (understood as agents of realpolitik and political calculation) and international actors (understood as champions of conscience and witnesses to truth). Much of the attention in internationalist literature exploring the nature and scope of the responsibility-to-protect concept has focused on the ways in which that concept justifies the expansion of international authority in situations where a state has failed to protect its population. International actors, particularly the UN, are portrayed as the protectors of life and welfare, with a newly unbounded jurisdiction and freedom to determine what forms of action are needed to protect those at risk of genocide, war crimes, crimes against humanity, and ethnic cleansing. There has been less attention paid in that internationalist literature to articulating the proper limits to the jurisdiction of those exercising international protective authority. Yet, as the task of international organisations and civil society shifts from representing the collective conscience of humanity to undertaking international police action in humanity's name, the need for a debate about the proper limits to the authority of such actors is becoming apparent. This chapter will explore some of the symptoms of the need to address those limits that have arisen through attempts to implement the responsibility-to-protect concept.

The UN and the collective conscience of humanity

The year 1999 was difficult for the UN. It was the year in which NATO circumvented the UN Security Council to intervene in Kosovo. NATO's action exposed the fault lines that divided world opinion on issues of international authority and intervention. While some states and commentators saw the NATO intervention as illegal and ineffective, others commented that there was strong 'moral or humanitarian justification for the action'.[2] Key to the division of opinion on the legitimacy of humanitarian intervention in general, and NATO's action in particular, was its link to realpolitik and great power ambition. Was it really possible to divorce the interests of powerful states from their role as humanitarian interveners? Did the UN and other humanitarian organisations lose their authority and their claim to impartiality if they aligned themselves with powerful states to defend human rights or end human suffering?[3] Yet, if humanitarian actors or international organisations did not create alliances with powerful states, how could they ensure a supply of the resources (whether financial, administrative, or military) necessary to bring about the social change or the end to suffering that they sought? This issue had particular resonance at the UN. For UN officials, the failure to respond in situations that 'shock the conscience of mankind' would mean abandoning what many had come to see as the mission of the organisation.[4] Kosovo (and later Iraq) represented a possible dystopian future in which powerful states or coalitions of the willing side-lined the UN and took its place as the representatives of humanity. Indeed, some commentators argued that if the UN failed to make the right decisions, failed to protect populations at risk effectively, and failed to conduct itself in conformity with fundamental human rights values, there was nothing wrong with coalitions of the willing, powerful states, or regional organizations taking its place as executive agents of the world community, particularly if they could do so more efficiently. The precedent represented by Kosovo thus threatened not only the authority of the sovereign state but also that of the UN. Revealing a keen understanding of the threat that the NATO action in Kosovo represented to UN jurisdiction, then Secretary-General Kofi Annan warned in his 1999 Annual Report to the UN General Assembly, 'If the collective conscience of humanity . . . cannot find in the United Nations its greatest tribune, there is a grave danger that it will look elsewhere for peace and for justice'.[5]

The year 1999 was also the year in which the reports of two UN inquiries were published – one into the responsibility of the UN for allowing genocide to unfold in Rwanda in 1994 and the other into the responsibility of the UN for the failure to protect the inhabitants of the UN-created safe haven of Srebrenica from genocide in 1995.[6] Many of the practical or operational challenges involved in international humanitarian action were exemplified by the disastrous effect of the attempts in Rwanda and Srebrenica to create 'safe havens' or humanitarian spaces in which the UN and humanitarian NGOs could protect the lives of civilians in situations of civil war or genocide. In the aftermath of those genocides, both internal and external critics questioned the viability of the long-standing commitment to impartiality and neutrality on the part of UN peacekeepers and humanitarian agencies in situations of mass atrocity. In the words of a major UN report on the future of UN peace operations, although impartiality should remain one of the 'bedrock principles' of peacekeeping, there are cases where 'local parties consist not of moral equals but of obvious aggressors and victims.'[7] In such situations, 'continued equal treatment of all parties by the United Nations can in the best case result in ineffectiveness and in the worst may amount to complicity with evil'.[8] The report called on world leaders 'to strengthen the capacity of the United Nations to fully accomplish the mission which is, indeed, its very *raison d'être*: to help communities engaged in strife and to maintain or restore peace'.[9] The massacre of civilians who had relied on the UN for protection in Srebrenica and Rwanda had shown 'how easy it was to declare land "safe", yet how difficult it was to persuade the major powers in fact to secure civilians'.[10] It was in light of this history that Kofi Annan famously asked the members of the General Assembly: 'if humanitarian intervention is, indeed, an unacceptable assault on sovereignty, how should we respond to a Rwanda, to a Srebrenica – to gross and systematic violations of human rights that affect every precept of our common humanity?'[11]

Despite the force of Kofi Annan's appeal, the idea that the UN might represent 'the collective conscience of humanity' was a controversial one. That idea was controversial for at least two reasons. The first involves the question of authority or jurisdiction. For much of its history, the UN had been largely concerned with more pragmatic and prosaic tasks of technical assistance and development aid, punctuated by limited forays into fairly modest forms of peacekeeping and civilian administration under more charismatic Secretaries General. Despite the role that human rights organisations played in the drafting of the UN Charter,[12] and the role that they would later come to play in shaping the expectations of international actors, human rights approaches did not inform the early forms of engagement with decolonised states by the UN. Indeed, Dag Hammarskjöld, who was the Secretary General at the time of the Suez and Congo crises, was quite hostile towards attempts to institutionalise human rights within the work of the organisation in the early years of decolonisation.[13] The many institutional discussions of the need to assist newly independent states that took place at the UN during the 1950s and 1960s involve strikingly few references to the protection of human rights as a major concern of international action. While independent states themselves sponsored support for the right of self-determination and the end of colonial oppression as core commitments of internationalism,[14] there was little or no support for the idea that the UN or great powers had a right to intervene within the affairs of Member States in the interests of protecting human rights or realising democratic values during the Cold War era. The ever-present threat of proxy wars and of nuclear annihilation that accompanied the heating up of the Cold War led government leaders and international lawyers to engage in fierce debates about the meaning and limits of the commitment to non-use of force and non-intervention in the internal affairs of states.[15]

Within that Cold War context, the claim that international actors might resort to force on behalf of the conscience of humanity received short shrift. Humanitarian intervention played a limited role both in official justifications for the use of force and in scholarly commentary. General Assembly resolutions passed during the 1970s unambiguously outlawed forcible intervention.[16] States themselves did not seek to justify their resort to force as humanitarian intervention.[17] Thus while India's intervention in East Pakistan, Vietnam's intervention in Cambodia, and Tanzania's intervention in Uganda have all since been justified by commentators as Cold War examples of humanitarian intervention, none of the intervening states justified their actions on humanitarian grounds at the time. This was not because the governments of India, Vietnam, or Tanzania lacked a sense of justice or an account of morality that was adequate to their actions, but because they considered the prohibition on unilateral intervention in the UN Charter as itself a moral state-ment.[18] Humanitarian intervention was 'not a doctrine that responsible states would want to espouse' because it was 'a doctrine capable of uncontrollable abuse'.[19] The notion that a powerful state or a coalition of allies might intervene to rescue or protect the people of another state could not easily be represented as an apolitical action. The Brezhnev doctrine of intervention to protect the self-determination of socialist countries in the face of capitalist threats and the Reagan doctrine advocating the legitimacy of pro-democratic invasion were met with pro-test and scepticism.

The second reason for the controversial nature of the idea that the UN represents the collective conscience of humanity is a more practical one. Is it possible for the UN to act *both* as the representative of collective conscience and as the guarantor of peace and security? For many centuries, the moral authority of conscience has been invoked in opposition to the activities of politicians and the world of state-craft – 'conscience' has been the enemy of 'sovereignty'.[20] The most influential modern representatives of this tradition of conscience as the enemy of sovereignty are the international human rights law and international criminal law movements. The question posed by Kofi Annan's appeal to conscience as a basis for mobilising military intervention was whether it would truly be possible for the UN to create order and maintain security while refraining from political calculation and from the more unsavoury aspects of statecraft, including collecting intelligence, using violence, and deciding who should be sacrificed to protect the greater good. If not, what were the implications of appealing to the moral authority of universal values to justify the exercise of power by international actors? These questions were to come to the fore with the development of the responsibility-to-protect concept as an institutional response to the humanitarian intervention debate.

The adoption of the responsibility-to-protect concept

In response to the challenges posed by Kofi Annan, the Canadian government announced at the General Assembly in 2000 its establishment of the International Commission on Intervention and State Sovereignty (ICISS), tasked with producing a report on the issues involved in debates about intervention. The subsequent ICISS report, titled *The Responsibility to Protect*, sought to transcend the per-ceived tension between sovereignty and humanitarian intervention that had divided international responses to the NATO intervention in Kosovo.[21] The report noted that while some saw the Kosovo intervention as 'a long overdue internationaliza-tion of the human conscience', others focused on the lack of authority for the intervention and the 'way in which the NATO allies conducted the operation', generating 'more carnage' than they averted.[22]

In order to find a way out of the broader 'intervention dilemma', the report's authors drew upon the work of Francis Deng on conflict management in Africa.[23] In *Sovereignty as Responsibility*, Deng and his co-authors had argued that responsibility rather than control should be seen as the essence of sovereignty.[24] *Sovereignty as Responsibility* explicitly raised the question of the lawfulness of state authority, arguing that if a government could no longer guarantee the security and welfare of the population, it might no longer be recognisable as the lawful authority over a territory. Sovereignty, understood in that sense of an obligation to preserve life, had become 'a pooled function'.[25] If local claimants to authority in Africa – whether they be 'governments, rebel leaders, militia leaders, civil society, or the general population' – fail to exercise the responsibility to protect citizens, 'they cannot legitimately complain against international humanitarian intervention'.[26] Indeed, a government that cannot protect its citizens may no longer even be recognizable as the lawful authority in a territory.

Following Deng's lead, the ICISS report argued that 'the changing international environment' required a rethinking of the fundamental notion of authority. ICISS proposed a 'necessary re-characterization' of sovereignty from '*sovereignty as control* to *sovereignty as responsibility*'.[27] According to ICISS, thinking of sovereignty in those terms facilitated a clearer focus upon the functions of state authorities. Sovereignty as responsibility 'implies that the state authorities are responsible for the functions of protecting the safety and lives of citizens and promotion of their welfare'.[28] That responsibility to perform the functions of protecting citizens and promoting their welfare 'resides first and foremost with the state whose people are directly affected'.[29] However, those functions are often not performed by the state, as evidenced by the fact that '[m]illions of human beings remain at the mercy of civil wars, insurgencies, state repression and state collapse'.[30] In such circumstances, where the state does not have the power, the capacity, or the will to meet its responsibility to protect, the need for international action arises. In that situation a 'residual' or 'fallback' responsibility to protect on the part of the 'broader community of states' is activated.[31]

The ICISS report envisaged that a broad range of techniques might be needed to ensure 'the provision of life-supporting protection and assistance to populations at risk',[32] involving not only a responsibility to react but also a responsibility to prevent and to rebuild. The report listed as potential techniques not only the much-discussed resort to military intervention but also many forms of preventive and rebuilding action short of force, including the provision of development assistance or support for 'local initiatives to advance good governance, human rights, or the rule of law', the deployment of 'good offices missions' or 'mediation efforts to promote dialogue or reconciliation', monitoring and reporting on human rights abuses, receiving and analysing 'sensitive information from member states', promoting better terms of trade for developing economies, reforming the military and state security services, and prosecuting 'perpetrators of crimes against humanity' before the ICC.[33] The report also envisaged that the responsibility to rebuild after military intervention 'may mean staying in the country for some period of time after the initial purposes of the intervention have been accomplished.[34] Two of the principal authors of the ICISS report, Gareth Evans and Ramesh Thakur, have since stressed that the humanitarian ambitions of the responsibility-to-protect concept require a continued commitment to the range of techniques beyond the resort to force. They argue that 'if interventions are genuinely motivated by humanitarian concerns as the primary goal . . . then their implementation implies solidarity across borders. Such solidarity, however, cannot begin and end with military intervention. It must also find expression at the pre-crisis point and be continued after the immediate crisis is over'.[35]

The responsibility-to-protect concept came of age in 2005 with its unanimous adoption by the General Assembly in its World Summit Outcome. The General Assembly there endorsed the notion that both the state and the international community have a responsibility to protect populations from genocide, war crimes, ethnic cleansing, and crimes against humanity. Though the General Assembly confined the situations in which the international community might intervene militarily to those in which a state was 'manifestly failing' to protect its population, it endorsed a broad range of preventive, early warning, and capacity-building actions to assist states 'before crises and conflicts break out'.[36] Member States also declared their preparedness 'to take collective action, in a timely and decisive manner, through the Security Council . . . on a case-by-case basis . . . should peaceful means prove inadequate' to protect populations.[37] The inclusion of the responsibility-to-protect concept in the World Summit Outcome 'transformed the principle, from a commission proposal actively supported by a relatively small number of like-minded states' to a concept 'endorsed by the entire UN membership'.[38]

Secretary-General Ban Ki-moon has since described his approach to operationalising the responsibility-to-protect concept as 'narrow but deep' – narrow in terms of the jurisdictional trigger of an international responsibility to protect, and deep in terms of the scope of the preventive, reactive and rebuilding techniques authorised to achieve protection.[39] According to the Secretary General, implementation of the concept involves 'utilizing the whole prevention and protection tool kit available to the United Nations system', with the aim of 'integrating the system's multiple channels of information and assessment',[40] adopting a 'unifying perspective', facilitating 'system-wide coherence',[41] and ensuring that the UN 'acts as one in the flow and assessment of information'.[42]

The most useful way to think about the modes of governance envisaged by these ideas of prevention, reaction, and rebuilding is in terms of *policing*. I mean here policing in the older sense developed in the police jurisprudence of the seventeenth and eighteenth century.[43] The jurisprudence of the police was concerned with the range of measures that the state might take to ensure the safety, prosperity, order, public health, and general welfare of the community. These measures could and did include the kinds of coercive acts that we have grown used to equating with modern police as the specialist enforcers of criminal laws, who are primarily responsible for locating offenders through surveillance and interrogation and having them punished for past misdeeds. However, as policing became identified with this more coercive function, the older sense of police science as part of political economy, involved in both the production of wealth and 'the administration of poverty', largely faded from view.[44]

That older sense of policing is of use in thinking about the work of protection envisaged by the responsibility-to-protect concept. It was oriented both to the past (punishing offenders for past actions),[45] and the future ('*shaping* the social body' according to the ends of the state or of new forms of economy).[46] Police worked 'as a sort of temporal-hinge word, allowing the governance of the past to be articulated with the governance of the future. Prevention and punishment are very different as logics of governance; "police" is the middle term that links them'.[47] The techniques for protection envisaged by ICISS and adopted by the General Assembly, including not just military intervention, but the creation of surveillance and early warning systems, economic intervention, development assistance, and aid work, can usefully be thought of as forms of international police action in that broader sense. Thinking of those techniques of protection as policing suggests new questions about the role being envisaged for international actors and how we might begin to address the proper limits to the power they exercise in the name of protection.

From human rights moralism to international police action

In the decade since the ICISS report was released, the responsibility-to-protect concept has colonised internationalist debates about conflict prevention, humanitarian action, peacekeeping, and territorial administration, and has garnered the support of a strikingly diverse range of states, international and regional organizations, and non-governmental organizations.[48] Its embrace is evidence of the increased influence of moral argument as a force in international relations, manifested particularly through the powerful role played by international civil society networks in shaping the language and focus of foreign relations. Yet, the techniques that have been envisaged as potential means of realising the responsibility to protect on the part of the international community suggest a radical departure from the role that human rights activists and other representatives of conscience have understood themselves to be playing in international politics over the past decades.

Before going further, it is important to differentiate between the perception that international human rights organisations and international humanitarian organisations have of their roles. While humanitarian organisations have understood themselves either as impartial or more recently as political actors, human rights organisations have often portrayed their role in the terms discussed above – as representing the conscience of humanity. Unlike humanitarian organisations, human rights activists do not see themselves as being 'impartial', but neither do they understand their role as 'political'. Since the end of the Cold War, many human rights organisations and faith-based civil society groups with an internationalist focus have understood their role as one that transcends politics. They reject the idea that it is appropriate to negotiate with leaders who are suspected of targeting civilians or repressing their populations, and they expect the UN to do the same.

To the extent that they see themselves as the judges of states and politicians, these human rights and faith-based organisations are part of a long conscience-based tradition of voluntary civil organisations that defined themselves against states. As the absolutist state emerged in Europe in a form that denied its subjects the capacity to participate in government, people endowed 'other concerns and pursuits – economic, cultural, moral – with an independent, and hence rival, authority'.[49] The effect of the growing moral authority of voluntary associations was that 'existing political societies came to be judged by standards' which took little account 'of the constraints which political men must inevitably take into account'.[50] Voluntary associations were treated as models for political society, while depending for their strength and security upon the statecraft that created the political order in which they could exist. The tradition of moralistic critique which they sponsored refused 'to take cognizance of its self-evidently political role'.[51] The creation of a distinction between an inner world of morals and an outer world of politics may have brought an end to the confessional wars of the seventeenth century, but many have argued that it threw the state into a permanent political crisis.[52]

> It created the crisis by giving private individuals authority to subject the moral deficits of politics and politicians to the critique of conscience. It concealed the crisis by disguising what was in effect a political endeavour as the exercise of purely moral faculties.[53]

Thus, in the modern world, 'sovereignty was declared to be absolute and subject neither to history nor positive law nor, above all, to any papal or imperial powers, but only to a natural law defined by a new science'.[54] That natural law found its champions in those who speak in the name of conscience. In the modern world, in other words, 'conscience' became the enemy of 'sovereignty'.[55]

The claim to the moral authority of conscience was taken up by Western human rights and faith-based NGOs during the 1990s and began to inform the way in which the public thought about the proper role of the UN and other representatives of the international community. The human rights and international criminal law movements, in concert with evangelist faith-based groups based largely in the US, turned towards more absolutist notions of right and wrong, and away from pragmatic accounts of nongovernmental action. For those activists, the world can be divided into good and evil, the act of distinguishing between the two is straightforward, and that simple fact has moral consequences – it is unacceptable to compromise or negotiate with evil and reprehensible to engage in political calculations when faced with the demands of conscience. The moral certainty of human rights and evangelistic civil society groups, particularly when compared with the more pragmatic approach taken by many humanitarian and aid organisations, became increasingly apparent during the 1990s, particularly in calls for increased resort to humanitarian intervention in situations where it was not clear that this would in fact help to protect local people. In contrast, humanitarian actors were much quicker to confront the political effects of their actions and influence in the post–Cold War world, and to reject more muscular forms of humanitarianism aimed at creating new world orders. In the words of Jean-Hervé Bradol, then President of Médicins Sans Frontières in France, '[t]he production of order at the international level – just as at national or local levels – demands its quota of victims'.[56]

Central to this new role claimed for international civil society in the post–Cold War era was its distance from governmental politics. In a short manifesto reflecting on the humanitarian internationalism of the 1990s, Michael Feher put the case for thinking about human rights and other non-governmental organizations as having quite different roles to those of state and governments.

> By definition, the purpose of a government is to govern, that is, to maximize its influence, both on its constituents and vis-à-vis other governing bodies, at a minimal cost. Insofar as nongovernmental activists intend to remain what they are – rather than embrace the alternative positions either of progovern-mental apologists, anti-governmental militants, or apolitical humanitarians – their sole purpose should be to raise the cost of those governmental policies that they consider objectionable. In other words, it is only by recognizing that governments are not meant to represent them that nongovernmental activists will be able to give precedence to their prevention of what they deem intoler-able over their stake in either redeeming or condemning the agencies that have the power to prevent it.[57]

Something resembling that worldview has informed much of the work done by human rights and faith-based organisations since the 1990s. The proper role of the UN and other humanitarian actors, like that of the church, is to represent con-science in a world of states, but not to govern.

The sense that political calculation is not the concern of human rights activists began to come under pressure as their influence expanded along with the scope of executive action being undertaken in the name of humanity. That pressure has further intensified with the embrace of the responsibility-to-protect concept. The promise to guarantee protection to people around the world necessarily leads to a politicisation of the role of international actors, including the UN and civil society groups, all of whom are now part of the machinery of protection and thus caught up in the project of 'seeing like a state'.[58] It is difficult to imagine how protection could really be guaranteed effectively by international actors without someone, somewhere, engaging in political calculation and strategic thinking, or resources allocated to one situation rather than another without some form of institution-alised decision-making process. Even in situations of genocide, the capacity to engage in protective action inevitably requires political decisions to be made relat-ing to logistics, personnel, and resources, let alone whether to risk the lives of national soldiers to protect the lives of foreign civilians. UN officials and officials of the states that contribute resources and troops to UN operations have no choice but to attend to domestic constituencies in reaching decisions about how to address those political questions. Yet, as Alex de Waal has argued, those human rights and faith-based organisations advocating for increased US military intervention in the twenty-first century still understand themselves as acting outside politics, in some kind of purely moral space. In relation to Darfur, for example, non-governmental organisations conducted the debate about the need for intervention 'in purely ethi-cal terms, with little regard to the hard-learned lessons of war fighting and peacekeeping'.[59]

> The interventionist position was the polar opposite of the deliberately apoliti-cal stand of relief agencies during war famines in the 1980s. Insofar as it was advocating robust actions aimed at dramatically changing a government's policy – and perhaps (though most Save Darfur leaders disavowed it) chang-ing that government itself – it was overtly political. But in terms of Sudanese realities, the Darfur campaign was curiously nonpolitical. It didn't want to engage in any of the complexities and compromises whereby political change occurs, incrementally, in a country such as Sudan. It wanted to remove the Sudanese state and its baleful influence from Darfur. Saving Darfur was a utopian project.[60]

The same could be said of liberal approaches to policing more generally – liberal states act as if 'administration and policing are somehow outside politics'.[61] Yet, the forms of police action authorised in the name of protection are deeply political, as is the work of those civil society organisations involved in fact-finding, lobby-ing governments to take action against evil, and campaigning to gather public support for forceful intervention. The actions envisaged by ICISS and by the UN General Assembly as techniques of prevention, reaction, and rebuilding are inti-mately related to broader political and economic issues, particularly when they involve international policing undertaken in a situation of uneven development and global inequality. Engaging in policing necessarily gives rise to significant fundamental questions, such as how the ends of international police actions will be determined, what kinds of constraints will be placed upon the capacity of inter-national actors to undertake surveillance and monitoring of populations considered to be at risk, how those exercising the responsibility to prevent and rebuild will deal with issues concerning control over land and resources in Africa and the Middle East, and whether international police action will lead to the adoption of pacification techniques aimed at insurgent groups.[62]

Limiting international police discretion

Much attention has focused on the use of the responsibility-to-protect concept to justify military intervention, but less attention has been paid to the use of the concept to consolidate established practices of international executive rule, such as surveil-lance, early warning, peacekeeping, and administration. Yet, thinking about the responsibility-to-protect concept as authorising new forms of international police action suggests the need to think more systematically about the proper limits of police powers. Let me conclude by briefly discussing four lines of inquiry that are opened up by thinking about the responsibility-to-protect concept in these terms.[63]

First, thinking about the responsibility-to-protect concept in these terms sug-gests that it is of normative significance, *not* because it imposes new obligations upon states but rather because it confers public powers and allocates jurisdiction. Commentators have tended to treat the inclusion of the responsibility-to-protect concept in the World Summit Outcome as a failed attempt to do the former, yet it seems clear that the responsibility-to-protect concept in the World Summit was carefully couched so as not to impose new legal duties upon states or international actors to take particular actions in specific circumstances.[64] The responsibility-to-protect concept should rather be understood as normative in the latter sense of providing legal authorisation for certain kinds of activities. The World Summit Outcome provides the international community, acting through the UN, with a discretionary mandate to take certain forms of executive or police action in situations where populations need protection. In that sense, the responsibility-to-protect concept has a similar character to the articles providing the legal basis for the political authority of the Secretary General, the Secretariat, and the Security Council under the UN Charter. It has long been accepted that Article 99 of the Charter, authorising the Secretary General to 'bring to the attention of the Security Council any matter which in his opinion may threaten the maintenance of international peace and security', does not impose a duty or obligation upon the Secretary General to exercise his political authority in a particular way, but rather provides a discretionary mandate to undertake executive action. Similarly, Article 24 vesting the Security Council with the 'primary responsibility for the maintenance of international peace and security' has not been interpreted as imposing an obligation upon the Security Council or its members to exercise that responsibility in preordained ways.

Second, thinking about the responsibility-to-protect concept as a form of law that allocates discretionary power to an international executive raises questions about the exercise of that discretion. To date, the discretionary mandate to undertake police action in order to further the goal of protecting civilians has been exercised in a selective fashion.[65] It seems almost banal to make the point that the responsibility-to-protect concept is unlikely ever to be invoked to authorise measures against a major ally of the P5, let alone against a Western European or North American state. Nonetheless, the concern with selectivity has been a recurring theme in Security Council debates in relation to Libya and more broadly in thematic debates about civilian protection since May 2011. Lawyers within domestic legal systems have long been concerned with issues of whether and how to constrain the broad discretionary powers vested in the executive arm of government. In the most extreme case, a political order that systematically differentiates between its subjects in the application and enforcement of laws may no longer be recognisable as a legal system and its dictates no longer capable of commanding fidelity or obedience.[66]

Third, justifying authority on the basis of the capacity to protect raises a new question: Who decides? Who decides whether a situation is one which triggers the jurisdiction of the international community, characterises particular conduct as legitimate attempts to secure order or illegitimate targeting of civilians, determines what protection means in a particular time and place, declares how protection can be realised, and decides which claimant to authority is best able to provide it? The power to make such decisions characterises police discretion and is central to the work of statecraft. The responsibility-to-protect concept vests the capacity to determine that a state has 'manifestly' failed to guarantee protection, along with the capacity to determine what protection means in a particular time and place, with representatives of the 'international community'. In terms of jurisdiction, it was essential to states that had experienced – or that might expect to be targets of – Western intervention, including the members of the Non-Aligned Movement, as well as to China, that this broad discretionary mandate was given to the international community acting through the UN, and in the case of the use of force, acting through the Security Council.[67] (Yet, this jurisdictional limitation has proved difficult to maintain. Again, the implications of this are illustrated by events in the Middle East, where many different political and military projects have been justified in terms of protecting civilians. In the context of Libya, for example, it was largely NATO, a regional organisation representing the security interests of Western Europe and North America, that exercised the power to make decisions during 2011 about how protection could best be realised in North Africa, and by whom.

Finally, grounding authority on the capacity to protect has historically tended to privilege certain kinds of institutions and certain forms of action over others. The turn to protection focuses upon creating institutions that privilege coherence, control, and centralisation. In that respect, authority justified in terms of its capacity to guarantee protection has had a tendency to become authoritarian. It might seem extreme to suggest that there could be any relation between the growth of authoritarian security states and the benign ambitions of the responsibility to protect concept. Yet, while much attention is currently being paid to building the international capacity to respond to protection challenges through developing more efficient and integrated forms of surveillance and policing mechanisms, there has been much less discussion of the legal limits to international action undertaken to guarantee protection. To take one example, the prospect of increased surveillance of foreign populations has been welcomed as a contribution to realising the promise that never again will genocide be allowed to occur, without any discussion of the threats that may pose to civil liberties or self-determination.

We are now beginning to see the emergence of an institutional discussion about the need to set limits on the power of international actors, for example, in the increasingly strong arguments put by the Brazil, Russia, China, India, and South Africa since May 2011 that NATO had exceeded its mandate to protect civilians in Libya both by bombing Gaddafi forces and by arming rebels. Of particular relevance is the debate inspired by Brazil's concept note of November 2011, titled 'Responsibility while Protecting'.[68] Brazil had already begun to express its concern about the conduct of the Libyan intervention as early as May 2011 in a Security Council thematic debate about civilian protection.[69] Brazil's statement there provides the background to the principles it later sought to develop in the concept note. Brazil directed its comments to what it described as 'the transformation of the civilian protection landscape over the past few months'.[70] It focused on four issues that have recurred in responses to the Libyan intervention: regime change, prioritising peaceful and preventive means over militarization, limits to the use of force, and impartiality.

> We must avoid excessively broad interpretations of the protection of civilians, which could link it to the exacerbation of conflict, compromise the impartiality of the United Nations or create the perception that it is being used as a smokescreen for intervention or regime change. . . .
>
> Wherever possible, the protection of civilians should be pursued through peaceful and preventive means. . . . We must take the greatest care to ensure that our actions douse the flames of conflict instead of stoking them.
>
> When the Council does authorise the use of force, such as in the case of Libya, we must hold ourselves to a high standard. The Council has the responsibility to ensure the appropriate implementation of its resolutions . . . Member States, too, must be clear on how they are fulfilling the mandate they have received from the Council.[71]

Finally, Brazil addressed the concept of impartiality and the importance of ensuring that UN forces 'are not perceived as parties to the conflict. Avoiding such a perception is crucial for the continued success of peacekeeping. Trust in the Organization's impartiality is indispensable for it to constructively contribute to sustainable political solutions to conflicts. . . . Protecting civilians is one of the most important ways in which the Organization gives expression to its ultimate objectives'.[72] Brazil's 'Responsibility While Protecting' note further stressed the issues of acting within the Security Council mandate, control by and accountability to the Security Council, and the preference for peace and prevention over militarisation as techniques of protection.[73] As India's Representative to the UN put this in the 2011 Security Council debate on civilian protection:

> I cannot but ask the question: *Quis custodiet ipsos custodes?* Who watches the guardians? There is a considerable sense of unease about the manner in which the humanitarian imperative of protecting civilians has been interpreted for actual action on the ground.[74]

Initially, the Secretary General responded to that push for international protectors themselves to be held accountable for their actions by arguing that while '[w]e all agree on the need for responsibility while protecting', we should 'not make the best the enemy of the good'.[75] The implication was that those who are on the side of the good should not be constrained in their use of force – an argument that has been made in other attempts to hold peacekeeping forces to account for alleged human rights violations.[76] In a later report, the Secretary General accepted the significance of the call for responsibility while protecting, linking it particularly to the need to ensure that 'early warning and assessment be conducted fairly, prudently and professionally, without political interference or double standards'.[77] The report noted the concerns expressed by Member States that those charged with implementing SC Resolution 1973 exceeded their mandate, and while not commenting on the specific merits of those arguments, declared that it is necessary that 'concerns expressed by Member States are taken into account in the future'.[78]

Conclusion

According to Secretary-General Ban Ki-moon, 'human protection is a defining purpose of the United Nations in the twenty-first century' and achieving it is 'a test of our common humanity'.[79] The UN is today understood both as the guarantor of protection and as the representative of humanity's collective conscience. These two ways of thinking about the proper role of the UN are not always easy to reconcile. What might it mean for the representatives of our common humanity to see and think like a state? Can the UN act as the guarantor of the protection and security of humanity while at the same time remaining aloof from the machinations of politics? The Secretary General bemoans the tendency of the responsibility to protect to become 'a minefield of nuance, political calculation and competing national interests', leading to 'hesitation or inaction' that 'we cannot afford'. Yet all the decisions involved in implementing the responsibility-to-protect concept are necessarily political, from deciding whether to characterise a situation as civil war or genocide to determining which lives should be sacrificed to achieve particular ends, allocating scarce resources to one situation rather than another, judging what protection demands in a particular time and place, or declaring which claimants to authority are best able to guarantee it.

The lack of attention to the institutional questions involved in transforming the UN and civil society groups into agents of human protection suggests that the implications of the expansion of international police action that we are witnessing with the embrace of the responsibility-to-protect concept are yet to be fully grasped and understood. Just as in the domestic context critical attention has tended to focus on the 'dramatic or even theatrical contexts surrounding police work' rather than 'the silent grinding of administrative mills (as in cataloguing, normalizing, data collection, and classifying)',[80] so too much of the focus, critical and otherwise, in the debate over the responsibility-to-protect concept has remained on the drama of military intervention. There has been much less critical attention paid to the far more prosaic and everyday practices involved in the institutional work of surveillance, fact-finding, prevention, capacity building, security sector reform, and administration. Nor has there been much attention paid to the subtle ways in which the language of protection has begun to authorise more expansive forms of intervention short of force, for example, in the demands made for increased access by Western media and NGOs to conflict situations or for a dramatic shift in the acceptability of providing logistical support and training to rebel groups. Yet, it in these routine practices of what we might broadly call 'international policing' that the political effects of the responsibility-to-protect concept will be determined.

Notes

1 UN Secretary General, '*Implementing the responsibility to protect: Report of the Secretary-General*', UN doc., A/63/677, 12 January, 2009.
2 International Commission on Intervention and State Sovereignty (ICISS), *Report of the International Commission on intervention and state sovereignty: The responsibility to protect* ,Ottawa: International Development Research Centre, 2001, p. vii.
3 David Rieff, *A Bed for the Night: Humanitarianism in crisis*, New York: Simon and Schuster, 2003; Fabrice Weissman (ed.), *In the Shadow of "Just Wars": Violence, politics and humanitarian action,* Ithaca: Cornell University Press, 2004.
4 ICISS (see n. 2), p. 31.
5 UN Press Release. *Secretary-General presents his annual report to General Assembly*, UN doc., SG/SM/7136, GA/9596, 20 September, 1999 (at http://www.un.org/News/Press/docs/1999/19990920.sgsm7136.html).
6 'Report of the Secretary-General pursuant to General Assembly Resolution 53/35: The fall of Srebrenica', 15 November 1999, UN doc., A/54/549, 1999.
7 *Report of the panel on United Nations Peace Operations* (Brahimi Report) (2000) UN doc., A/55/305-S/2000/809 , 21 August 2000, p. 9.
8 Ibid, p. ix.
9 Ibid. p. xv.
10 Samantha Power, *Chasing the Flame: Sergio Vieira de Mello and the fight to save the world*, London: Penguin Books, 2008, p. 206.
11 Millennium Report: 48 Millennium Report of the Secretary-General of the United Nations, *We the Peoples: The role of the United Nations in the 21st century*, UN doc., A/54/2000, 2000, p. 48.
12 Felice Gaer, 'Reality check: Human rights NGOs confront governments at the UN', in Thomas G. Weiss and Leon Gordenker (eds.), *NGOs, the UN and global governance*, Boulder: Lynne Reinner, 1996, pp. 51–52.
13 Jeff King and Alan Hobbins, 'Hammarskjöld and human rights: The deflation of the UN human rights programme 1953–1961', *Journal of the History of International Law*, 5, 2003, pp. 337–386.
14 Samuel Moyn, *The Last Utopia: Human rights in history*, Cambridge: The Belknap Press, 2010.
15 Anne Orford, 'Moral internationalism and the responsibility to protect', *European Journal of International Law*, 24, 2013, pp. 83–108.
16 *Declaration on Principles of International Law Concerning Friendly Relations and Co-operation Among States in Accordance with the Charter of the United Nations* (Friendly Relations Declaration), UN doc., GA Res 2625, 1970; and, *Declaration on the Definition of Aggression*, UN doc., GA Res 3314, 1974.
17 Christine Gray, *International law and the use of force* (3rd ed.), Oxford: Oxford University Press, 2008, p. 33–5.
18 Orford, 'Moral internationalism' p. 94.
19 Muthucumaraswamy Sornarajah, 'Power and Justice: Third world resistance in international law', *Singapore Yearbook of International Law*, 10, 2006, pp. 19–57.
20 Constantin Fasolt, *The limits of history*, Chicago: Chicago University Press, 2004, p. 28.
21 International Commission on Intervention and State Sovereignty (ICISS), *Report of the International Commission on Intervention and State Sovereignty: The Responsibility to Protect* ,Ottawa: International Development Research Centre, 2001,
22 Ibid, p. vii.
23 Gareth Evans, 'From humanitarian intervention to the responsibility to protect', *Wisconsin Journal of International Law*, 24, 2006, pp. 703–22.
24 Francis Deng, Sadikiel Kimaro, Terrence Lyons, Donald Rothchild, and William Zartman, *Sovereignty as Responsibility: Conflict management in Africa*, Washington, DC: The Brookings Institution, 1996.

25 Ibid, pp. 1–2.
26 Ibid, p. xvi.
27 ICISS, *Report of the International Commission*, p. 13.
28 Ibid.
29 Ibid, p. 17.
30 Ibid, p. 11.
31 Ibid.
32 Ibid, p. 17.
33 Ibid, pp. 19–24.
34 Ibid, p. 39.
35 Gareth Evans and Ramush Thakur, 'Correspondence: Humanitarian intervention and the responsibility to protect', *International Security*, 37, 2013, p. 203.
36 World Summit Outcome, UN doc., GA Res. 60/1, 24 October 2005. paras 138–9.
37 Ibid, para. 139.
38 Alex J. Bellamy, *Responsibility to Protect: The global effort to end mass atrocities,* Cambridge: Polity Press, 2009, p. 95.
39 UN press release, *Secretary-General defends, clarifies '"responsibility to protect" at Berlin event on "responsibility to protect: International cooperation for a changed world"'*, UN doc., SG/SM/11701, 15 July, 2008.
40 Ibid.
41 UN Secretary-General, *Implementing the responsibility to protect,* p. 7.
42 UN Secretary-General, *Early warning, assessment and the responsibility to protect: Report of the Secretary-General*, UN doc., A/64/864, 14 July.2010, p. 4, 8.
43 Michel Foucault, *Security, Territory, Population: Lectures at the Collège de France 1977–1978,* trans. G. Burchell, Hampshire: Palgrave MacMillan, 2007, and Pasquale Pasquino, 'Spiritual and earthly police: theories of the state in early-modern Europe', in Markus D. Dubber and Mariana Valverde (eds.), *The New Police Science: The police power in domestic and international governance*, Stanford: Stanford University Press, 2006, pp. 42–72.
44 Robert Reiner, 'Policing a postmodern society', *Modern Law Review*, 55, 1993, p. 762.
45 Markus Dubber and Mariana Valverde, 'Perspectives on the power and science of police', in Markus D. Dubber and Mariana Valverde (eds.), *The New Police Science: The police power in domestic and international governance*, Stanford: Stanford University Press, 2006, p. 4.
46 Mark Neocleous, *The Fabrication Of Social Order: A critical theory of police power*, London: Pluto Press, 2000, p. 26.
47 Dubber and Valverde, *The New Police Science*, pp. 4–5.
48 Ann Orford, *International authority and the responsibility to protect,* Cambridge: Cambridge University Press, 2011, pp. 17–22.
49 Victor Gourevitch, 'Foreword', in Richard Koselleck, *Critique and Crisis: Enlightenment and the pathogenesis of modern society,* Cambridge: The MIT Press, 1988, p. viii.
50 Ibid, p. viii.
51 Ibid.
52 Richard Koselleck, *Critique and Crisis: Enlightenment and the pathogenesis of modern society,* Cambridge: The MIT Press, 1988.
53 Fasolt, *The limits of history*, pp. 35–6.
54 Ibid, p. 25.
55 Ibid, p. 28.
56 Jean-Hervé Bradol, 'The Sacrificial international order and humanitarian action', in Fabrice Weissman (ed.), *In the Shadow of "Just Wars": Violence, politics and humanitarian action,* Ithaca: Cornell University Press, 2004, p. 4.
57 Michel Feher, *Powerless by Design: The age of the international community,* Durham: Duke University Press, 2000, pp. 134–5.
58 James C. Scott, *Seeing Like a State: How certain schemes to improve the human condition have failed,* New Haven: Yale University Press, 1988.

59 Alex de Waal, 'An emancipatory imperium?: Power and principle in the humanitarian international', in Didier Fassin and Mariella Pandolfi (eds.), *Contemporary States of Emergency: The politics of military and humanitarian interventions*, Brooklyn: Zone Books, 2010, p. 311.

60 Ibid, p. 309.

61 Mark Neocleous, 'Theoretical foundations of the "New Police Science"', in Markus D. Dubber and Mariana Valverde (eds.), *The New Police Science: The police power in domestic and international governance*, Stanford: Stanford University Press, 2000, p. 104.

62 Orford, *International authority and the responsibility to protect*.

63 See further: Orford, *International authority and the responsibility to protect*.

64 Orford, 'From promise to practice? The legal significance of the responsibility to protect concept', *Global Responsibility to Protect*, 3, 2001, pp. 400–24.

65 Ibid.

66 Orford, 'What kind of law is this? Libya and international law', *London Review of Books Blog*, 29 March 2011 (at http://www.lrb.co.uk/blog/2011/03/29/anne-orford/what-kind-of-law-is-this/).

67 Ortner, *International authority and the responsibility to protect*.

68 Permanent Representative of Brazil, *Responsibility while protecting: Elements for the development and promotion of a concept*, Annex to the letter dated 9 November 2011 from the Permanent Representative of Brazil to the United Nations addressed to the Secretary-General, UN doc., A/66/551–S/2011/701, 11 November 2011.

69 UN Security Council, UN doc., S/PV.6531, 10 May 2011.

70 Ibid, p. 11.

71 Ibid.

72 Ibid, p. 11.

73 Permanent Representative of Brazil, *Responsibility while protecting*

74 UN Security Council *Responsibility while protecting* , p. 10.

75 UN Secretary-General, *Address to the Stanley Foundation Conference on the responsibility to protect*, New York, 18 January 2012.

76 Orford, 'The passions of protection: Sovereign authority and humanitarian war', in Didier Fassin and Mariella Pandolfi (eds.), *Contemporary States of Emergency: The politics of military and humanitarian interventions*, Brooklyn: Zone Books, 2010, pp. 346–8.

77 UN Secretary-General, *Responsibility to protect: Timely and decisive response*, UN doc., A/66/874–S/2012/578, 25 July 2012, p. 14.

78 Ibid.

79 Secretary-General's address to Stanley Foundation Conference on the Responsibility to Protect, New York, 18 January 2012.

80 Klaus Mladek, 'Introduction', in Klasu Mladek (ed.), *Police Forces: A cultural history of an institution*, New York: Palgrave Macmillan, 2010, p. 5.

2 Understanding the gap between the promise and the reality of 'the responsibility to protect'

David Chandler

Introduction

One of the most striking aspects of the Responsibility to Protect (R2P) doctrine appears to be the gap between the promise and the reality. In 2001, when the International Commission on Intervention and State Sovereignty (ICISS) published its report 'The Responsibility to Protect', there was little doubt that, as stated in the 'Foreword', the concept of R2P was 'about the so-called "right of humanitarian intervention" – the question of when, if ever, it is appropriate for states to take coercive – and in particular military – action, against another state for the purpose of protecting people at risk in that other state'.[1] The ICISS was tasked with trying to develop a global political consensus on the question of humanitarian intervention, which it believed it had achieved through reformulating the problem in terms of the 'responsibility to protect'. Today, the relationship between the R2P and the right of humanitarian intervention appears to be much less clear. This shift in the meaning of R2P will be the subject of this chapter and is at the heart of the apparent gap between the 'promise' of R2P and the policy realities, which has been facilitated by the fact that it would appear that R2P's universal acceptance has come at a cost to both its meaning and application.

For the advocates of R2P, its endorsement at the UN General Assembly 2005 World Summit is taken as a fundamental turning point. For Gareth Evans, former Australian foreign minister and primary architect and leading authority on R2P, the summit marked 'the really big step forward in terms of formal acceptance of R2P'.[2]

For Alex Bellamy, the summit marked a transformation of R2P from a 'concept' – an idea – to a 'principle' – a 'fundamental truth' based upon a 'shared understanding' and a 'sufficient consensus' – making the right of intervention no longer subordinate to the other key international principle: the right of sovereignty.[3] Yet, even its advocates argue that the summit 'achieved much less than had been envisaged', with leading proponents of the cause expressing a 'deep disappointment' with what had been achieved, and many stating a need for the Summit Outcome to be 'reaffirmed', to be 'operationalised', and for the 'shaky consensus' to be hardened.[4]

Gareth Evans argues that the work of establishing R2P is still to come and involves taking on 'three big challenges'.[5] The first challenge is conceptual: defining the concept – the meaning – of R2P. One would have thought that this was pretty fundamental. In fact, it is strange to talk about R2P as if it had some real existence despite the fact that there is no clarity about what it might actually entail. The second challenge is the institutional one: what institutions are necessary or have the task of carrying 'it' out (whatever the 'it' of R2P might be). The third challenge is the political one: mobilising the political will for the institutions (as yet undecided) to act on R2P (once it is clear what that might mean). This chapter seeks to explain why there should be such a gap between claims of the importance of R2P and the lack of certainty of what the R2P even means, let alone how it might be turned from an 'idea' into established policy 'practice'.

The problems of relating its advocates' ideal of R2P with policy practice will be addressed, first, through a consideration of the R2P on its own terms. It will be argued that the ICISS report should be understood as recognition of the deeper problems of building consensus around the concept of 'humanitarian intervention' rather than as a solution to the problem. In fact, it was the ICISS report itself which sowed the seeds of confusion and evasion which seem to have dogged the concept of R2P. Second, this chapter will put R2P in the broader context of international disengagement and the desire to shift political responsibility away from leading Western states. The gap between the promise and the reality of today's R2P consensus will be located in the fact that it implies less responsibility for Western states to act and to intervene and reflects the broader context of post–Cold War lack of strategic concern with large areas of the world, such as sub-Saharan Africa.

R2P and the ICISS report

In terms of the contrast between the international consensus for R2P at the United Nations Summit and the lack of practical clarity or political obligations, unravelling the gap between rhetoric and reality is made easier when we understand the concept in the context of post–Cold War international relations. The advocates of R2P tend to take R2P out of context and believe that R2P only starts with the ICISS report, without which it is alleged, the idea 'would never have been given birth'.[6] These advocates understand R2P as born in the wake of the UN failure to agree on military intervention for humanitarian purposes, and therefore as inspired by the failures of Rwanda and Srebrenica, and therefore as about saying 'never again' in the face of mass atrocities.

In fact, this view of R2P – understood as the establishment of an international consensus on humanitarian intervention – was a fiction in the heads of a few ICISS commissioners and activists. As Gareth Evans himself states, when the ICISS report was published, shortly after 11 September 2001, international policy and academic focus was elsewhere and 'the report seemed likely to disappear without a trace'.[7] Bellamy goes further to argue that the unpopular US-led invasion of Iraq killed off the desire for discussion of humanitarian intervention and that the war in Iraq was wrongly associated with the R2P.[8] This exaggerates the links being made and conflates the ICISS report opinions with those of international society more broadly, as a reflection of the desire for humanitarian intervention post-Kosovo which is then allegedly muted by Iraq.

In fact, it was international disarray over Kosovo which heralded the first steps away from the 1990s declarations of Western mission and humanitarian responsibility. The ICISS report itself reflected the problems of humanitarian intervention, recasting the 'right of intervention' accruing to Western military actors, as the 'Responsibility to Protect' and shifting the focus away from the interveners to the objects of intervention. The difficulty of justifying Western military intervention was also reflected in the report's shift of focus away from non-consensual military intervention in its argument for a continuum of responsibility: 'to prevent', 'to react' and 'to rebuild'.

While a small group of liberal interventionists saw the ICISS report as a resolution to the problems of gaining international consensus for coercive intervention in the cause of human rights, there is no evidence that this was actually achieved. As Bellamy notes, little consensus was achieved for the argument for giving institutional backing to the concept of humanitarian intervention outside the Canadian government and a few prominent ICISS commissioners themselves.[9] What the report did do was set up a moral case for more engaged regulation and consensual intervention in the domestic policy processes of non-Western states: a framework which the US was keen to promote, especially in relation to sub-Saharan Africa and the newly reconstituted African Union. The R2P continuum implied that few areas of domestic policy-making were now 'out of bounds' once it was established that the international community had a duty to assist potentially 'weak' or 'failing' states in carrying out their responsibility to prevent 'mass atrocity crimes'. The desire to take the edge off the focus on Western-led military intervention and to focus on more indirect mechanisms of 'conflict prevention' was further encouraged by the international policy problems of Western responsibility in the Global War on Terror – most specifically, the war and occupation of Iraq.

In fact, rather than seeing the invasion and occupation of Iraq as nearly ending the R2P discussion, it should be seen as clarifying the dynamic behind R2P. The R2P which emerged post-Iraq reflected more acutely the crisis of confidence about Western intervention, which began to emerge with the ICISS report itself. Where the ICISS report begins to restore the credibility of the UN, highlighting the difficulties Western states faced in mustering the legitimacy for non-consensual intervention if the UN Security Council failed to agree strict criteria, today's framework of R2P is even less confident in a non-bureaucratic and non-legalistic justification for intervention. Where the inability to win a consensus around the Kosovo intervention enabled the UN to regain ground, the discrediting of unilateral action in the international sphere after the Iraq invasion strengthened the UN's hand further and encouraged successive Secretary-Generals to regain the upper hand over the moral agenda of ending mass atrocity crimes.[10]

R2P beyond ICISS

In September 2003, the UN Secretary-General Kofi Annan gave new life to R2P by selecting Gareth Evans to be on the High Level Panel on Threats, Challenges and Change, charged with preparing the ground for the 2005 World Summit declaration. The panel's report, *A More Secure World: Our Shared Responsibility*,[11] released in December 2004, was then used as a basis for the Secretary General's report to the summit, *In Larger Freedom: Towards Development, Security and Human Rights for All*, published in March 2005.[12] Annan took over the R2P language of the ICISS report but distanced it from the use of coercive force, putting the recommendations in different sections of the report. While the discussion on the criteria for coercive intervention was to be a subject for the Security Council and the potential reform of their decision-making powers, the R2P was clarified as a matter of state capacity, as a normative moral principle requiring a state to protect its own citizens.[13]

The separation between the R2P and the use of coercive force continued the shift of focus of the ICISS report; moving further from an emphasis on Western state responsibilities of intervention and towards an emphasis on the responsibilities of the 'failing' state. For the advocates of humanitarian intervention, this was a major shift which, as Evans notes, 'resulted in them being seen as quite separate, rather than inherently linked, proposals when they came to be debated at the World Summit'.[14] Evans was clearly 'unhappy' that Annan's delinking of coercive intervention and R2P had resulted in the failure of the World Summit to adopt any criteria which could legitimise the use of force independently of a Security Council decision.[15]

If we take R2P at face value as 'ending mass atrocities once and for all',[16] then it appears paradoxical that the one thing that did not occur was any international commitment on this precise point. Despite the reproduction of the language of the International Criminal Court, in the construction of mass atrocities as justiciable crimes – 'Each individual State has the responsibility to protect its populations from genocide, war crimes, ethnic cleansing, and crimes against humanity'[17] – there are no institutional obligations which flow from this, other than those which pre-existed the declaration.

Article 138 of the World Summit Outcome declaration asserted that individual states accepted their responsibility to prevent such crimes. Article 139 asserted that the UN General Assembly members were committed 'to helping States build capacity to protect their populations . . . and to assisting those which are under stress before crises and conflicts break out'. The same article went further in declaring that 'the international community, through the United Nations' has the responsibility to protect populations through 'appropriate diplomatic, humanitarian, and other peaceful means, in accordance with Chapters VI and VIII of the Charter'.

Article 139 clarifies that the international community is 'prepared to take collective action, in a timely and decisive manner, through the Security Council, in accordance with the Charter, including Chapter VII, on a case-by-case basis . . . should peaceful means be inadequate and national authorities are manifestly failing to protect their populations from genocide, war crimes, ethnic cleansing, and crimes against humanity'.[18] There is no discussion here of any ICISS-inspired independent criteria which could justify the use of military force independently of the Security Council and the UN Charter framework. The Secretary General's follow-up report, in January 2009, 'Implementing the Responsibility to Protect'[19], confirms this, asserting that: 'the responsibility to protect does not alter, indeed it reinforces, the legal obligations of Member States to refrain from the use of force except in conformity with the Charter'.[20]

In this context, the application of R2P seems little different from a non-R2P response to international crisis situations where mass atrocities are occurring or seem possible. This was highlighted in Kenya, at the end of 2007, where disputed elections led to ethnic-related violence, with 1,000 people killed and 300,000 displaced. UN Secretary-General Ban Ki-moon publicly characterised this as an R2P situation.[21]. Here, R2P was seen to facilitate international pressure on the Kenyan government and to provide a discursive framework for international diplomatic involvement. Even, in the case of Darfur, it was alleged that becoming classed as an R2P situation did not mean that non-consensual force would be used, or that R2P had 'failed' because military coercion was not deployed.[22]

In fact, it appears that the more that R2P has been disassociated from the ICISS focus on justifying military intervention the more confusing the pronouncements of its leading advocates have become. Under ICISS, R2P could justifiably be seen as a concept designed to make humanitarian intervention more acceptable.[23] Yet, in 2008, Gareth Evans was seemingly right to assert that the biggest misunderstanding about R2P was the belief that 'R2P is just another name for humanitarian intervention'.[24] (2008: 56). As Alex Bellamy states, counter-intuitively perhaps, the World Summit Outcome position 'is seemingly at odds with the concerns which animated those most closely associated with the ICISS and with the concerns which have animated most of the commission's commentators'.[25]

R2P 'lite'?

It would appear that all that remains of the R2P is the moral focus on the centrality of the potential victims of 'mass atrocity crimes'. As Gareth Evans states, without the R2P focus on potential atrocity victims, the legitimacy of external intervention in the domestic affairs of 'vulnerable' states would be much more disputed:

> The whole point of embracing the new language of "the responsibility to protect" is that it is capable of generating an effective, consensual response to extreme, conscience-shocking cases in a way that "right to intervene" language simply could not. We need to preserve the focus and bite of "R2P" as a rallying cry in the face of mass atrocities.[26]

Evans seeks to resist the apparent watering-down of the R2P concept, arguing that without the focus on the potential victims of mass atrocities it will not be possible to garner international support for external intervention. Diplomatically, rather than challenge the UN Summit Outcome from a more open position – asserting that the UN has retreated from the assertive military interventionism of the ICISS report – Evans seeks to argue that – in broadening the conception of R2P too far, 'to embrace what might be described as the whole human security agenda' – the UN risks inviting opposition from many states and commentators 'who see it as the thin end of a totally interventionist wedge – as giving an open invitation for the countries of the North to engage to their hearts' content in the *missions civilisatrices* (civilizing missions) that so understandably anger those in the global South, who have experienced it all before'.[27]

He raises the concern that, in this way, the possibility of military intervention would be opened up in a 'whole variety of policy contexts', such as that of the Burmese/Myanmar government's failure to react adequately to Cyclone Nargis, inevitably giving the concept of R2P a bad name. Here, Evans' argument that R2P should be primarily about 'prevention' but also strictly limited in application to 'atrocity situations' becomes a contradiction in terms. Evans himself admits that: 'of course, it is true that some full-fledged R2P mass atrocity situations evolve out of less extreme human rights violations, or out of general conflict environments'.[28] This makes it difficult to understand Evans' determination to have his cake and eat it, concerning prevention (which only makes sense at a general level) and the focus on mass atrocities (where reaction or 'humanitarian intervention' only occurs in specific isolated cases).

At this level, the lack of clarity over R2P, both in conceptual and institutional terms, is an inevitable consequence of its development out of the ICISS report which attempted to muddy the waters over the right of intervention. It is not conceptually possible to consider R2P in terms of prevention, no matter how often the advocates of R2P repeat the mantra that 'prevention is the single most important dimension of the responsibility to protect'.[29] It is not possible to draw the line that makes R2P a tenable concept once it is no longer about legitimising coercive military intervention. Even the language used by Evans to describe the conundrum is contradictory. For example, in relation to Mynamar/Burma, is the situation 'best characterized and responded to as a human rights and democracy problem, requiring whatever mix of pressure and persuasion will best work, or as an R2P situation in the making'?[30] Here, the intimation is that 'an R2P situation' involves the need for military intervention if necessary, but Evans has already stated that not all 'R2P situations' require military intervention; some can be dealt with by international 'pressure and persuasion'. How can a judgement be made in advance about the potential for mass atrocities, in order to enable R2P prevention to take place as some discreet set of practices, separate from international responses to 'a human rights and democracy problem'?

The contradictions multiply as Evans tries to dig himself out of the hole which he has created here. For Evans, the solution to the conundrum is 'the need for some further criteria to be developed and properly applied if any kind of credible "R2P watch list" is to be prepared'.[31] On the basis of a set of indicators, which Evans admits are 'an art rather than a science' and 'essentially seat of the pants judgements', he suggests we can draw up a list of countries which, without mass atrocities 'obviously occurring', are nevertheless of 'R2P concern'.[32] The poverty of the argument is clear, for Evans asserts: first, that these indicators, yet to be properly thought through – such as history of mass atrocities, persistent tensions, poor coping mechanisms, receptivity to external influence and poor leadership – can clearly distinguish a select list of countries; that, second, any such list and labelling could generate a consensus around this classification; and, third, that, once clarified and consented to, some set of discrete policy measures could be set in place to prevent 'mass atrocities' as a distinct sphere of policy intervention.

There is no possibility that a discrete range of prevention, intervention and rebuilding mechanisms can be instituted which address such limited concerns. Mass atrocities do not arise *de novo* but in a context of inequalities and conflict. Some R2P advocates, such as Alex Bellamy, are more aware of this problem. However, even Bellamy tends to underestimate the conceptual vacuum created by shifting the focus of R2P to prevention rather than intervention. He argues that:

> Much work needs to be done on clarifying the responsibility to prevent and identifying the measures required. . . . The first, and perhaps most important, task is to identify precisely what it is that the responsibility to prevent is seeking to prevent and what measures are necessary to achieve that goal.[33]

It appears inevitable that, in shifting the emphasis from intervention to prevention rather than establishing an international consensus on coercive action, we are left merely with a set of questions as to what R2P could mean or how it could be 'operationalised'.

The R2P is dead. Long live R2P

The Secretary General's 2009 follow-up report seeks to evade the problems with the ICISS view of a continuum of responsibility beginning with prevention. Despite the declarations of Gareth Evans, it is clear that in the ICISS formulation the idea of a continuum of intervention, the '3Rs' – 'the responsibility to prevent', 'the responsibility to react' and 'the responsibility to rebuild' – is conceptually problematic, merely developed as an 'add-on', tactically designed to win greater support for the core concern of enabling military intervention.[34] The Secretary-General's report substitutes the ICISS report's 'three pillars' with its own 'three pillar strategy', summarising the World Summit Outcome: Pillar one is 'the protection responsibilities of the State'; Pillar two is 'international assistance and capacity-building' for the State; Pillar three is 'timely and decisive response' by the international community.

Rather than focusing on the responsibilities of Western states to prevent, react and rebuild, the reshaped R2P is focused on the responsibilities and capacities of the 'weak' or 'failing' state, held to be in need of assistance. It is the non-Western state which is at the centre of today's R2P. This is clear in the Secretary General report's reinterpretation of the fundamental cause of mass atrocities: taking the emphasis away from the context of war and conflict and shifting an understanding of causation towards the institutional framework of the state concerned:

> The twentieth century was marred by the Holocaust, the killing fields of Cambodia, the genocide of Rwanda and the mass killings of Srebrenica . . . the brutal legacy of the twentieth century speaks bitterly and graphically of the profound failure of individual States to live up to their most basic and compelling responsibilities.[35]

This shift is of fundamental significance for the 'operationalisation' of R2P today. Framing mass atrocities as occurring as the result of failings at the level of the 'individual State' concerned, implicitly takes these abuses out of any international context of war and conflict and is an interesting re-reading of the history of these events which all occurred in the context of war and intervention and a question over the nature and borders of the state.

The focus on the responsibility of the non-Western state, while having a shaky basis in any historical understanding of the context of mass atrocities, distances the discussion from overt and coercive Western intervention. The R2P of the 2009 follow-up to the World Summit inverses the problematic at the heart of the 2001 ICISS report – the problem is seen to be the weak institutional capacity of some sovereign states not the legal barrier of sovereignty itself:

> As the assembled Heads of State and Government made absolutely clear, the responsibility to protect is an ally of sovereignty not an adversary. It grows from the positive and affirmative notion of sovereignty as responsibility, rather than from the narrower idea of humanitarian intervention. By helping States to meet their core protection responsibilities, the responsibility to protect seeks to strengthen sovereignty, not weaken it.[36]

Where 'humanitarian intervention' put the emphasis on leading Western states overtly intervening to take responsibility for stopping mass atrocities, the new-look R2P argues that Western responsibility is much more limited. Essentially, the role for Western powers is an indirect one, providing support to the 'weak' and 'failing' state in enhancing its 'sovereignty'. Rather than the R2P being a coda for direct humanitarian intervention it has become the key normative justification for the more indirect forms of intervention associated with international state building.[37]

Beyond the rhetoric of its advocates, the R2P appears to be no more about a focus on mass atrocities than it is about establishing a right of humanitarian intervention. Something else would appear to be going on in the gradual transformation from the 'right of humanitarian intervention' of the 1999 Kosovo war to the R2P of the 2001 ICISS report and the R2P of the 2005 World Summit. It seems that successive Secretary Generals have sought to use the ethical or moral consensus around mass atrocities to facilitate a broader strengthening of UN institutions and mandates. For the UN, and for R2P as it exists today, it is not the intervention (or reaction) aspect which is central but the institutionalisation of international cooperation coordinated through the UN. The UN has turned the issue of humanitarian intervention, which in the 1990s threatened to undermine its authority – by questioning the sovereign rights of member states and UN Security Council authority over intervention – into an issue of international governance which asserts the UN's moral authority over major Western powers and post-colonial states. Key to this has been the UN's assertion of an administrative and technocratic agenda of 'good governance' as the solution to a range of problems from development to conflict prevention.

Good governance, bad governments

Today's framework of R2P shifts responsibility away from direct Western solutions, whether economic, political or military, and towards indirect Western engagement, which is held to be able to ameliorate problems but cannot be expected to prevent them:

> The responsibility to protect first and foremost, is a matter of State responsibility, because prevention begins at home and the protection of population is a defining attribute of sovereignty and statehood . . . the international community can at best play a supplemental role.[38]

'Pillar one' of the Secretary-General's 2009 report therefore foregrounds the non-Western state as the bearer of responsibility for mass atrocities.

'Pillar two' asserts that the problems of scarcity and conflict in the non-Western world can be understood through the framework of state institutional capacity. The 2009 Report asks the question 'why one society plunges into mass violence while its neighbours remain relatively stable'? The answer it provides is the neoliberal rational choice perspective which argues that the institutional framework of the state is the key to paths of development or conflict, asserting that this abstract schema is one based on principles which 'hold across political and economic systems' and hold 'regardless of a country's level of economic development'.[39]

This liberal institutional approach understands mass atrocities outside of any concern with economic and social relations, focusing merely on the institutional structures which are held to shape the behaviour of individuals, either providing opportunities and incentives for mass atrocities or limiting the possibility of these occurring:

> Genocide and other crimes relating to the responsibility to protect do not just happen. They are, more often than not, the result of a deliberate and calculated political choice, and of the decisions and actions of political leaders who are all to ready to take advantage of existing social divisions and institutional failures.[40]

The understanding of mass atrocities as a product of institutional shortcomings then sets the agenda for international preventive engagement to assist in institutional capacity-building that would make states 'less likely to travel the path to crimes relating to the responsibility to protect'.[41]

> Experience and common sense suggest that many of the elements of what is commonly accepted as good governance – the rule of law, a competent and independent judiciary, human rights, security sector reform, a robust civil society, an independent press and a political culture that favours tolerance, dialogue and mobility over the rigidities of identity politics – tend to serve objectives relating to the responsibility to protect as well.[42]

These policies flow less from evidence linking institutional frameworks to mass atrocities[43] than from the desire to lower expectations about both Western willingness and capacity to make a substantial difference to ongoing conflicts and instability. Here, the best that the international community can do is to indirectly work to facilitate good governance mechanisms and capacity-build state institutions which are the ultimate solution, rather than the direct provision of expensive social, economic and military resources.

The R2P concept depends upon the conceit that non-political, technical and administrative experts, coordinated through the UN, can understand, prevent and resolve conflict. This conceit only works through reducing social, economic and political problems to technical and administrative questions of institutional governance. At the core of R2P is the assertion that: 'Achieving good governance in all its manifestations – representative, responsive, accountable, and capable – is at the heart of effective long-term conflict and mass atrocity prevention'.[44] R2P's reinterpretation of 'mass atrocities' in the framework of neoliberalism or liberal institutionalism is explained by Gareth Evans in this way:

> Some conflicts that may appear at first sight to be clear-cut examples of loot seeking or a contest over resources – in Sierra Leone and the Democratic Republic of the Congo, for example – were more fundamentally driven by the failures of basic governance: decades of misrule and corruption by parasitic state elites and associated socioeconomic deterioration and institutional decay. These made their ruling regimes extremely vulnerable to both general popular discontent and the specific ambitions of rebels and various external actors, with poor governance not only fuelling political and economic grievances but reducing the risk and cost of mounting violent challenges to it.[45]

However we might understand the proximate causes of conflict – rebel groups or exploitative rulers or external actors seeking to gain resources – the structural causes of conflict and therefore the possibilities of 'mass atrocities' are located in the failing institutions of the state and the lack of good governance.

Liberal institutionalism provides a convenient framework of understanding for the UN, for the answers are not to be found in large scale measures of economic and social transformation nor merely in the prosecution of individuals (as with the ICC), but in the institutional framework of states held to be at risk of 'failing' or of failing to take on 'their most basic and compelling responsibilities'. If the cause of 'R2P situations' is at heart the lack of 'good governance' the solution would appear to be the inculcation of the practices and norms of 'good governance' which are seen to be open to understanding and export, through either the 'carrot' of aid, loans and membership of international institutions or the 'stick' of sanctions and the threat of more coercive forms of intervention. Through marshalling these 'carrots' and 'sticks' with the cooperation of the international financial institutions, regional organizations and associations and the UN's own institutions, the UN is seen to be the key to the coordination of the necessary tasks of prevention and the similar 'good governance' responsibilities of post-conflict rebuilding.

The underlying assumption is that the more that the institutions of the 'failing' or the 'post-conflict' state are engaged with by international institutional actors, the more secure their sovereignty and their capacity to take up their 'responsibilities' will be. In the words of the Secretary-General's follow up report: 'The State . . . remains the bedrock of the responsibility to protect, the purpose of which is to build responsible sovereignty, not to undermine it.[46] Far from a discourse of military intervention – undermining sovereignty – the revamped R2P is understood to be a framework of state capacity-building. As Alex Bellamy notes, the R2P, as endorsed by the World Summit and subsequently by the UN Security Council, is essentially about 'international assistance to help build responsible sovereigns with appropriate capacity'.[47]

The only problem the UN faces in turning the liberal institutionalist perspective into workable policy practice is the fact that even reducing the problem of 'preventing mass atrocities' to a problem amenable to technical and administrative intervention at the level of the 'failing' state is unlikely to prove successful on its own terms. The international state-building literature questions the assumption that greater external engagement can strengthen and cohere states, either in terms of prevention or rebuilding.[48] Many experts argue that international support for states is just as likely to have unintended consequences, whether it is the risk of preventive intervention encouraging conflict or of post-conflict intervention undermining country ownership and creating dependencies. While the best liberal institutional frameworks may well ensure that conflicts can be mitigated or prevented, it seems that there is no clear framework of policy which can ensure that these liberal institutions take root.[49]

Nevertheless, the reposing of economic, social and political problems at the level of institutional frameworks and the solutions at the level of external mechanisms of intervention to assist in creating viable liberal institutions, achieves one important benefit: taking the responsibility for social, economic and political crises away from both international power inequalities and from Western states as policy actors. All that external actors can do is attempt to assist institutional reform: there is no 'illusion' that greater levels of economic aid will work or that democracy is a magic solution. The focus on state institutions of the 'failing state' shifts the policy and coordination responsibility away from Western states and international institutions.[50]

R2P: Divesting Western responsibility

While the R2P was certainly resuscitated by the disastrous invasion and occupation of Iraq, the policy discourse is not one of intervention but of recasting the framework of international regulation. The ICISS report itself could be seen, as above, as less about seeking to ensure that Western powers had a blank cheque for intervention and more as a way of evading the focus on Western responsibility. In the post–Cold War world, it appeared that the more the West declared its responsibility for dealing with conflict and crises, the more Western governments were stuck in the cleft stick of either standing on the side-lines or sending in the marines and coping with body-bags returning home as well as being saddled with responsibilities for outcomes, often in parts of the world where they had little long-term strategic interests. While Kosovo clearly exposed the awkwardness of the 'damned if we do and damned if we don't' dilemma for Western politicians,[51] it was the earlier failure of intervention in Somalia which should be signalled as heralding the start of the policy discussion of R2P.

At the heart the discourse of the Responsibility to Protect appears to be the desire to divest Western responsibility rather than to take it on. As Francis Deng *et al.* noted in the mid-1990s, when the concept of 'sovereignty as responsibility' was first developed, it was necessary as a response to super power withdrawal from Africa:

> It is important to explore the implications of this shift in great power roles for the management of conflict in Africa. In the changing world context of the 1990s, Africa has little choice but to confront a wide variety of clashes on the continent and to do so increasingly on its own. . . . [T]he 'aggravating external factor' had been removed, but so had 'the moderating role of the superpowers both as third parties and as mutually neutralizing allies'. Given Africa's resource constraints, who can assume the mantle of peacemaker when state actors fail to govern responsibly.[52]

In the wake of US disengagement from Africa, understood to have been hastened by the disastrous direct military intervention in Somalia, the question for the policymakers was how to develop a new set of relations emphasising the need for strengthened regional institutions in enforcing stability, with Western states playing a much less directly interventionist role: 'With the great powers reducing their involvement in Africa, further US peacemaking initiatives will most likely emphasize the leading role of local actors and taken an indirect form'.[53] At the end of the 1990s, only around 25 per cent of UN peacekeeping troops were contributed by major Western powers, by the beginning of 2008 this figure was down to 10 per cent.[54] As Bellamy notes: 'there is a vast difference between the states which mandate peace operations and advocate R2P, robust doctrines and civilian protection, and the states which actually contribute most of the troops to UN peace operations'.[55]

In fact, rather than juxtaposing intervention and withdrawal, it would be better to see R2P as a process of relationship management where regulatory frameworks are reshaped under a desire to internationalise regulation in areas which are no longer considered to be of vital security interest. The central area of R2P concern is the regulation of sub-Saharan Africa, and in this guise the policy practice has not lagged behind the declarations of R2P intent. In 2003, the African Union was formally established as a replacement for the Organization of African Unity, reflecting the changing nature of African security. Rather than an organization expressing solidarity between African states against external intervention, the AU was established as a mechanism for external intervention. In this context, the power and authority of the AU was drastically enlarged, with a right of intervention in cases of war crimes, genocide and crimes against humanity.[56]

Bellamy notes that the organisational capacity behind R2P is being built not by Western states or international institutions, like the UN, but by the African Union. The AU's African Stand-By Force (ASF) is being given international funding to build five regional brigades capable of deploying 20,000 troops by 2010. The US aims to train 75,000 African peacekeepers by 2020 through its Global Peace Operations Initiative, and Britain and France are also both heavily involved in training African troops for peacekeeping operation.[57] Bellamy asserts that far from a licence for Western states to take responsibility for 'ending mass atrocity crimes' in sub-Saharan Africa, it appears that the emphasis on "'African solutions to African problems permits the [Security Council] P5 to defer its responsibilities to the AU in cases where the former lacks the political will to act'".[58]

The R2P of the 2005 World Summit Outcome and the Secretary-General's follow-up report in 2009 can only be understood in the wake of the broader shift in the framework of international regulation and intervention since the end of the Cold War. Rather than seeing the mass atrocities of Rwanda and Srebrenica as marking the birth and transformation of R2P, it would therefore make more sense to see Somalia, Kosovo and Iraq as the turning points in the problematisation of Western responsibility and the mutual desire on behalf of both the UN and leading Western states to internationalise responsibility for relationship management with the post-colonial world on the basis of indirect forms of regulation: through intervention at the level of the institutions of the non-Western state and, failing that, at the level of regional organisations. Ironically, this R2P is a far cry from the liberal interventionist fantasy which claimed that Western leaders and Western states would take direct responsibility for intervening in the cause of protecting human rights.

Conclusion

What we are seeing in the shift to liberal institutionalist perspectives, highlighted by the shifting discourse of R2P, is, in fact, a shift away from responsibility. In effect, no one becomes responsible. While the ICC approach of laying responsibility at the feet of individual government leaders and army officials is clearly inadequate as a way of grasping the causes of conflict or of preventing it, the R2P approach suggests even less responsibility. For the R2P, implicitly – as long as state institutions fail to create a framework which enables conflicts to be ameliorated and the rule of law and human rights to be enforced – it is inevitable that political actors will attempt to take advantage and that the incentive, to assume state responsibilities of protection, will be lacking. In this framework, actors in 'failing' states have less responsibility for outcomes, as they are seen to be shaped by their institutional context, with little capacity to overcome these structural constraints.

Even more counterintuitively, international institutions have less responsibilities. The emphasis on 'good governance' as prevention and on institutional reform takes the emphasis away from any broader transformative vision of social, economic and political change. In this context, external Western actors appear to be powerless to influence events and can only 'at best play a supplemental role'.[59] In effect, any external responsibilities are removed once 'mass atrocities' are understood to be structured by institutional frameworks. The blame for recurring crises is located narrowly at the level of post-colonial state societies and political elites rather than in any policy interventions (intended or unintended) by external actors.

The institutionalist perspective of the R2P is both conceptually and institutionally a reflection of the evasion of Western responsibility for others. Conceptually, it denies the economic, social and political frameworks which would inculcate Western powers in the problems and underdevelopment of post-colonial regimes. Institutionally, it seeks to relieve Western states of direct responsibility to respond to crises, through establishing indirect mechanisms of policing and military intervention, as illustrated with the development and training of the African Union. The gap between the promise and the practice of R2P becomes narrowed once the intention to evade Western responsibility is clarified. This makes the calls from R2P advocates for a struggle to muster the political will to turn the R2P from an idea into a practice particularly misleading. It would appear that it is not political will which is lacking here but political understanding.

Notes

1 International Commission on Intervention and State Sovereignty, *Report of the International Commission on Intervention and State Sovereignty: The Responsibility to Protect* (Ottawa: International Development Research Centre, 2001), p. vii.
2 Gareth Evans, *The Responsibility to Protect: Ending Mass Atrocity Crimes Once and For All* (Washington, DC: Brookings Institution, 2008), p. 44.
3 Alex Bellamy, *Responsibility to Protect: The Global Effort to End Mass Atrocities* (London: Polity, 2009), p. 6.
4 Bellamy, *Responsibility to Protect*, pp. 91–3.
5 Evans, *The Responsibility to Protect*, p. 54.
6 Evans, *The Responsibility to Protect*, p. xiiii.
7 Evans, *The Responsibility to Protect*, p. 5.
8 Evans, *The Responsibility to Protect*, p. 70.
9 Bellamy, *Responsibility to Protect*, pp. 70, 95.
10 Evans, *The Responsibility to Protect*, p. 69.
11 *Report of the High Level Panel on Threats, Challenges and Change: A More Secure World: Our Shared Responsibility* (New York: United Nations, 2004).
12 *In Larger Freedom: Towards Development, Security and Human Rights for All*, Report of the Secretary General (New York: United Nations, 2005).

13 Bellamy, *Responsibility to Protect*, p. 76.
14 Evans, *The Responsibility to Protect*, p. 46.
15 Evans, *The Responsibility to Protect*, p. 140.
16 Evans, *The Responsibility to Protect* passim.
17 *UN General Assembly 2005 World Summit Outcome Document*, A/60/L.1, UN doc, 15 September 2005b, Art. 138.
18 *UN General Assembly 2005 World Summit Outcome Document*, Art 138.
19 *Implementing the Responsibility to Protect: Report of the Secretary-General*, A/63/677. UN doc, 12 January, 2009.
20 *Implementing the Responsibility to Protect*, §3.
21 Evans, *The Responsibility to Protect*, p. 51.
22 Evans, *The Responsibility to Protect*, p. 61.
23 Bellamy, *Responsibility to Protect*, p. 52.
24 Bellamy, *Responsibility to Protect*, p. 56.
25 Bellamy, *Responsibility to Protect*, p. 4.
26 Evans, *The Responsibility to Protect*, p. 65.
27 Evans, *The Responsibility to Protect*, p. 65.
28 Evans, *The Responsibility to Protect*, p. 69.
29 Evans, *The Responsibility to Protect*, p. 79.
30 Evans, *The Responsibility to Protect*, p. 73.
31 Evans, *The Responsibility to Protect*, p. 74.
32 Evans, *The Responsibility to Protect*, p. 74.
33 Bellamy, *Responsibility to Protect*, p. 130.
34 Bellamy, *Responsibility to Protect*, p. 52.
35 *Implementing the Responsibility to Protect*, §5.
36 *Implementing the Responsibility to Protect*, §10a.
37 See David Chandler, *Empire in Denial: The Politics of International State-building* (London: Pluto Press, 2006), for more details.
38 *Implementing the Responsibility to Protect*, §14.
39 *Implementing the Responsibility to Protect*, §15.
40 *Implementing the Responsibility to Protect*, §21.
41 *Implementing the Responsibility to Protect*, §44.
42 *Implementing the Responsibility to Protect*, §44.
43 *Implementing the Responsibility to Protect*, §44.
44 Evans, *The Responsibility to Protect*, p. 88.
45 Evans, *The Responsibility to Protect*, p. 88.
46 *Implementing the Responsibility to Protect*, §13.
47 Bellamy, *Responsibility to Protect*, p. 4.
48 For example: Simon Chesterman, Ramesh Thakur and Michael Ignatieff, *Making States Work: State Failure and the Crisis of Governance* (Tokyo: United Nations University, 2005) and Roland Paris and Timothy Sisk, *The Dilemmas of Statebuilding: Confronting the Contradictions of Postwar Peace Operation*s (London: Routledge, 2009).
49 Paris and Siske, *The Dilemmas of Statebuilding*, and Douglass North, *Institutions, Institutional Change and Economic Performance* (Cambridge: Cambridge University Press, 1990).
50 See further: Ashraf Ghani and Clare Lockhart, *Fixing Failed States: A Framework for Rebuilding a Fractured World* (Oxford: Oxford University Press, 2008) and David Chandler, *Hollow Hegemony: Rethinking Global Politics, Power and Resistance* (London: Pluto Press, 2009).
51 Ramesh Thakur and Albrecht Schnabel, 'Unbridled humanitarianism: Between justice, power and authority', in A. Schnabel and R. Thakur (eds.) *Kosovo and the Challenge of Humanitarian Intervention* (Tokyo: UN Press, 2000), p. 497.
52 Francis, M. Deng *et al.*, *Sovereignty as Responsibility: Conflict Management in Africa* (Washington, DC: Brookings Institution, 1996), p. 168.

53 Deng *et al., Sovereignty as Responsibility,* p. 189.
54 Bellamy, *Responsibility to Protect,* p. 161.
55 Bellamy, *Responsibility to Protect,* p. 161.
56 Bellamy, *Responsibility to Protect,* p. 78.
57 Bellamy, *Responsibility to Protect,* p. 161.
58 Bellamy, *Responsibility to Protect,* p. 79.
59 *Implementing the Responsibility to Protect,* §14.

3 The rise and fall (and supposed rise again) of the responsibility to protect (R2P) as a norm of international law

R2P in the human rights landscape

Jeremy Sarkin

Introduction

For some, since 2001, the responsibility to protect (R2P) has become an accepted and useful norm of international law. For others, it has never been accepted, has not been used, and will never be used, in the form that some seek for it to be used, humanitarian intervention. For those people and those states that accept R2P, 2005 was a watershed in its development and application. They argue that from 2005, the year the World Summit adopted its basic premises, R2P became an important part of the global legal landscape. These proponents argue that from 2005 R2P has played a crucial role in ensuring that massive human rights violations are prevented and halted, wherever, and by whomever, they occur. In this context some believe that the intervention in Libya in 2011 is proof that R2P is an accepted component of international law, and that it will now be used routinely. However, until the Libya intervention in 2011, it is more accurate to say that from 2005 R2P as an available concept to be used on the international stage appeared to have clearly been on the decline. Indeed, it was already a waning concept *by* 2005.[1] In fact, until the Libyan intervention, even the theory of R2P was being narrowed; never mind the practice, to the detriment of the original goals. These goals were to ensure that massive human rights violations would be prevented, and steps taken to halt them wherever they were occurring. At present, it is a concept whose future remains murky. What is clearer is that its potential use will remain dependent on the tides of international relations and the processes and issues that play out in international fora, and on the global stage.

This chapter explores the rise, the fall, and now the possible rise again, of R2P. It examines why these fluctuations have occurred over a decade. It argues that while R2P has its direct origins in attempts to reclassify the notion of sovereignty and to shift it away solely as a right so to also include responsibilities, its real source is the Hague Convention of 1899 and its Martens Clause. This clause codified the legal principles of 'laws of humanity, and the requirements of the public conscience'. The source of R2P is also linked to the 1948 Genocide Convention as well as other human rights instruments.

The chapter further explores what R2P means and why even those who believe in it have used different language to describe it variably as a concept, a norm or a principle, and what the implications of this have been for R2P. This is important as the language used by its proponents reflects the shifting understanding of what role(s) R2P could play, what support it enjoys and whether it is on the ascendancy or decline. I also examine the reasons why those who had supported R2P shifted their attitude, before 2011, concerning the meaning of R2P. I assess as well the debate about strategy in the context of fighting for principle, versus the strategy of being pragmatic, and thus constructing a narrower version of R2P in the hope of achieving some level of consensus.

In addition, the decade's developments in international human rights law related to human protection are also examined. The shifting patterns in regional bloc's views concerning human rights as seen in their voting patterns are also interrogated as this is determinative to some extent of what may happen when events occur that provoke efforts to apply R2P, as with Libya in 2011.

The Security Council's role in the protection of human rights in this period is examined, both generally, and with specific respect to decisions on Myanmar/ Burma (2007), Zimbabwe (2008), and Libya (2011) to see what can be deduced as to the role that R2P has played and could play in the future. It is argued that voting patterns in the Security Council on human rights issues concerning these countries, as well as voting patterns at the UN in general, reflect shifting dynamics among member states with regard to support for traditional human rights principles and human rights enforcement mechanisms specifically. It is argued that these shifts have occurred as a result of the ascendency of various regional blocs, and that this alignment and voting on human rights issues have changed as a result of these new patterns. It is argued that between 2005 and 2011, even proponents and supporters of R2P narrowed what they argue R2P meant, and should mean. They did so as a strategy to try and ensure that R2P, even in a more limited version, gets more widespread acceptance. There has, however, been a shift again in 2011 with those in favour of R2P again being stronger in the advocacy around the norm.

While some have seen the norm back on the ascendancy since 2011 because of the UN Security Council resolution on Libya (UNSC Resolution 1973) and the decision to take action there, it will be argued here that it remains largely to be seen whether Libya reflects the upward mobility of R2P, or whether Libya was a rare application of the norm in practice, and thus just a blip on the radar of its application in reality. The Libyan example, it is argued, is probably not the start of a new trend, but rather an isolated or rare example of R2P being used in practice and beyond the rhetoric. It is also argued that the factors unique to the Libyan situation galvanized action in a way that may rarely occur again. Further it will be argued that the fact that action was taken in Libya may actually be a reason why achieving consensus, especially amongst the permanent five of the Security Council, may be more difficult in the future. There may be concern by some states that the application of R2P may have negative consequences for them or in their sphere of influence. The presently ambiguous case of Syria, for example, demonstrates that it is too early make absolute predications. The fact that continuing attempts to take even limited action against the Syrian regime should leave supporters of R2P at best cautiously optimistic.

The emergence and importance of R2P

In the first few years of the twenty-first century there was tremendous optimism and progress, at least in the rhetorical sense, in regard to the development of R2P. This was especially so in the years directly after R2P's adoption in 2001 by the International Commission on Intervention and State Sovereignty.[2] There was even more optimism and hope about its possible role after it was included in the 2004 report of the UN High-Level Panel on Threats, Challenges and Change: *A More Secure World: Our Shared Responsibility*.[3] There was even greater fanfare after it was adopted unanimously as part of the World Summit Outcome document in 2005. The fact that the then UN Secretary-General Kofi Annan proposed using the doctrine in his *In Larger Freedom* reform package and that R2P was included, at least implicitly, in various Security Council Resolutions: in 2006, 2007 and 2008, amongst others resulted in many seeing it as a doctrine whose time had come.[4]

The conceptual substance of R2P, however, emerged specifically in the 1990s in the wake of the Rwandan genocide because it was seen that the international community as a whole, and the Security Council in particular, had not been responsive to massive human rights abuses that had been occurring in various places around the world.[5] Particularly in the wake of the Rwandan genocide, familiar questions were asked about why the world had let genocide occur, especially when there were so many warning signs, and why when it did occur, so few steps were taken until it was too late.

Thus, in the mid-1990s a reassessment began of the role and obligations of the international community with regard to human rights abuse, particularly when they were occurring inside a state and with respect to internally displaced persons.[6] A reformulation of the issue of sovereignty thus came to the fore to ensure that the international community had a framework to 'prevent and respond to gross and systematic violations of human rights where the sovereign state is either unwilling or unable to do so. . . '.[7] As former Secretary-General Kofi Annan stated,[8] 'when we read the [UN] Charter today we are more than ever conscious that its aim is to protect individual human beings, not to protect those who abuse them'.[9] Despite these normative developments, the UN High-Level Panel on Threats, Challenges and Changes stated, 'The Security Council has been neither very consistent nor very effective in dealing with these cases, very often acting too late, too hesitantly or not at all'.[10]

Yet still for many, the addition of the R2P doctrine in 2001 was a sign of a new commitment by the international community to dealing with grave violations, even if committed by a state on its own citizens. Todd Lindberg saw it as a 'revolution in consciousness in international affairs, a departure in the relationship between sovereignty and human rights'[11] while Gareth Evans has noted that 'it has taken the world an insanely long time, centuries in fact, to come to terms conceptually with the idea that state sovereignty is not a license to kill'.[12]

Is R2P a new concept?

R2P as an idea, or even as a part of international law, is not entirely new. For the most part, it is a novel concept in name only. Humanitarian intervention, which for many is the most important, and indeed the most contentious, part of R2P,[13] has its origins at least in the nineteenth century. R2P also has substantive connections to human rights instruments such as the Convention on the Prevention and Punishment of the Crime of Genocide (Genocide Convention) adopted in 1948 and a range of other instruments, including the African Charter on Human and Peoples' Rights.

The real problem is not that the world did not have the tools or have the concepts to take the necessary steps to end mass atrocity. The key issue was, and in fact still is, a universal political unwillingness[14] to take the necessary steps to enforce the earlier concepts that have been available in international law at least from the 1899 Hague Convention with its Martens Clause. This clause codified the legal principles of 'laws of humanity, and the requirements of the public conscience'. It provided additional legal protection to individuals and groups during war and peace, and, as such, the Martens clause is a bedrock of positive international human rights law. Even though positive principles date back thousands of years to the origins of natural law, the clause has shaped the course of customary international humanitarian and human rights law. For instance, the clause's unanimous adoption at the Hague conferences, and acceptance by various international courts, reflect international consensus with regard to non-treaty humanitarian law. Many regard the clause as the official basis, in codified international law, for protection against 'crimes against humanity'. Its 'laws of humanity' and 'requirements of the public conscience' forms the backdrop for states' duties and responsibilities even today. Clearly, R2P has its origins from at least a century ago.[15] Already in 1914 the international community told Turkey that it was committing international crimes in Armenia and that it would be held accountable for those atrocities.

Though the connection of R2P to humanitarian intervention seems on the surface rather clear, whether humanitarian intervention constitutes a critical part of R2P remains a point of contention. For its part, the ICISS sought assiduously to divorce R2P from the concept of humanitarian intervention by changing the terms of the debate.[16] Following ICISS, the UN in its 'A More Secure World' document notes 'the primary focus should be on assisting the cessation of violence through mediation and other tools and the protection of people through such measures as the dispatch of humanitarian, human rights and police missions. Force, if it needs to be used, should be deployed as last resort'.[17]

It is not the availability of the legal means to take steps where abuses are occurring, it is rather the political will to reign in those who commit massive human rights abuses that remains suspect. While the world has embarked on a number of international processes recently to hold individual perpetrators, especially leaders, accountable, holding states accountable and taking steps against a state seems far more out of the reach of the international community in general. However, the case of *Bosnia v. Serbia* before the ICJ shows that even this might be changing.

Many human rights activists, as well as concerned citizens around the world, saw the developing notion of R2P in the twenty-first century as a major positive step by the international community to take steps to prevent human rights abuse. This must be seen in the context of the atrocities committed in the twentieth century when about 170 million people were killed as a result of the 250 conflicts that occurred since World War II.[18] Problematically, while civilian casualties were only about 5 per cent in World War I, by the 1990s, civilian casualties accounted for about 90 per cent of the total.[19]

International legal developments over the last decade

Only with recent developments of the last decade or so in international law have the effort to reduce levels of impunity been really significant. While some domestic trials have taken place since the Nuremburg and Tokyo trials of the 1940s, until 1993, when the International Criminal Tribunal for the former Yugoslavia (ICTY) and 1994, when the International Criminal Tribunal for Rwanda (ICTR) were established, no international criminal tribunal existed to punish those responsible for international crimes.[20] But starting with the two ad hoc tribunals there has been a developing commitment to dealing with gross human rights violations. Indeed, it can be argued that with the fight against impunity, there has been some degree of practical commitment to R2P's central concern, ending mass atrocities once and for all.[21]

Obviously, the most momentous of these achievements was the coming into being of the International Criminal Court, which resulted from the 1998 Rome Conference. That year also saw former Chilean dictator General Augusto Pinochet, who stepped down from power in 1990, after enacting an amnesty law absolving him of criminal liability, being arrested in London on a Spanish arrest warrant. This arrest, under notions of universal jurisdiction, has been significant for the development of international criminal justice and the rule of law. Critically, many of those who committed gross human rights abuses have remained beyond the law. But, the developments of the 1990s make it more likely that those who commit gross human rights abuses will not be able to escape prosecution, especially if they leave their own countries. As a result, a whole range of former leaders, who have committed the most heinous of crimes, live today in their own countries or in exile in greater fear of prosecution than ever before. The ratification of the international criminal court statute by 120 states has influenced those countries to import the statute's standards as well as international legal principles into domestic law.

At another level, it can be argued that R2P has become more relevant with the establishment of the Human Rights Council, in 2006, in that it now conducts Universal Periodic Review for all UN member states, and not only for those states that have ratified specific human rights instruments that have treaty bodies. In this way a step forward has occurred in reviewing the "domestic affairs" of a state. Thus, sovereignty again has been blunted and states cannot necessarily claim that matters in their countries are internal matters that are not subject to international scrutiny. In this regard there is no claim that only serious international crimes are available for review in the UPR process. All human rights matters are subject to oversight during the interactive dialogue process. While this is a weakened form of oversight, and does not permit the international community to do anything to prevent human rights abuse or take steps where such abuse is occurring, UPR at least provides a greater degree of oversight than before. However, the mechanism of states reviewing other states in a very short period, has major limitations, and is subject to the political process that exists amongst states.

The application of R2P in the international context

The issue of the role, acceptance and application of R2P must be understood in the context of an international human rights system which remains largely dependent on voluntary state compliance, and where enforcement – even when there are massive human rights atrocities – remains limited.[22] Within this milieu, which institution is able to wield authority and determine when steps are taken to prevent or respond to human rights abuse, is important. The institution responsible for authorizing the use of force has been the Security Council, but the Council remains a highly politicized institution whose composition reflects the world as it was in 1945. Its five permanent members wield the veto, often to protect their own interests, often at the expense of preventing massive human rights violations. The Russian and Chinese veto of a draft resolution regarding Syria in February 2012 is the latest case in point. For some, the replacement of the UN Human Rights Commission, by the Human Rights Council, has done little to advance a less politicized human rights process.

Circumstances at the birth of R2P had nevertheless seemed auspicious. Anthony Lewis spoke for many when he argued that the ICISS report 'captured the international state of mind'.[23] (As a result of that normative symmetry, R2P's early life was nothing less than meteoric. In fact, Tom Weiss famously argued, 'With the possible exception of the prevention of genocide after World War II, no idea has moved faster or farther in the international normative arena the Responsibility to Protect (R2P)'.[24] Evans was equally sanguine when he argued in 2007 that 'in the space of just five short years [the concept of R2P] evolved from a gleam in a rather obscure international commission's eye, to what now had the pedigree to be described as a broadly accepted international norm, and one with the potential to evolve further into a rule of customary international law'.[25]

Today, however, these claims of a linear upward trajectory of R2P as a practical and valuable additional international law tool seem somewhat precipitate. As a result, the present status of R2P is decidedly ambiguous. While it may have been true as late as 2005 when it was claimed that R2P reflected 'a profound shift in international law, whereby a growing sense of global responsibility for atrocities is increasingly encroaching upon the formerly sanctified concept of state sovereignty', [26] the reality is that R2P has, for at least half of its time in the normative arena, been on a negative trajectory. Between 2006 and 2011, much of the early momentum enjoyed by R2P and its advocates was checked or reversed. As a result of these declines, Patricia O'Brien, Under-Secretary-General for Legal Affairs at the UN noted that R2P 'is still fragile'.[27] Similarly, Alex Perry, referring to the principles of R2P, such as contingent sovereignty adopted at the 2005 World Summit, has opined, 'That's the theory. It's pretty optimistic. It assumes that the world agrees on the primacy of human rights over national sovereignty and has the resolve to impose that consensus – another heady assumption – on the wayward few'.[28] As he notes – R2P is about theory. But for R2P to be meaningful it must be applicable on the ground in places such as the Democratic Republic of Congo.[29]

The rise and fall of R2P

At the beginning of 2011, R2P was no longer the concept it had been in 2001. While the ICISS in 2001 recognized that there are three specific responsibilities within the concept: the responsibility to prevent, the responsibility to react and the responsibility to rebuild, what this means and even whether these issues are still a part of R2P are unclear.[30] It has been noted, for example, that there is no language of rebuilding in the World Summit Outcome document.

The ICISS stipulated that '[w]here a population is suffering serious harm, as a result of internal war, insurgency, repression or state failure, and the state in question is unwilling or unable to halt or avert it, the principle of non-intervention yields to the international responsibility to protect'. On this footing is predicated the three primary elements embodied in the original R2P:

1 the responsibility to *prevent* (to tackle the causes of conflict and other human-created crises);
2 the responsibility to *react* (to take appropriate action where there are compelling circumstances, including coercive steps such as sanctions or even military intervention as a last resort where there are reasonable prospects of success, taking due regard of the issue of proportionality); and
3 the responsibility to *rebuild* (after an intervention, to provide assistance in dealing with the causes of the conflict, and to assist in reconstruction, reconciliation, and so forth).

With respect to the all-important responsibility to react, various criteria for military intervention were laid out. It was argued that there must be a just cause, there must be the right intention, proportional means are required; it must be the last resort; there must be reasonable prospects of success; the authority to exercise HI must be obtained (from the UN Security Council).

Even then there were sceptics and critics of the ICISS report. Some argued that even the original report, written by those favourable to R2P, overly limits the notion itself because of the compromises in the process which gave too much to those opposed to the very concept itself. Thus, even the ICISS Report was a compromise, and though negotiated and accepted by the likeminded, it was nonetheless narrower than those who proposed a much wider version of R2P. It must also be noted that the ICISS Report left issues purposely vague in order to achieve consensus. This has allowed critics (and even supporters) to read various meanings into the report and where necessary narrow what the intent of the Commission was.

Thus, some have seen the ICISS Report as limiting R2P unduly. Some see that the goal was to allow humanitarian intervention in ways not permitted to occur before. However, even the authors of the ICISS Report realized the massive political connotations of what they were recommending. The report noted that

> as a matter of political reality, it would be impossible to find consensus . . . around any set of proposals for military intervention which acknowledged the validity of any intervention not authorized by the Security Council or General Assembly.[31]

While the 2001 ICISS report specifically stated that the responsibility to prevent has the utmost importance and stated, 'Prevention is the single most important dimension of the responsibility to protect',[32] this is now really what R2P means, for many, in practice. Thus, the responsibility to protect in this guise addresses 'both the root causes and direct causes of internal conflict and other man-made crises putting populations at risk'.[33] While the responsibility to react means 'to respond to situations of compelling human need with appropriate measures, which may include coercive measures like sanctions and international prosecution, and in extreme cases military intervention', this is not seen by many today to be a critical part of R2P. Finally, the responsibility to rebuild provides, 'particularly after a military intervention, full assistance with recovery, reconstruction and reconciliation, addressing the causes of the harm the intervention was designed to halt or avert'. [34] However, as military intervention has really been avoided in the recent debates about the theory of R2P and certainly in the practice of it, it is hardly relevant at all today in the scope of R2P in the majority of circumstances.

Where there was excitement and vibrancy about what the (emerging) norm may mean for human rights protection, by 2011, there was a much more tepid response to using the doctrine to establish peace and prevent human rights abuse. R2Psuffered the consequences of a variety of issues that had occurred in the years between 2005 and 2011. These include the US invasions of Iraq[35] and Afghanistan,[36] the growing strength of the African, Asian and other regional or global blocs and the concomitant reduction in the positions of the North American and European regional blocs in the UN system, particularly as regards human rights issues.[37]

These developments were effected by a range of political relations. These included concerns about the composition of the Security Council, viz. its undemocratic composition. This relates principally to the fact that only the permanent five members of the Security Council have the veto, to the identity of the permanent five and to their often inconsistent use of the veto. Other developments must also be seen to have played a part in concerns about international justice, including the growth of universal jurisdiction and the first indictment of a sitting head of state, Sudanese president Omar Al-Bashir. While his indictment was accepted by some states, it has been roundly criticized by many states in Africa and elsewhere, as well as by the African Union (AU). The AU accused the ICC of 'pouring oil on the fire' by attempting to indict the President. The former President of Algeria, Ahmed Ben Bella, who chaired the AU Panel of the Wise, also criticized the indictments, warning of their 'dangers', including that they could cause an unconstitutional removal of the government. The dispute between France and Rwanda over the Rwandan genocide (related to French complacency and the role of the Rwandan Patriotic Front in the commission of atrocities) and between Spain and Rwanda (related to the presence in the UN peacekeeping mission in Darfur of a Rwandan commander alleged to have had a role in killings after the 1994 genocide) added to the negative reactions to issues such as R2P.

R2P also suffered from a debate between principle and pragmatism. Those who supported and believed in R2P after the ICISS conference in 2001 believed they had to make a choice. They could fight a hard, long, drawn-out, impossible-to-win fight because of things like the composition of the Security Council, or accept the political realities of the international community, including the strengths and composition of those opposed to R2P, and try and get widespread acceptance of a more limited version of it. Many in positions of influence opted for the latter approach, at least until 2011.

Bellamy has argued that in the wake of the Iraq invasion debate, R2P was watered down in crucial areas, indeed Iraq affected R2P to such a degree that it looked like a 'stillborn concept'.[38] Because of the very strong negative reaction to the US intervention in Iraq, many have argued that the exercise of military power should be based on UN authority instead of US capacity.[39]

Why even the 2005 world summit was a setback for R2P

There was a great deal of exuberating at the World Summit in 2005 when R2P was included in the final document. Bellamy notes that the 'adoption of R2P was one of few real achievements of the 2005 World Summit'.[40] But as has been noted, I don't know how the U.N. ever passed that resolution', says Anthony Holmes, head of the Africa program at the Council on Foreign Relations 'maybe all the delegates had a great champagne reception before they signed, but I suspect that many of the countries that voted for it then would never vote for it again'.[41]

While the inclusion of R2P in the World Summit document was hailed as significant, what was missed or ignored was that the language used might in future be used to limit its availability. This is because in order to get R2P included in the World Summit Outcome document the conceptual and operational breadth was significantly reduced. Whereas the original ICISS document prescribed international action in the face of 'serious harm, as a result of internal war, insurgency, repression or state failure' in a more limited way, the Outcome Document recognized that the international community, as a collective, has the 'responsibility to protect' populations only from genocide, war crimes, ethnic cleansing and crimes against humanity.[42] The focus on these specific crimes clearly narrows when R2P may be used. Thus, traditional notions of state sovereignty and non-interference will apply as long as these enumerated crimes are not involved.[43] Thus, while some have sought to extend R2P to cover such human security challenges as HIV/AIDS, proliferation of nuclear weapons, global warming and poverty, these are now not seen to be on the same level as the listed crimes.[44] The General Assembly did, however, find that the Security Council would examine the issues and decide when and if humanitarian intervention should occur 'should peaceful means be inadequate'.[45] What was the inability or unwillingness of a state to protect its citizens became a 'manifest failure'.[46] Thus, the threshold when R2P comes into operation became when the 'national authorities manifestly fail to protect their populations from genocide, war crimes, ethnic cleansing and crimes against humanity'.[47] Thus, this version of R2P has been aptly named 'R2P lite'.[48]

Gareth Evans has thus argued that 'the 2005 General Assembly position was very clear: When any country seeks to apply forceful means to address an R2P situation, it must do so through the Security Council'.[49] However, this is not so clear.[50] The African Union, and some of the various sub-regional actors in Africa, seemingly decided that on a specific occasion, where necessary, they will intervene even without UN Security Council authorization.[51] Thus, who authorizes R2P has become part of the debate about when R2P exists, who applies it and under what circumstances.[52] For some, limiting who authorizes it may mean that more states might support it. It encourages those states that are most critical of R2P, such as Russia and China, to be more likely to support it if they have the power to control its use by using the veto in the Security Council. This issue will be returned to later.

The decline in the role and importance of R2P from 2006

It has been noted that the progressive development of R2P in the first half of the first decade of the twenty-first century did 'not trigger the same alarm bells in Africa as it does in other regions of the world'.[53] Many African states, including South Africa and Tanzania, were initially supportive of R2P.[54] They were in some ways led by Rwanda who, for obvious reasons then related to the 1994 genocide, was committed to advancing the R2P agenda.[55] Now, however, a number of these countries have backtracked on their endorsement of the World Summit document, and in particular their support for R2P, and are joining with, at least as far as what R2P means in practice, countries that have in the past generally opposed the use of R2P.[56] As a result, Gareth Evans has concluded that 'there has been a falling-away of overt commitment to the norm in sub-Saharan Africa (although in substance still remaining a significant theme in the doctrine of the AU and some of the sub-regional organizations)'.[57] Even countries such as Uganda, which supported international justice for their own political interests, have seemingly reversed course. A greater divergence between the West and African countries is particularly noticeable in the case of Zimbabwe. While the United States and Britain were attempting to use the R2P to address a cholera outbreak there, their attempts were blocked by other permanent members of the Security Council, with the support of other African states. African states have, in fact, accused those wishing for intervention in Zimbabwe of using R2P 'as a cover for colonial-style interference'.[58]

Thus, while the European and African positions on international justice and human rights in genocide were largely in agreement in the year following the Rwanda genocide and the development of the justice cascade, a reversal in such unanimity has occurred of late. This can be seen in a number of developments, such as the Fifth Committee of the General Assembly's (Administrative and

Budget) refusal to accept the appointment of a special adviser to the Secretary General to focus on R2P. The committee only agreed to appoint Edward Luck when the term R2P was removed from his title.[59] concerned are those who support R2P that they believe the present climate is so hostile to R2P that it might well suffer consequences simply from being listed as an agenda item for discussion in the General Assembly.[60]

International relations and R2P

The debate about R2P and when it can be applied must be understood in the context of a tremendous reluctance by some, particularly some states whose human rights records have long been subject to criticism, to accept R2P. Some of those states deeply opposed to R2P have argued that it will be used as a 'pretext for political or military domination, or selective enforcement for discriminatory or political motives, and that as a result it could compound a humanitarian crisis'.[61] Some link R2P to the interventions in Kosovo in 1999 and Iraq in 2003, which occurred without Security Council authorization. Others see it as a pretext for regime change.

Even the language used to describe R2P suffers as a result of the larger controversy about the status of R2P. It is described by some as a *norm*, others as a *concept* and even others as a *principle*.[62] The term chosen reflects a person's belief about what the status of R2P is or ought to be. Thus, those who believe that R2P has a high status in international law use the term, principle, norm or emerging norm. In this regard some have questioned how a concept supposedly designed in 2001 could so quickly become a legal norm and an integral part of UN procedures. For their part, both the ICISS and the UN High-Level Panel saw R2P as an 'emerging principle of customary international law'.[63] On the other hand, those who see R2P as having a diminished status, or those who want to imply that there should be less concern by those who fear R2P, use the term *concept*. Surprisingly, however, the World Summit did not refer to the R2P as a concept. It recognized that R2P was more than a concept or an idea.[64]

R2P has been attacked or criticized by those who disapprove of the very idea itself but also by those who are concerned by the possible breadth of R2P. Some are also concerned about the whole R2P as a legal obligation. Even those in favour of the protection of human rights have argued in favour of narrowing its application for a variety of reasons, including the belief that doing so may improve the chances of the norm's acceptance.

As noted earlier, in the years around the World Summit, understanding the difficulty in getting a broad version of R2P accepted a number of States and others around the world who were committed to R2P believed they had to confront a difficult choice. They believed they could fight either to get R2P accepted as a broad concept or for a more "realistic" option – as a narrower version of R2P that had more chance of widespread acceptance. One country that proceeded with the 'realist approach' was Canada, which had sponsored the original ICISS Commission. It adopted a 'long-term approach'. Thus, the Prime Minister of Canada, Paul

Martin, in a speech to the UN General Assembly in September 2004, blinked and argued for a 'watered-down version' of the responsibility to protect. He argued that that 'the responsibility to protect is not a license for intervention; it is an international guarantor of political accountability'. Canada has attempted to win over those against R2P by setting the threshold for intervention very high and that the Security Council ought to authorize any such action. A proposal for a 'code of conduct' for the permanent members of the Security Council was dropped. The code of conduct was seen to be critical in making the Security Council work more effectively, but with it came the probability of less support precisely from those quarters.

Canada was not alone in this strategy. Besides the number of countries that have seen the value in this approach, a number of high-profile norm entrepreneurs have adopted a similar strategy. Ramesh Thakur, one of the most well-known ICISS Commissioners, adopted the approach of trying to get acceptance of a narrower version of R2P. UN Secretary-General Special Advisor Ed Luck's language when he referred to R2P, at least in the past, also seems to narrow what R2P meant. Luck referred to R2P as a concept, a lesser connotation than a norm, or even an emerging norm. In this regard he has noted that 'it is, in fact, a political concept, not a legal one'.[65] Luck, in 2010, argued that R2P only applies to four crimes and that it is not about humanitarian intervention. He argued: 'The concept of the responsibility to protect was developed precisely to provide an alternative to the largely discredited notion of unilateral coercive intervention for humanitarian purposes'.[66]

UN Secretary-General Ban Ki-moon took a similar approach. In 2008 he argued that

> RtoP is not a new code for humanitarian intervention. Rather, it is built on a more positive and affirmative concept of sovereignty as responsibility. . . . RtoP should be also distinguished from its conceptual cousin, human security. The latter, which is broader, posits that policy should take into account the security of people, not just of States, across the whole range of possible threats. . . . Our conception of RtoP, then, is narrow but deep. Its scope is narrow, focused solely on the four crimes and violations agreed by the world leaders in 2005. Extending the principle to cover other calamities, such as HIV/AIDS, climate change, or response to natural disasters, would undermine the 2005 consensus and stretch the concept beyond recognition or operational utility.[67]

In 2010 Ban Ki-moon further told the General Assembly's Interactive Dialogue on the Responsibility to Protect that discussion of R2P must now focus on early warning and assessment. While the Secretary-General's report in 2009 was titled 'Implementing the Responsibility to Protect', in 2010 it was titled 'Early Warning, Assessment and the Responsibility to Protect'. In his 2010 speech he noted: 'Today, we are gathered to exchange views on early warning and assessment. This is the right place to start for several reasons'. In other words, let's deal with the issue of prevention and not the issues of reaction. Thus, the message was clear – let's deal with the preliminary and less-contentious issues and not the more difficult ones, at least for now.

Regardless of outcome, the strategy of attempting to build a consensus by limiting the reach of R2P has been criticized. Referring to the original search for a means of intervening to stop mass atrocities when the Security Council is unable to act, Byers argued that 'unilaterally conceding your most important point is hardly the optimal way to commence negotiations, since the other side will invariably seek further concessions'.[68] The result of this, however, is that, as Bellamy notes, when governments, regional organizations and the UN talk about R2P they mean not the concept put forward by the ICISS but the principle endorsed by world leaders at the 2005 World Summit and reaffirmed by the Security Council in 2006'. As Ed Luck argues, it is important not to confuse what we would like the R2P principle to be with what it actually is.

For many, though, this fundamentally undercuts what R2P was supposed to be about and calls into question the international community's will to take the necessary steps where human rights abuses occur. Certainly, the extent of R2P remains ambiguous. While the International Commission contained fairly clear notions of the duties to prevent, react and rebuild, today questions concerning when the R2P applies, when the R2P begins, who has the responsibility to protect and who should exercise it all remain clouded in the controversy and ambiguity. The issue of the attack on R2P as a concept, as well as on it so as to achieve a reduction in its breadth and application, must also be seen in the context of a wider attack by some on human rights protection in general, and on the mechanisms that can, and do, provide human rights oversight, or attempt to enforce human rights standards globally. Thus, the last few years have seen attempts by some states to reduce the efficacy of mechanisms and standards that promote human rights promotion and protection around the world. The concept of R2P has been seen by those wishing to limit human rights protection as a problem, and the mechanisms that promote such rights as obstacles. Thus, these groups have seen the need to limit R2P's availability and value.

Thus, the attempts to reduce the usefulness and breadth of the R2P must have been part of a much larger effort to effect the protection of human rights standards by some. As this occurs there are those who see compromise as a means to obtain consensus. As a means to obtain greater support, or to get even those opposed to the very idea of R2P itself to be supportive to at least some degree, some are trying to limit what the concept means, and where and how it ought to be practically relevant. This may ensure that R2P itself becomes just a broad concept, rather than having the practical effect of obligating the international community to take specific and definite steps when gross human rights occur. Thus, the limiting of R2P to only four crimes is a major limitation on the protection of human rights. Where atrocities do occur the struggle will be on what types of crimes are occurring, as occurred with Darfur. It will also be used to rationalize when R2P ought to apply to the detriment of the concept itself. This can be seen during the recent Georgia–Russia conflict when the Russian Foreign Minister invoked R2P as one of the justifications for Russia's use of force.[69] In this regard it was noted that

President Dmitry Medvedev, Prime Minister Vladimir Putin and UN Ambassador Vitaly Churkin have described Georgia's actions against the local population in South Ossetia as 'genocide', while Foreign Minister Sergey Lavrov explicitly argued that Russia's use of force was an exercise of the 'responsibility to protect', which applied not only 'in the UN when people see some trouble in Africa' but also under the Russian constitution when its own citizens were at risk.[70]

Thus, limiting which crimes fall into R2P and the specific steps that ought to be taken tries to ensure that few steps will be taken in practice, as can be seen over the last few years.

The issue of who supports R2P and who does not has major implications for human rights in general. Thus, the human rights agenda globally and at the UN has shifted over the last few years. This can be seen through a variety of issues and in a number of events through which a shift can be ascertained in the way human rights issues are viewed and handled. In September 2008 a study found that while EU positions on human rights positions in the General Assembly received more than 72 per cent support in the 1990s they received only 48 per cent support in the years 2006–2007 and 55 per cent support in 2007–2008.[71] The rise in the regional bloc system and the shifting support of these blocs from the EU to the Chinese and Russian positions is blamed for these changes. Thus, the European Council on Foreign Relations found that the EU had lost a lot of support from many of the African states it previously enjoyed.[72] Latin America too has diverged from the European and North American position on issues of Human Rights and international law, pushing a stronger development agenda.[73] While there was a strong alliance in the 1990s between Western and Muslim States, especially during the conflict in the Former Yugoslavia, now countries like Egypt and Pakistan are 'among the staunchest opponents of international action of the UN to protect individual rights (while the US and EU avail criticizing them for fear of losing alliances in the "war on terror")'.[74]

The United States State Department has also noted that support for US positions at the UN has fallen from 50.6 per cent in 1995 to 23.6 per cent in 2006. While these numbers are challenged by some who criticize the methodology used in arriving at these numbers,[75] it has been argued that the voting score for the US on human rights issues fell from 77 per cent is 1997–1998 to 30 per cent in 2007–2008.[76]

The European Council Report notes that the UN agenda is increasingly being shaped by China, Russia and their allies or supporters on a particular issue. Support for the positions of China and Russia in the same period went from 50 per cent to 74 per cent. In other words, the debate is increasingly being shaped by those who are anti-R2P. The implications of this the Report notes are that

if Europe can no longer win support at the UN for international action on human rights and justice, overriding national sovereignty in extreme cases, it will have been defeated over one of its deepest convictions about international politics as a whole. This is particularly true in cases involving the Responsibility to Protect against genocide and mass atrocities, when the humanitarian consequences of inaction are most severe.[77]

This is not isolated to the GA, as at the Human Rights Council the EU position has been defeated in more than half the votes. It has also been argued that at the Human Rights Council there have been attempts to end the Council's oversight of the various country human rights situations. Only the threat by European states to withdraw from the HRC, and the agreement to end human rights monitoring of Belarus and Cuba, ended this attempt.

It is in the Security Council (SC) where there has been the most dramatic developments for human rights in general and R2P specifically. At the SC the Chinese and Russians used the veto on two important human rights resolutions (Burma in 2007 and Zimbabwe in 2008). These events were important tests for R2P. Arguing why Russia used the veto, Yuri Fedotov, the Russian Ambassador to the UK, wrote: 'UN Security Council resolutions exist as a mechanism to address global peace and security issues. It is in clear contravention of the UN Charter to use them to deal with domestic concerns within individual states'.

To this the non-governmental organization iR2P responded:

It is surprising that the Ambassador is more worried about the charge of 'inconsistency' than that of abetting widespread and systematic political violence in Zimbabwe, or indeed that of further discrediting the UN Security Council. As he points out, Russian diplomats have been remarkably consistent in blocking attempts by the Security Council to put pressure on regimes that persecute their own citizens. I'm sure they have some legitimate concerns, but to pass off the crisis in Zimbabwe as a mere 'domestic concern' and not 'an urgent peace and security issue' appears deeply cynical.[78]

Thus, Burma and Zimbabwe were in many ways tests of whether R2P may be implemented in practice in the future. The fact that China and Russia used their vetoes (and used them jointly) on both these occasions is significant. They have very important implications for R2P.

The use of the veto is an interesting issue in this context. The veto power has been exercised 269 times in the UN since 1946.[79] Some of these vetoes have been exercised on the same resolution so the actual number of resolutions vetoed is actually much less. Further the bulk of the vetoes were exercised in the period between 1946 and 1995, when 244 out of the total of 261 vetoes were exercised. Between 1996 and 2008, the veto was only used nineteen times, again at times, on the same resolution. Between 1946 and 2008 Russia used the veto on 124 occasions, the United States eighty-two times, the United Kingdom thirty-two times, France eighteen times and China only on six occasions. It must be remembered though that the seat now held by China on the Security Council was occupied by Taiwan between 1946 and 1971. Taiwan only used the veto once.

High-profile cases, such as the China–Russia joint veto of a recent draft resolution concerning the humanitarian crisis in Syria tend to obscure the fact that the use of the veto has declined in recent years. The veto only has been exercised on seventeen occasions over the last ten years. In fact, the US has exercised about half of the last twenty-one vetoes. The last time before 2007 and 2008 that Russia and

China jointly exercised the veto was in 1972. The veto has thus been used spar-
ingly and has been used jointly by Russia and China on very few occasions. However, it is not only the use of the veto which is important but also the threat of the
veto. This often ensures that resolutions do not even make it to a vote. In addition,
resolutions that are adopted have been watered down as a result of the threat of the
use of the veto.[80] The use of the veto has had significant impact. Today, the veto is
rarely exercised, but when it is, its use is significant. The use of the veto in the
cases of Syria, Burma and Zimbabwe must be seen to be another blow in R2P
becoming realizable and a practical part of international law. However, it must be
noted that developments in 2011 around Ivory Coast saw the Security Council
move towards R2P implementation. The next section evaluates whether that is the
beginning of a trend towards R2P becoming a more used doctrine going forward
or whether what has happened is exceptional hardly to be repeated again.

Libya and R2P

The events of 2011 have had some dramatic effects on the world. Most importantly, the Arab Spring was seen to be a defining moment. Many around the world
saw it as a major change in what was possible and what could occur. It gave hope
to many about what was possible both internationally and domestically. This was
especially true for R2P.

Emboldened by events around the world, including the Arab Spring and the
intervention in Libya, the 2011 report of the Secretary General on R2P, a report
delivered yearly, was now titled 'The Role of Regional and Sub-regional Arrangements in Implementing the Responsibility to Protect'.[81] The link from this title is
clear as to how it was being imagined and how and when R2P could be used. As
Mona Rishmawi has argued, R2P can be useful as a concept if it can rally political
support for human rights protection. Another way of looking at this is that R2P
may be applied if political support for it in a particular context can be obtained.
R2P will probably not be able to be applied again in the future if there is no
regional support for its application in that part of the world. This was a reason why
UN Security Council resolution 1973[82] allowing 'all necessary means' in Libya
came to occur.[83] The region broadly supported action against Libya. Publically the
Gulf Cooperation Council (GCC) called for all available means to be used against
Libya on 8 March 2011. About a day later, the Organization of the Islamic Conference (IOC) joined this call. Thus, the role of the regions, and the need to get them
on board before any action can be contemplated in a specific part of the world, is
now accepted as an imperative, if R2P is going to be applied again in the future.

When the Secretary-General's report was discussed, it was taking place after the
Security Council resolution on Libya and action had been taken in that country.
On this occasion the Secretary General argued that 'we need to sharpen our tools
for prevention and for protection'.[84] It is interesting to note that in the report of the
interactive dialogue the mood change is very apparent. In this regard, a summary
of that meeting notes: 'A majority of statements pointed to the evolution of R2P
from what was seen as a controversial concept when endorsed in 2005 to an

evolving norm that had in the last year become an "operational reality"'. While this is probably a stretch as there are still many states still opposed to it, or who seek to limit R2P's expansion, there seems to be a greater tolerance for R2P than there was even a year previously. However, world events, and the way things play out at various institutions, especially the Security Council, will determine whether R2P is a norm whose time has come or whether the steps taken in 2011 were ones not to be repeated, or only to be taken in really exceptional circumstances.

While some such as Gareth Evans[85] see the intervention in Libya as the indication that R2P is now part of the legal lexicon and that the international community has shown that its application will become the norm, time will tell whether this is true. However, the intervention in Libya may, rather than extending the opportunities for R2P to be applied, have the opposite effect. In this regard, it has been noted that and has been argued by various countries, including India, China, Brazil, Russia and South Africa, that Libya has given R2P a bad name.[86] While the actions and comments of the states that have always opposed R2P are to be expected, what may be problematic is the fact that countries such as Brazil and South Africa may be unwilling to support R2P initiatives in the future. Global politics, the strategic (and particularly commercial) interests of members of the Security Council, particularly the permanent five, and the politics between members of the Security Council, are important in this regard. There is also a fear about what the implications are for them, or their allies, in future. In a very telling statement, Lindiwe Zulu, South African President Jacob Zuma's special adviser on foreign relations, argued that South Africa abstaining on the resolution on Syria: 'We did the right thing. This is because of complications arising from global politics. We weighed our options. But this does not mean we condone what's happening in Syria'.[87]

Critically, the position taken on R2P, by the non-permanent members of the Security Council are important. Brazil for example has noted:

> The protection of civilians is a humanitarian imperative. It is a distinct concept that must not be confused or conflated with threats to international peace and security, or with the responsibility to protect. We must avoid excessively broad interpretations of the protection of civilians, which could link it to the exacerbation of conflict, compromise the impartiality of the United Nations or create the perception that it is being used as a smokescreen for intervention or regime change. To that end, we must ensure that all efforts to protect civilians be strictly in keeping with the Charter and based on a rigorous and non-selective application of international humanitarian law.[88]

In this context, it is important to take account of what occurred concerning the massive human rights violations that were taking place in Syria during 2011.While there had been long discussions about what ought to occur, the memory of what had occurred in Libya was apparent. Thus, agreement about what the Security Council ought to do about the situation could not be achieved between the members of the Council. No resolution was voted on until 4 October 2011. At that vote China and Russia double vetoed that draft. Nine countries supported the resolution

(Bosnia and Herzegovina, Colombia, France, Gabon, Germany, Nigeria, Portugal, the United Kingdom and the United States) which would not have imposed any measures on Libya. Most importantly South Africa, India, Brazil and Lebanon abstained on the resolution. Thus, the power of the newest global BRICS (Brazil, Russia, India, China, South Africa) must not be underestimated in general, and for R2P in particular.

Conclusion

There have been massive changes in the world and developments in the promotion and protection of human rights over the last two decades. As a result of the formation of the various international courts since 1993, international law in general, and international criminal law specifically, have dramatically grown in substance and stature. However, these developments have really been to ensure that individuals are held accountable and not states. Where state accountability has become important is in the various regional systems. However, it is really only the Inter-American and European court systems that are functional in the judicial sense, although the Inter-American Commission and African Commission are playing very useful roles on their respective continents. The African court has only dealt with a few cases, and the ASEAN and Arab systems still do not have such institutions. The role of the sub-regional court systems should not be forgotten, although there have been some regressions in the last year or two with the Sothern African Development Community tribunal being suspended and other courts not hearing many cases.

R2P has benefitted from these developments to some degree, although it has suffered at the same time. The reason being that those who commit violations, especially leaders in repressive states, fear what such a concept might mean in practice. This has impacted R2P significantly.

Nevertheless, the effects of the justice cascade are that major perpetrators of human rights abuse are being held accountable to a greater degree. This is true not only in the international arena but also as a result of universal jurisdiction, where courts in a number of countries are holding perpetrators liable for the human rights crimes they have committed even where there is no connection to the country where the prosecution occurs. While there is some room for optimism about the developments on a range of human rights norms and standards – such as the adoption of the Convention on the Rights of Persons with Disabilities (2006), the International Convention for the Protection of All Persons from Enforced Disappearance (2006), the Declaration on the Rights of Indigenous Peoples (2007), a protocol to the International Covenant of Economic Cultural and Social Rights – other developments are not so positive. The lack of progress on events in Zimbabwe, together with a lack of action on Sudan, Burma, Syria, Belarus and elsewhere, indicate that there is much that needs to be done.

At one level, R2P has, however, more meaning in practice. While in 2002 there were 31,000 peacekeepers on the ground in Africa (from the UN and AU), by 2007 the number was more than 60,000.[89] The total of UN peacekeepers around the world now stands at more than 110,000, at a cost of $8 billion annually.

Significantly, the number of conflicts around the world is assessed to have declined 40 per cent between 1992 and 2005.[90]

Critically, it is Security Council politics which is the major factor determining when and what steps are taken where massive human rights violations are occurring. This in future may be impacted by processes to reform the Security Council.[91] It does remain to be seen if it occurs, and if it does how it will affect these issues, and R2P in particular. If reform does occur, these issues may be impacted by the determination as to how large the Council will be, how many will be permanent members, who they will be, and crucially, who will have the veto. The issue of whether the permanent five will continue to have the veto will be decisive in any negotiations. It is this issue which is likely to hold up any agreement. If agreement is reached on reform the new composition of the Security Council and the powers that that these states have will play a critical role in shaping the developing of R2P, and the international community's response to massive human rights violations.

Prior to 2011 there was a backtracking by some proponents and supporters of R2P. These people supposedly saw the writing on the wall for the development and widespread acceptance of R2P and therefore saw that limiting what R2P was, and narrowing when it could be used, was in the long-term interests of ensuring that R2P remained viable, even if it had to be in a more limited form.

The year 2011 might be a watershed moment for R2P, but the global situation ensures that this is probably not going to occur. In fact, the future of R2P does not look rosy. The commitment that came in the wake of the genocide to never let such events occur again has never been completely been in tune with the political will to do so.[92] Events seem to have bypassed the notion of R2P becoming the norm it was destined to be. If R2P is to become a practical and realizable goal, then much needs to be done by those who support it. A shift in the membership of the Security Council will probably not bring greater support to R2P or mean that it is used more often in practice. It is likely that the rhetoric of R2P will continue to be contained in SC resolutions, and that it will be referred to often. However, the events seem to indicate that the political will to take action is not as widespread as is necessary to take action. The determination not to take action, in cases such as in Burma, Zimbabwe and Syria, seem to indicate that the possibility of R2P being realized in its full form, beyond the rhetoric, are slim. It is possible though, that some cataclysmic event may again shift support towards realizing the goal of international action where massive human rights violations are occurring. At present, though, it does not seem to be sizeable enough to warrant R2P in the form of humanitarian intervention where these events are occurring.[93] When such intervention does occur by the Security Council in a part of the world where security council member states have an interest, or where it occurs into a first world country R2P will be seen to have arrived.

Notes

1 Alex J. Bellamy, 'Libya and the Responsibility to Protect: The Exception and the Norm', *Ethics & International Affairs*, Vol. 25, No. 3, 2011, pp. 263–269, Simon Chesterman, S., 'Leading from Behind: The Responsibility to Protect, the Obama Doctrine and Humanitarian Intervention after Libya', *Ethics & International Affairs,* Vol. 25, No. 3, 2011,

pp. 279–285, and Thomas G. Weiss 'RtoP Alive and Well after Libya', *Ethics & International Affairs*, Vol. 25, No. 3, 2011, pp. 287–292.

2   See: http://responsibilitytoprotect.org/ICISS%20Report.pdf

3   United Nations, High-level Panel on Threats, Challenges, and Change, *A More Secure world: Our Shared Responsibility*. New York: United Nations, 2004.

4   UN Security Council (2006) S.C. Res. 1674, U.N. Doc. S/Res/1674, Apr. 28, 2006, UN Security Council (2007) S.C. Res 1755, U.N. Doc. S/Res/1755, Apr. 30, 2007, UN Security Council (2008) S.C. Res. 1828, U.N. Doc. S/Res/1828, July 31, 2008, see also Jennifer M. Welsh, J.M. (2010) 'Implementing the Responsibility to Protect: Where Expectations Meet Reality', *Ethics & International Affairs*, Vol. 24, No. 4, 2010, pp. 415–30.

5   Gareth Evans, 'The Responsibility to Protect: An Idea Whose Time Has Come . . . and Gone?' *International Relations*, Vol. 22, No. 3, 2008, pp. 283–298, and Thomas G. Weiss, 'The Sunset of Humanitarian Intervention? The Responsibility to Protect in a Unipolar Era', *Security Dialogue*, Vol. 35, No. 2, 2004, pp. 135–153.

6   Deng, F. M. and Cohen R. (1998), *The Forsaken People: Case Studies of the Internally Displaced*, Washington: Brookings Institution Press.

7   Brian Barbour and Brian Gorlick, 'Embracing the "Responsibility to Protect": A Repertoire of Measures Including Asylum for Potential Victims', *International Journal of Refugee Law*, Vol. 20, No. 4, 2008, p. 533.

8   See further, David Chandler, 'The Responsibility to Protect? Imposing the "Liberal Peace"', *International Peacekeeping*, Vol. 11, No. 1, 2004, pp. 59–81.

9   Kofi Annan, 'Two Concepts of Sovereignty', *The Economist*, 18 September 1999, pp. 49–50.

10 UN High-Level Panel on Threats, Challenges and Change, *A More Secure World*, 2004, p. x.

11 Todd Lindberg 'Protect the People', *Washington Times*, September 27, 2005; available at washingtontimes.com/op-ed/20050926–092335–2083r.htm, in Alex J. Bellamy, 'Whither the Responsibility to Protect? Humanitarian Intervention and the 2005 World Summit', *Ethics & International Affairs*, Vol. 20, No. 2, 2006, p. 144.

12 Gareth Evans, 'Delivering on the Responsibility to Protect: Four Misunderstandings, Three Challenges and How To Overcome Them', address to the *StiftungEntwicklung und Frieden*, Development and Peace Foundation, Symposium, 20 Nov. 2007 in Bonn (at www.crisisgroup.org/home/index.cfm?id=5190&1=1)

13 Though the Responsibility to Prevent mass atrocity crimes is given rhetorical pride of place in the original ICISS document, it has been noted that the lion's share of the text deals with the reaction responsibility.

14 Simon Chesterman, *Just War or Just Peace? Humanitarian Intervention and International Law*, Oxford: Oxford University Press, 2003.

15 Jeremy Sarkin, 'The Historical Origins, Convergence and Interrelationship of International Human Rights Law, International Humanitarian Law, International Criminal Law and International Law: Their Application from at Least the Nineteenth Century', *Human Rights and International Legal Discourse,* Vol. 1, No. 1, 2007, p. 137.

16 Gareth Evans, *The Responsibility to Protect: Ending Mass Atrocity Crimes Once and For All,* Washington DC: Brookings Institution Press, 2008.

17 UN High Level Panel on Threats, Challenges and Change, *A More Secure World*, 2004, para. 201.

18 M. Cherif Bassiouni, 'The Normative Framework of International Humanitarian Law: Overlaps, Gaps, and Ambiguities', *Transnational Law and Contemporary Problems*, Vol. 8, No. 2, 1998, pp. 199–276.

19 Simon Chesterman, *Civilians in War,* Boulder: Lynne Rienner Press, 2001, p. 2.

20 Kai Ambos and Mohamed Othman Ambos (eds), *New Approaches in International Criminal Justice: Kosovo, East Timor, Sierra Leone and Cambodia.* Freiburg: Max Planck Institut für ausländisches und internationales Strafrecht, 2003.

21 Evans, *The Responsibility to Protect*, 2008.
22 Penrose, M.M. (1999), "Lest We Fail: The Importance of Enforcement in International Criminal Law," *American University International Law Review,* 15: 321–394.
23 Anthony Lewis, 'The Challenge of Global Justice Now', *Daedulus* Vol. 132, No. 1, 2003, p. 8.
24 Thomas G. Weiss, 'R2P after 9/11 and the World Summit', *Wisconsin International Law Journal*, Vol. 24, No. 3, 2006, p. 741.
25 Evans, 'Delivering on the Responsibility to Protect'..
26 Mark Turner, 'UN "Must Never Again be Found Wanting on Genocide"', *Financial Times*, Sept. 15, 2005 (at http://www.ft.com/cms/s/0/545f929a-2618–11da-a4a7–00000e2511c8.html?nclick_check=1)
27 Patricia O'Brien, '"Responsibility to Protect": United Nations Torino Retreat 2008', *International Journal of Refugee Law*, Vol. 20, No. 4, 2008, p. 714.
28 Alex Perry, 'Congo Seeks Protection', *Time,* 29 January, 2009, p. x.
29 Perry, 'Congo Seeks Protection', 2009, see also Autesserre, this volume.
30 International Commission on Intervention and State Sovereignty (ICSS), *The Responsibility to Protect*, Ottawa: International Development Research Centre, 2001.
31 ICSS, *The Responsibility to Protect*, 2001, para. 6.37.
32 ICSS, *The Responsibility to Protect*, 2001, p. xi.
33 ICSS, *The Responsibility to Protect*, 2001, p. xi.
34 ICSS, *The Responsibility to Protect*, 2001, p. xi.
35 Nicholas J. Wheeler and Justin Morris, 'Justifying the Iraq War as A Humanitarian Intervention: The Cure Is Worse Than the Disease', in R. Thakur and W.P.S. Sidhu (eds), *The Iraq Crisis and World Order*, Tokyo: UN University Press, 2006.
36 Joseph S. Nye, Jr. 'U.S. Power and Strategy After Iraq', *Foreign Affairs*, Vol. 82, No. 4, 2003, pp. 60–73.
37 On the role of regional human rights institutions, see Jeremy Sarkin, 'The Role of Regional Systems in Enforcing State Human Rights Compliance: Evaluating the African Commission on Human and People's Rights and the New African Court of Justice and Human Rights with Comparative Lessons from the Council of Europe and Organisation of American States', *Inter-American & European Human Rights Journal,* 2009, pp. 1–40.
38 Bellamy, *Ethics & International Affairs*, 2006.
39 Weiss, *Security Dialogue*, 2004.
40 Alex J. Bellamy, *The Responsibility to Protect: The Global Effort to End Mass Atrocities*, London: Polity Press, 2009, p. 2.
41 Cited in Perry, *Time*, 2009.
42 Barbour and Gorlick, *International Journal of Refugee Law*, 2008, p. 533.
43 Barbour and Gorlick, *International Journal of Refugee Law*, 2008, p. 533.
44 Barbour and Gorlick, *International Journal of Refugee Law*, 2008, also Evans, *StiftungEntwicklung und Frieden*, 2007.
45 UN General Assembly, *2005 World Summit Outcome*, New York: United Nations, 2005. A/RES/60/1, para. 139.
46 UN General Assembly, *2005 World Summit Outcome*, para. 139.
47 UN General Assembly, *2005 World Summit Outcome*, para. 139. The 26 April 2006 United Nations Security Council Resolution 1674, adopted by the United Nations Security Council, 'Reaffirm[ed] the provisions of paragraphs 138 and 139 of the 2005 World Summit Outcome Document regarding the responsibility to protect populations from genocide, war crimes, ethnic cleansing and crimes against humanity' and commits the Security Council to action to protect civilians in armed conflict.
48 Thomas G. Weiss, *Humanitarian Intervention: Ideas in Action,* Cambridge: Polity Press, 2007, pp. 116–117. See also Alex Bellamy, 'The Responsibility to Protect and the Problem of Military Intervention', *International Affairs*, Vol. 84, No. 4, 2008, pp. 615–639.

49 Evans, 'Russia in Georgia: Not a Case of The "Responsibility to Protect,"' *New Perspectives Quarterly*, Vol. 25, No. 4, 2008, pp. 53–55
50 Alicia Bannon, 'The Responsibility to Protect: The UN World Summit and the Question of Unilateralism', *Yale Law Journal*, Vol. 115, No. 5, 2006, pp. 1156–65.
51 Jeremy Sarkin, 'The Role of the United Nations, the African Union and Africa's Sub-Regional Structures in Dealing with Africa's Human Rights Problems: Connecting Humanitarian Intervention and the Responsibility to Protect', *Journal of African Law*, Vol. 53, No. 1, 2009, pp. 1–33
52 See Yevgeny Primakov, UN process, Not Humanitarian Intervention, Is World's Best Hope', *New Perspectives Quarterly*, 2 Sept. 2004.
53 Greg Puley, 'The Responsibility to Protect: East, West and Southern African Perspectives on Preventing and Responding to Humanitarian Crises', *Project Ploughshares Working Paper*, 05–5, September 2005, p. 19.
54 Bellamy, *The Responsibility to Protect*, 2009.
55 Some of the other influential countries supporting R2P were Argentina, Canada, Chile, Guatemala, Mexico and the United Kingdom.
56 Alex J. Bellamy, "The Responsibility to Protect and the Problem of Military Intervention," *International Affairs*, Vol. 84, No. 4, 2008, pp. 615–639.
57 Evans, *International Relations*, 2008, p. 283.
58 Richard Gowan and Franziska Brantner, 'A Global Force for Human Rights? An Audit of European Powers at the UN', Policy Paper, London: The European Council on Foreign Relations, September 2008, p, 15.
59 UN General Assembly, Fifth Committee, cited in Bellamy, *International Affairs*, 2008.
60 Bellamy, *International Affairs*, 2008, p. 616.
61 Barbour and Gorlick, *International Journal of Refugee Law*, 2008, p. 550.
62 Bellamy, *The Responsibility to Protect*, 2009.
63 Bellamy, *The Responsibility to Protect*, 2009, p. 6.
64 Bellamy, *The Responsibility to Protect*, 2009, p. 5.
65 Edward Luck, 'Taking Stock and Looking Ahead – Implementing the Responsibility to Protect' in *UN Security Council and the Responsibility to Protect: Policy, Process, and Practice*, special issue of *Favorita Papers*, 1/2010, p. 62.
66 Luck, *Favorita Papers*, 2010, p. 62.
67 Ban Ki-moon, 'Secretary-General Defends, Clarifies, "Responsibility to Protect" at Berlin Event on "Responsible Sovereignty: International Cooperation for a Changed World,"' SG/SM/11701 Department of Public Information, News and Media Division, New York, 15 July 2008 (at www.un.org/News/Press/docs/2008/sgsm11701.doc.htm)
68 Michael Byers, 'High Ground Lost on UN's Responsibility to Protect', *Winnipeg Free Press*, 18 Sept. 2005, p. B3.
69 Global Centre for the Responsibility to Protect, *The Georgia–Russia Crisis and the Responsibility to Protect: Background Note*, 2008 (at http://globalR2P.org/pdf/related/GeorgiaRussia.pdf).
70 Evans, *New Perspectives Quarterly*, 2008, p. x.
71 Gowan and Brantner, A *Global Force for Human Rights*, 2008.
72 Gowan and Brantner, A *Global Force for Human Rights*, 2008, p. 4.
73 Gowan and Brantner, A *Global Force for Human Rights*, 2008, p. 15.
74 Gowan and Brantner, A *Global Force for Human Rights*, 2008, p. 15.
75 Gowan and Brantner, A *Global Force for Human Rights*, 2008, p. 18.
76 Gowan and Brantner, A *Global Force for Human Rights*, 2008, p. 25.
77 Gowan and Brantner, A *Global Force for Human Rights*, 2008, p. 1.
78 iR2P, 'Russian Ambassador Challenges R2P Principle', 2008 (at http://www.ir2p.org/2008/07/18/Russian-ambassador-challenges-R2P-principle/).
79 Global Policy Forum, (2015), "UN Security Council" accessed July 20, 2015. https://www.globalpolicy.org/security-council.html.
80 Gowan and Brantner, A *Global Force for Human Rights*, 2008.

81 UN General Assembly, Security Council, 'The role of regional and sub-regional arrangements in implementing the responsibility to protect', Report of the Secretary-General, Un doc. A/65/877–S/2011/393, 2011.

82 The resolution was adopted by a vote of ten in favour and none against. There were five abstentions: Brazil, China, Germany, India and Russia; see UN Security Council, 'Security Council Approves 'No-Fly Zone' over Libya, Authorizing 'All Necessary Measures' to Protect Civilians, by Vote of 10 in Favour with 5 Abstentions', Press Release SC/10200, 17 March 2011.

83 Similar language had been used for the intervention in Somalia in 1992.

84 UN Secretary-General, 'Secretary-General's Remarks to General Assembly Informal Interactive Dialogue on the Responsibility to Protect', Latest Statements (at http://www.un.org/sg/statements/?nid=5410).

85 Evans, 'Ending Mass Atrocity Crimes: The Responsibility to Protect Balance Sheet After Libya', Second Renate Kamener Oration, The Australian Jewish Democratic Society, 31 July 2011 (at www.gevans.org/speeches/speech443.html).

86 Bolopion, Philippe, 'After Libya, the Question: To Protect or Depose?' *LA Times* 25 August 2011.

87 C. Molele, 'SA Defends "Ambivalent" Stance on Syria', *Mail and Guardian*, 8 October 2011 (at http://mg.co.za/article/2011–10–07-sa-defends-ambivalent-stance-on-syria).

88 UN Security Council, 'Security Council Approves "No-Fly Zone", 2011

89 UN Department of Peacekeeping Operations, 'Background Note' (at: www.un.org/Depts/dpko/dpko/bnote.htm) [last accessed 14 April 2008].

90 Human Security Research Group, *Human Security Report 2005: War and Peace in the 21st Century*, New York, Oxford: Oxford University Press, 2005, p. 22.

91 See further, Anne-Marie Slaughter, 'Security, Solidarity, and Sovereignty: The Grand Themes of UN Reform', *American Journal of International Law*, Vol. 99, No. 3, 2005, pp. 619–631.

92 Rajan Menon, 'Pious words, puny deeds: the "international community" and Mass Atrocities', *Ethics & International Affairs*, Vol. 23, No. 3, 2009, pp. 235–246.

93 Jeremy Sarkin and C. Fowler, 'The Responsibility to Protect and the Duty to Prevent Genocide: Lessons to be Learned from the role of the International Community and the Media During the Rwandan Genocide and the Conflict in the Former Yugoslavia', *Suffolk Transnational Law Review*, Vol. 33, No. 1, 2010, pp. 35–86.

4   Africa

Is there a state? Implications of statelessness for a state-centric human protection norm

Brett R. O'Bannon

We might begin with a story

The equipment needed for a research project here in Kounghany, a riverside village a few kilometers downstream from Mali and across the border from Mauritania, was due to arrive weeks ago. It has, however, disappeared into the bureaucratic equivalent of a singularity. To look into the matter we seek to phone colleagues and friends in Dakar as well as the company in Britain that shipped the equipment. That, however, requires a functioning cellular network that has not, in fact, functioned for several days. Fortunately, in addition to the cell phone purchased here, which is wed to the inoperative Senegalese network, whose failure, it is important to note, has raised hardly an eyebrow among the many here who are equally isolated by its failure, I also have a "smart" phone. As I consider turning on the wildly expensive data roaming option that might allow me to e-mail my inquiries to Dakar and abroad, I notice that there is an additional cellular network within reach – not Senegalese, but Mauritanian.

By switching to a network originating in a neighboring state I can now do what I have not been able to do using the Senegalese *réseau* – call the capital city from within the State's own borders. Doing so, however, is how I learn that my equipment has fallen victim to the infinite gravitational pull of the customs bureaucracy. As I seek to phone for assistance from a colleague at the Université Gaston Berger, the Mauritanian cellular network also fails. I recall with greater understanding a remark made 10 years earlier by an elder in a neighboring village. He said, 'when you return to Senegal, tell them about us.' That neighboring village is on the *Senegalese* side of the border.[1]

When I leave here next week, I will likely go back the way I came, on N1, the auto-route that links Dakar with its neighbor Mali. As we approach the city of Kaolack we will encounter a stretch of N1 that only 10 years after it was opened suffers from such severe degradation that for a stretch of about 50 kilometers we will be diverted back and forth across the highway onto such rough terrain that a 4×4 is really required (or a donkey cart). This is still an improvement, however, from the preceding year when the trip out to the village required travel by a completely different – and 300 kilometers longer – route, because the N1 was fully closed at this stretch. For what appeared to be the privilege of using the road, our driver on the way out this year had to pay an internal customs agent African

Financial Community (CFA) 3,000 francs, which the agent explained to me was a fine for driving with an expired license. As we pulled away, the driver showed me his license. It was three weeks from expiration. As to the road itself, the government of then President Abdoulaye Wade had been trying to force the Senegalese construction firm that was awarded the construction contract – and an advance of CFA 10 billion – to fix what it said was poorly constructed. The head of the firm, Bara Tall, however, has said the road's problems result from the state's failure to regulate the country's payload limits. Whatever the cause, the government has not had much success in securing improvements to the road, nor in collecting the CFA 20 million daily fine for delays the president imposed on the construction firm. As the driver explained to me – and as has been well covered in the Senegalese press – the firm has demanded payment of the rest of the contract before it will take restorative action, but the state has refused to pay the remaining sum until the road is repaired. It is a vicious circle of failing governance that leaves those who would use the road seeking alternatives to the public good the state has failed to provide.

Near the end of our journey back to the capital we will travel just south of the city of Thiès. Not long after the historic victory in 2000 of the perennial opposition, the Parti Démocratique Sénégalais (PDS), Thiès became the center of a major political storm when its mayor, and by then *former* Prime Minister – and also the 'political son' of former President Wade – found himself in jail awaiting trial on corruption charges stemming from, *inter alia*, embezzlement of funds allotted for construction and improvements of that principal highway out of the Dakar peninsula. To this observer, who was here at the time of Idrissa Seck's arrest, it first appeared as exemplary good governance (i.e., effective executive and judicial oversight of servants of the commonwealth). The president was even quoted in papers as saying that he could not acquiesce to calls from Seck's supporters demanding his release, for doing so would violate the principal of separation of powers. These events were, however, universally known, I came to see, as but a rupture within the ruling party resulting from the president's fears of the Mayor/Minister's growing popularity.

What, one might ask, do cell phones, highways and allegedly corrupt government officials have to do with the considerably more significant subject of our book, a norm intended to protect people from genocide and other mass atrocity crimes? The answer is that one sees in this vignette the struggle of a state to perform some of the most basic functions associated with contemporary statehood. And the norm we are exploring, and its supporters, make certain assumptions about the universal presence of states as that concept is generally understood. This suggests the need to question that which R2P takes wholly for granted – the universal presence of modern states.

Long before the idea of a 'failed state' became commonplace, Crawford Young dared to ask, 'Is there a State in Zaire?'[2] His question did not suggest that there were no public institutions of authority. He found, in fact, the presidency, its security apparatus and even public education notable for their lingering significance, the first two especially so for their rapacity. He also found significant the emerging societal networks of exchange enabling Zairians to employ survival strategies and secure outside the formal public sphere what the state did not provide. He deemed these budding institutions apolitical, but presciently saw that 'they will not necessarily always remain so.'[3] His analysis did suggest, however, that the 'aberrations of Zaire, which undermined so many conventional assumptions over the years, now challenge established concepts of the state.'[4]

Senegal is no Zaire, of course. On the contrary, despite being home to the continent's longest running rebellion in the southern Casamance region, it is widely seen to be among the most viable of Africa's states. Yet, there is a clear connection between this account of *l'État Sénégalais* and Young's analysis. His research led him to conclude that there were three vectors of decay that seriously compromised the conceptual integrity, to say nothing of the continuing empirical viability, of that matrix of public institutions of sovereign authority we call the State. The first was its *competence*, or the declining ability 'to relate material means to policy ends' (e.g., providing public goods such as transport and communications infrastructure). The second was its *credibility*, or the 'loss of the belief of the citizenry in the capacity of the state to perform its accustomed functions' (as might be evidenced, for example, in a complete lack of surprise among a populace when such basic services as phones, electricity and highways become unusable). The third was its *probity*, or the 'systemization of corruption . . . from petty survival venality at the lower echelons to kleptocracy at the summit'[5] – such as illicit traffic fines amounting to about US \$6.50 or alleged criminal behavior of a minister of state arrested, but never indicted, for stealing more than \$30 million of public money.

The Congolese state, once known as *Bula Matari,* or "the crusher of rocks", named so after its progenitor, Henry Morton Stanley and the brutally efficient manner in which he pursued his objectives, had been left by those pathologies mere 'fragments of institutional reality in a sea of make-believe.'[6] Though far from a failed state as that concept is generally understood, one can see in Senegal essentially the same vectors of decay that ultimately led to Zaire's demise. They certainly leave those living outside the center of gravity of Senegal's political economy feeling so abandoned by the state that they speak as if they no longer live within its borders. And it is worth reiterating that though the rebellion in southern Senegal in no way approaches in scale the horrors of Africa's "first World War" centered on the Congo, after 30 years Senegalese governments now seem content merely to contain the rebellion to the southern region. So at the risk of overgeneralizing about conditions in a continent that should be known more for its diversity, I call into question for Africa that which Young questioned 25 years ago in Zaire, a name, of course, no longer found on the political map. Given the set of conventional assumptions about what constitutes a state, I explore the question of whether Africa can be said to have states in any meaningful sense of the word.

The implications for R2P are significant because despite it being a *human* protection norm, R2P remains a decidedly *state-centric* framework. It is, according to ICISS co-chairs, 'aimed at providing precise guidance for *states* faced with human protection claims in other *states*.'[7] Its state-centrism can be seen in the 'basic principles,' which include: '*state* sovereignty implies responsibility, and the primary responsibility for the protection of its people lies with the *state* itself' and when a people face serious harm 'and the *state* is unwilling or unable' to take action the international community must respond.[8] The Secretary General's "three pillars" of R2P, as articulated in paragraphs 138 and 139 of the 2005 World Summit Outcome Document,[9] are equally statist: 1) The State has the primary responsibility for protecting populations from mass atrocity crimes, 2) the international community has a responsibility to assist States in fulfilling their responsibility and 3) if a State manifestly fails to protect its populations, the international community must be prepared to take collective action.

Any relevance to the human suffering that R2P purports to alleviate or prevent presupposes, therefore, a Westphalian universe of sovereign states. The premise that R2P resolved formerly intractable debates through the conceptual shift from Battati and Kouchner's[10] 'Right to Intervene' to Francis Deng's[11] 'Sovereignty as Responsibility' turns on the assumed presence of states that can first assume (or fail to assume) the responsibility for preventing or responding to mass human suffering. On Deng's view, it is only in the presumably *rare* occasion of a state being unable or unwilling to uphold its sovereign responsibilities for the maintenance of human welfare, that its responsibility, its sovereignty, can be said to transfer to the international community. There has not, however, been adequate concern in the R2P community for whether implicit assumptions regarding normal conditions of state agency are sound.

The central questions thus opened here are what does R2P mean for Africa if what Young found for Zaire, that the state had ceased to exist in any meaningful sense of the word, is true for the continent more generally? For one, it has been said that R2P was designed with Africa as the essential canvass that it emerged out of the African experience.[12] If conditions in contemporary Africa so undermine our basic assumptions about statehood, where does sovereignty (as responsibility or otherwise) presently lie? Some might fear that absent states essential to the norm's conceptual and operational framework, one could reason that African sovereignty lies already with the international community. That is to say, in the absence of the requisite universe of sovereign states, R2P's state-centrism – its presumption regarding the presence of states as they are both juridically and empirically understood – might be constitutive of a wholesale transfer of sovereignty from Africa back to the states from which it was hard won only a half a century ago. Beyond these important conceptual or legal matters are equally important operational questions. Who, or what institutions, in the absence of meaningful state structures, should be recognized as "responsible" parties within the framework of the Responsibility to Protect? Must a human protection norm such as R2P remain wed to formal institutions of state when there is good reason to argue that doing smacks of bad faith?

To explore these ideas I organize the rest of this chapter as follows: I briefly lay out in the second section the contours of what I refer to as the "classical model" of the modern state – a purportedly universal form of organizing a country's public institutions of governance. I construct this model by drawing on the corpus of works from early social theorists of the modern state (e.g., Comte, Hegel, Marx, Durkheim and Weber). One finds in the contemporary global political imaginary a clear resonance of these early voices and a clear reaffirmation of their ideas. Thus by drawing on foundational theories of the state as a basis for analysis of contemporary statehood one can attest to the power of the imaginary's representational forms by seeing that, even in the face of widespread evidence that challenges them, the modern state's genealogical origins remain the basis for contemporary state-centric theorizing. In the third section I explore contemporary research on the state in Africa – despite the difficulty of generalizing in such a diverse context – in order to juxtapose the conditions of contemporary African statehood against the state of the global political imaginary, which is implicit in the Responsibility to Protect. In addition to secondary sources on the African state, I offer a brief analysis of Failed States Index data and cursory references to several years of primary research on statehood and governance in Senegal – that alleged oasis of statehood in a desert of statelessness. Because it is so widely seen as such a viable state it constitutes a "least likely case" to affirm the working hypothesis that there may be no state in Africa. As such, it is a reasonable case from which to make certain generalizations. Having selected secondary sources that examine statehood in all regions of sub-Saharan Africa, I conclude by reflecting on the implications of the stark divergence between the classical model of the modern state and contemporary politics in the place that served as R2P's inspiration.

The state in the contemporary political imaginary

As noted, proponents of R2P make a critical set of assumptions about statehood. They are, in effect, ideas about what constitutes a modern sovereign state. These are not unreasonable assumptions; they logically follow from classical works on the modern state – the corpus of state theory from Comte, Hegel, Marx, Durkheim, Weber and others. Just as importantly, these ideas are rearticulated and reinforced in today's global political imaginary (GPI). The GPI is, at the level of international society, and in reference to contemporary sovereign states, what Montrose refers to in his analysis of Elizabethan politics and Tudor political culture as that 'collective repertoire of representational forms and figures – mythological, rhetorical, narrative, iconic – in which beliefs and practices' are forged.[13] The GPI abounds with state myths that ostensibly explain its origins, its universal form, and the functions, rights and responsibilities international society holds for its members.

Quintessentially iconic in the constitution of states of the global political imaginary is the United Nations, in particular, its General Assembly. Signifying the modern state as the constitutive member of international society, the Assembly is the representational form (and forum) of the ideal type of statehood. Each seat being equal, sovereign equality is not just narrated in textual forms, such as the UN Charter or its 1970 Declaration on Principles of International Law Concerning Friendly Relations and Cooperation Among States, but also in the very architecture of the institution's physical presence. Performances of sovereign equality constitute the business of the Assembly. Juridically equal sovereign heads of state occupy equally spaced seats that enjoy equal voting power and that are arranged to provide a uniform view of the rotating president for which they vote annually. From that mass of uniformity rise to the dais co-equal sovereigns to make pronouncements on behalf of peoples over whom they are presumed to exercise supreme authority. Meanwhile, outside the great hall, the grounds are adorned with regalia doing more of the rhetorical work of the political imaginary. Equal-sized state flags fly at symbolically equal height. There is, in all of that regalia and theater, a classical model of statehood that is being efficiently rearticulated. That it belies the existential verities of political life is seemingly lost in the pomp. It is only obscure academic discourses about states that vary in strength, centralization and secularity that suggest that the emperor might be under-clad. The "classical" model of the modern state that its early theorists forged and that is sustained in this global imaginary is comprised of the following elements.

First, though Comte, in his *Système de politique positive,* was perhaps among the first to make much of this issue,[14] and Marx after him would make even more, it is Durkheim in *Division of Labor*[15] who explores most fully the societal origin of the modern state. For Durkheim, loss of the primordial ties of kinship groups and so forth, which constituted the connective tissue of pre-modern society, gives rise to the modern state. Critical is the need for authoritative sanctioning of society's increasingly complex "contractual" relationships being forged among its increasingly divided laborers and merchants seeking to secure the goods and services they no longer provide for themselves. Contracts never being self-enforcing, the state emerges in an organic relationship to society as that authority responsive to the enforcement needs of society.

Second, having so emerged, the state becomes an independent, autonomous agent able to act both domestically and internationally for itself and/or as a trustee on behalf of the interests of society, or for its hegemonic elements. Hegel is unequivocal on this point. The very 'idea of the state' is 'the individual state as a self-dependent organism.'[16] Weber's conception of the modern state turns squarely on the distinct separation of the means of administration from society and from even those who employ them.[17] Durkheim's functionalist argument for the emergence of the state is also the basis for why it becomes an autonomous, spontaneous power in social life. As pre-modern society's *conscience collective* exercises less and less power over its "directive organ" the state is freed from its earlier, more binding sources of authority.

Third, from what is manifestly a multitude of vertically and horizontally separated institutions of power and authority arises something of an emergent property that is effectively unitary and rational. Hegel, again, is unequivocal: 'The state is absolutely rational . . .'.[18] For Durkheim, rationality is the *raison d'être* of the state: 'its principal function is to think.'[19] The state is, as expressed so commonly today, a rational, unitary actor whose decision-making capacity and ability to act on those decisions reflect *raison d'état*.

Fourth, in what is one of the most commonly cited references from this corpus of social theory, the state is that which lays a successful claim to 'the monopoly of the legitimate use of physical force within a given territory.'[20] Oddly, this most frequently cited conception of the state is not something about which the other early social theorists had as much to say. It is, however, critical to operationalizing

R2P. Comte somewhat begrudgingly concedes the point in his (later) criticism of the state's concentration of power over its territory[21] while Marx, of course, comes to see the state as the instrument of force/violence necessary to maintain the politico-economic order that suffers from its ultimately lethal internal contradictions.

Finally, though the discourse about R2P and Deng's contingent sovereignty suggests that the modern state is only recently endowed with responsibilities of an ethical or moral order, it has, in fact, always been represented as an agent with clear moral imperatives; that is, the state is a moral agent. 'The march of God in the world, that is what the state is' Hegel states, 'the ethical whole.'[22] For Durkheim, the social origin, the division of labor in society, is itself a moral phenomenon. Jones argues that in Durkheim's analysis

> we are led to see the division of labor in a new light – the economic services it renders are trivial by comparison with the moral effect it produces. Its true function, the real need to which it corresponds, is that feeling of solidarity in two or more persons which it creates.[23]

There is thus, 'a social solidarity derived from the division of labor' and given the state's relationship to that division of labor, the state's emergence from societal differentiation is a moral imperative.

In sum, the modern state as theorized in its early form and as it is rearticulated in the contemporary global political imaginary is a rational, unitary actor with moral responsibilities for the increasingly differentiated society whence it emerged. This origin and subsequent moral obligation requires, and therefore functionally endows the state with, an independence of resources, action and thought necessary to successfully exercise the claim to a monopoly on the use of physical force (violence) throughout the territory associated with a given political society. It is about this Weberian notion of a state monopoly on force that human rights activists make particular assumptions as they engage in the business of advancing a human protection norm. A state is a state, for example, *because* it enjoys such a monopoly. But the point made here is that it is time to recognize merely juridical states for what they are not. They are not the state of the global political imaginary. They are not well described by its terms of reference. They do not have its history. They do not execute its functions. They do not, therefore, easily square with states that might be more appropriately subject to a contingent sovereignty. For if they are so subject, they might be said, for all practical purposes, to be seen already as wards of international society.

Let us now consider these elements of modern statehood in light of contemporary African politics.

The juxtaposition

The African State is, of course, a post-colonial state – but it is not just any post-colony. The post-colonial state in Africa is the legacy of 500 years of evolution in the technology or the art of colonial governance. Mere embryos were the enclave sites of penetration of the Venetian Maritime Empire in comparison to that which exploded onto Africa in the 19th century.[24] 'The professionalization and specialization of [Bula Martari's] formal apparatus was far removed from the polity that began the imperial age five centuries before.'[25] Young sees in the state what many see in institutions of all kinds – a power to recreate themselves over time. In particular, '[a] state, once institutionalized, has a formidable capacity for its own reproduction across time and in the face of systematic efforts by new regimes to uproot prior forms and build new blueprints.'[26]

So to what degree can it be said that the African state emerged from societal differentiation (e.g., division of labor)? In only one distinct, and distinctly non-Durkheimian, way, does it seem possible. And in this view it is not *African* societal differentiation that explains its emergence. On the contrary, Boone found considerable European opposition to allowing such a socio-economic phenomenon to occur in the colonies, much less leaving it to determine the nature of the colonial state.[27] Instead, the nature of the colonial state was determined by contests among competing *metropolitan* interests. In the French debate between merchant and industrial capital about capitalist development in the colonies, the former argued that 'we must not create a colonial proletariat . . . which will rapidly become a danger to French sovereignty.'[28] This argument against creating conditions in the colony that would give rise to an industrial division of labor such as Durkheim and others were witnessing in their home countries, 'found support in the political affairs division of the colonial ministry' and thus won the day.[29] The result was a state postured to oppose indigenous, especially rural, interests through a state-enforced *économie de traite*, in which institutions designed to implement protectionist measures assured maintenance of the 'principle of buying African commodities cheap and selling French manufactured goods dear.'[30]

At independence, the state was still essentially the same set of institutions that had long been captured by metropolitan mercantile interests. There was no semblance of an organic state–society relationship. During the colonial period, the critical regime structures had been the great trading houses acting as the state's principle agents of the *économie de traite*. After independence, state opposition to the emergence of contractual exchange relationships among peasant producers and urban consumers remained formal policy. Marketing boards in Dakar, Abidjan and Kampala simply replaced the *maisons de commerce* in Bordeaux and London, and producer prices were kept below market price in furtherance of the urban-bias characteristic of nearly all African states.

African societal differentiation? Indeed. Africa was and is not the undifferentiated mass of Conrad's nightmares. But this differentiation was not meaningfully state determining; it is more accurate to suggest that, in fact, it was state determined. The state was inorganic in origin and thus remains fundamentally alienated from African society. It is, therefore, rather uniformly across Africa despotic in nature. Mbembe emphasizes how, 'the general practice of power has followed directly from the colonial political culture and has perpetuated the most despotic aspects of ancestral traditions, themselves reinvented for the occasion.'[31]

Regarding its autonomy and independence of agency, Weber held that in the modern state . . . no single official personally owns the money he pays out or the buildings, stores, tools and war machines he controls. In the contemporary state – and this is essential for the concept of the state – the "separation" of the administrative staff, of the administrative officials, and of the workers from the material means of administrative organization is complete.[32]

To what degree does the state in Africa enjoy this independence and autonomy of agency? Not having had the requisite origins, attaining such a status would have required a reform of the state's structures of power that merely re-sited the despotism characteristic of the colonial state. There is, thus, after five decades of political analysis of the African post-colony, something of a consensus on the essential nature of governance, or the exercise of power, in contemporary Africa, at least in its broad contours. Though regimes have been formally labeled according to, *inter alia*, pronounced ideologies (radical, conservative, African socialist, etc.), the means by which power was obtained and maintained (e.g., military regimes) or by reference to formal rules about political participation (e.g., multiparty, single-party dominant, one-party and no-party systems), in the end a system of governance commonly referred to as 'personal rule remains prominent' throughout sub-Saharan Africa.[33]

Joseph, in contrasting the exercise of power in Nigeria directly against the Weberian model, found 'patterns of political behavior which rest on the justifying principle that [state] offices should be competed for and then utilized for the personal benefit of office holders as well as of their reference or support groups.'[34] This is the personal appropriation of the means of administration, or the privatization of the state. But what he referred to as 'prebendalism' (aka *clientelism, factionalism, neopatrimonialism* or *"big man" rule*) is not about mere *personal* aggrandizement, though in cases such as Zaire's Mobutu it devolved into little more than that. It is, rather, a mode of governance, of state-building even, that, however dysfunctional and conflict producing it might be, rests upon expectations of reciprocity that patrons will enrich themselves with public resources but shall also share their (privatized) public wealth with their clients.[35] Achebe captured this deeply legitimated practice in his scathing critique of that "Man of the People". In seeing the school-teacher-turned-minister of state returned to his natal village an extraordinarily wealthy man, the protagonist laments,

> Tell them that this man had used his position to enrich himself and they would ask you – as my father did – if you thought that a sensible man would spit out the juicy morsel that good fortune placed in his mouth.[36]

Those villagers, did, however, expect that this man of the people should deliver to them the patronage that was theirs by right.

More is made of this model of power, but far from an independent agent, this mode of governance has been said to have rendered the African polity an *entrêpot* state – a resource, or store of wealth to be appropriated by "big men" and "big women" and distributed as private wealth down through clientelist networks in exchange for political support.[37] Referring to this deeply entrenched mode of governance in Cameroon, citizens of the one-party regime imparted new meaning to the acronym of the ruling Rassemblement Démocratique du Peuple Camerounais by chanting at rallies with just the tonal quality needed to reformulate RDPC into the French verb *redépécer* – or 'cut it up and dole it out!'[38] Seen in this light, the state is endowed with next to none of the autonomy and independence deemed 'essential to the concept' of the modern state. The *longue durée* reveals that not being organically linked to society, having emerged from, at best, European societal differentiation, the state remains but that key prize on which all eyes remain intently focused, in hopes of enjoying a turn at appropriating the common wealth and the opportunity to share it with privileged groups.

Lacking the requisite societal origins that would have linked state to society in the organic way early social theorists envisioned and absent the autonomy of an independent agent, what can be said for seeing the African state as a rational, unitary actor whose decision-making reflects *raison d'état*? Robert Bates, in his landmark work, *Markets and States in Tropical Africa*, lamented that '[p]ublic institutions no longer embody a collective vision but reinforce a pattern of private advantage that may often be socially harmful.'[39] Not content to chalk this apparent lack of public spiritedness up to an inherently African flaw, his analysis of agricultural policy in Africa began by making it a question; 'Why should reasonable men adopt public policies that have harmful consequences for the societies they govern?'[40] In answer he held that 'while acknowledging the importance of public purposes and reasons of state in motivating agricultural policy, we also recognize that more personal motives animate political choices.'[41] For political elites, economically bad policies may represent the soundest political choices. In the context of an *entrepôt* state, and personal or prebendal systems of rule, such choices are those that maximize the rent-seeking capacity of elites, which allow them to maintain their position as "'men of the people". Bates' work made the case that Africans, peasants or elites, were no less rational than anyone else. The structure of incentives in African polities was merely such that bad policy choices made good sense. The state's apparent irrationality belied the opposite.

As influential as this work proved to be, the assumption of state elites acting with an autonomous capacity to determine political outcomes, such as a state crafting its agricultural policies and institutions, has not proved an entirely sound one. Boone's analysis of the ever-contingent nature of the state's central power vis-à-vis local elites demonstrates how badly a "unitary" (an by extension "rational") conception of statehood explains the curious 'political topography of African states,.[42] She demonstrated how the state's institutional "choices" (e.g., land tenure) are not choices at all, but rather the unavoidable result of the central government bargaining with local elites. Because these local elites vary in their capacity to confront the center with demands, the array of center-local relationships delivers institutions that are highly uneven across a state's territory. Seen in this light, the state can be said to enjoy only a contingent internal sovereignty. Beck has noted that these center-local bargaining relationships can actually determine the nature of the regime itself.[43] This means that the formal rules of politics will vary across a state's territory in reflection of the power of local elites to stake claims to preferred modes of governance. Thus some regions of the state may be quite democratic, while others remain considerably less so.

Again, the state must be seen in this light as enjoying but a contingent internal sovereignty and thus far from a unitary entity whose central purpose is, as Durkheim held, "to think". There is much "thinking" going on in the African body politic. Hyden describes a 'fundamental social logic' driving an 'economy of affection' in which distributing personal 'wealth is more rewarding than investing in economic growth';[44] Chabol and Daloz speak of an 'instrumentalization of disorder' by political and economic elites;[45] Reno finds that when rulers of weak states are confronted by challengers to their rule, the former 'intentionally cripple the arms of the state' so as to deny the latter the institutional wherewithal to pursue their aim.'[46] Creativity and ingenuity are as important in African politics as anywhere else. There is simply not much conceptual leverage in packaging this political and economic reasoning as *raison d'état* – the *national interest*.

If the African state, having been forged in the late imperial era, remains estranged from society, and thus cannot determine on its own the nature of its institutions, nor even the kind of regime that will structure state-society relations, what can likely be expected of its capacity to stake a claim to 'the monopoly of the legitimate use of physical force within a given territory?'[47] It would be easy to refer to any of Africa's so-called failed states to attest to this best-known sovereign shortcoming. But what about Africa's *other* states? Consider again Senegal, once described as a 'quite remarkable success story' with a 'uniquely effective political apparatus'[48] and which has, in fact, dispatched military forces to peacekeeping missions in over 20 countries and, at the time of this writing is participating in eight such missions. It is home to a rebellion launched by southern insurgents in 1982 – making this the longest running rebellion on the continent. Though former president Wade came into office in 2000 with the Casamance rebellion high on his list of priorities, no serious effort to bring it to an end appeared anywhere on the government's agenda.

Likewise, it might be hard for new students of Africa to imagine, but only a short time ago Côte d'Ivoire was held to be a model state. Catherine Boone, herself a leading theorist of African statehood, in cautioning against facile generalizations about states in Africa, argued persuasively that

> it will be hard to go back to easy generalizations about 'the African state' if that means we must place Liberia, now decayed beyond the point of recognition, in the same category as neighboring Côte d'Ivoire, which seems to have found strategies for regime survival in the political and economic reforms of the 1990s.[49]

General Robert Guéï, of course, toppled that regime the following year. Three years on, civil war would take the country to the brink of collapse. In 2005 it occupied the top spot in the Failed States Index.

Having relied since independence on a strong French military presence to maintain the regime of Félix Houphouët-Boigny, it is a darkly ironic twist of fate that this critical means of the state's hegemony would be turned so squarely against its successor. In November 2004, the government of Laurent Gbagbo gave up on the peace process and launched operation 'Dignity,' which according to the force commander was intended 'to re-conquer our territory and reunify Côte d'Ivoire.'[50] In what the government insisted was the result of the fog of war, eight French soldiers were killed when their base was bombed by Russian-made and Belarusian-piloted Sukhoi Su-25s. In retaliation, and in what is striking evidence of a state lacking a claim to a monopoly on the legitimate use of force, French President Jacques Chirac 'gave the order to destroy the entire air fleet of a sovereign state [and] in a matter of hours the Ivoirian military lost the entirety of its air force, purchased only a few months earlier.'[51] A sovereign state's air force was utterly destroyed by foreign forces that had been stationed on its territory for over 40 years.

Côte d'Ivoire's fate is indeed ironic, but hardly unique. It is, rather, consistent with Will Reno's conclusions about the struggles of Africa's weak states more generally to claim their sovereign monopoly on violence. He notes that the experience of weak states in Africa 'turns on its head the Weberian notion that a state's viability is proportional to its capacity to monopolize the exercise of violence.'[52] When, for example, the United States, following the end of the Cold War, began to reduce its support for Liberia, 'this monopoly became a liability to [President Samuel] Doe when he ran out of external funds to maintain it and his associates turned this state "strength" into a weapon against him.' Furthermore, Reno notes, 'Sierra Leone's rulers avoided a similar fate for a time by privatizing violence' – contracting out the work of the armed forces to the private military-for-hire company Executive Outcomes.[53] By putting the legitimate means of violence into the hands of foreign, non-state actors the government in Freetown was able to shore up its position vis-à-vis indigenous challengers. But only, of course, for a time.

Whether it is a collapsed state such as Somalia, in which numerous militias vie for control of the remnants of the structures of juridical sovereignty, or the continent's most stable polities, only tenuous claims to Weber's monopoly can be asserted. Reno notes, 'an actuarial calculation showed that as of 1991 the 485 postcolonial African rulers faced a 59.4 percent chance of dying, being imprisoned or being exiled as a consequence of holding office.'[54] The study cited does not make comparisons with non-African states, but we can do so with the Failed States Index. The picture is grim. Not only do African states occupy the top five spots of the current Failed States Index (FSI), but 23 of the most troubled 35 countries are African. Though the continent accounts for only 28% of the world's countries, it constitutes 60% of the states in the highest category of political instability. Not only do African states presently represent the core of a deeply troubled political space, but matters also appear to be getting worse in Africa at a more significant rate than anywhere else. So while the period 2006–2009 registered a *worldwide* trend toward greater instability, African countries suffered a mean increase in their FSI scores (signifying a movement toward state failure) *nearly three times* that of non-African states. Considering only the world's countries that moved toward failure, that is, excluding those registering net improvement, African states still experienced a pace of demise *one and a half times* that of non-African states. It would seem, then, that African states not only suffer a higher probability of succumbing to instability, they also seem to fail faster than non-African states once on the track to failure.

Finally, if the state does not have the origins that would have linked it organically with society, and if, as a result, it does not enjoy the autonomy and independence presumed essential to the concept of the state, and, therefore, it cannot be said to be a rational, unitary actor in any meaningful way, and thus has been shown to have nearly no claim to a monopoly on legitimate force within its territory, can the state in Africa be expected to act as the moral agent described in the classical model, re-articulated in the political imaginary, and as demanded by the Responsibility to Protect?

One of the most influential statements about the moral constitution of the African body politic is Peter Ekeh's analysis of the implications of colonialism. That experience, he argues 'led to a unique historical configuration in modern postcolonial Africa: the existence of two publics instead of one public, as in the West.'[55] Ekeh explains,

> the distinction between public and private realms as used over the centuries has acquired a peculiar Western connotation, which may be identified as follows: the private realm and the public realm have a common moral foundation. That is, what is considered morally wrong in the private realm is also considered morally wrong in the public realm. Similarly, what is considered morally right in the private realm is also considered morally right in the public realm.[56]

The issue is that

> when one moves across Western society to Africa, at least, one sees that the total extension of the Western conception of politics in terms of a monolithic public realm morally bound to the private realm can only be made at conceptual and theoretical peril.[57]

According to Ekeh, there is in Africa a *primordial* public, 'which is moral and operates on the same moral imperatives as the private realm' and a *civic* public, constituted by the legitimating strategies of the colonial era. The civic public 'is amoral and lacks the generalized moral imperatives operative in the private realm and in the primordial public.'[58] We have already discussed the key moral element of the private realm and primordial public in the context of prebendalism. This is the set of reciprocal obligations among kin – however large that group might be construed. Thus, the public realm that is the state lacks the moral foundation that animates private affairs in Africa.

Kin-based moral imperatives and the dialectic between the two publics offer an elegant explanation for prebendalism. The civic public, what Western analysts would see as the state and/or political society, simply reflects the amoral, extractive functionality of the colonial state and the violent and ideological legitimating strategies employed by *Bula Matari* to secure the collaboration of those Bayart identified as the 'active agents in the *mise en dependence* of their own societies.'[59] Ultimately, for Ekeh, 'the most outstanding characteristic of African politics is that the same political actors simultaneously operate in the primordial and the civic publics'[60] and that the 'civic public is starved of badly needed morality.'[61]

On what responsibilities should a state so constituted be expected to deliver? This chapter began with a story about a driver robbed of $6.50 – three days wages for 2.5 billion people in the global South. It also told of a former prime minister charged with stealing from the civic coffers enough money to vaccinate every child in Africa against measles. Coming, as these stories of probity do, from what the CIA *World Factbook* refers to as 'one of the most stable democracies in Africa" is not without meaning.[62] Blundo and Olivier de Sardan, in fact, argue that one cannot begin to understand how politics works in Africa until one accepts the fact that the state in Africa is fundamentally characterized by its *everyday* corruption, from – as Young put it 25 years ago – the highest levels of the state and its connections to industry to the quotidian affairs of all people's lives.[63] Following exacting comparative ethnographic protocols designed to deliver 'first hand' qualitative data on corruption in Africa, they found 'the same "dominant tendencies" everywhere: the same procedures of corruption (and corruption of procedure), the same unwarranted fees, the same "arrangements", the same "tricks".'[64] 'Furthermore,' they argue 'all of these practices were embedded in the same weakness of the official state, the same widespread clientelism and the same impotence – and in part abdication – on the part of the political elites.'[65]

This is not a mere restatement of prebendalism. What they and others have found suggests something deeper. Indeed, current work on the state bespeaks what one might say is a *moral polity* of corruption – a systemic arrangement for the constitution of power and authority reflecting what Ekeh sees as the interaction between the primordial and civic publics. This, I argue, is the ethical and historical (rather than cultural) foundation of prebendalism. The result is as Englebert has said; most African states 'have caused their people much havoc, misery, uncertainty and fear. With some exception, African states have been, mildly or acutely, the enemies of Africans.'[66]

In the moral polity of corruption informal and formal institutions do not run parallel to each other but rather crisscross and interpenetrate each other. The choice is not to focus on the formal or the informal, but rather on their engagement with each other. Reno sees something new emerging in the worst cases of state "failure". The *Shadow State* is forged in the context of warlordism, from the dialectical entanglement of formal and informal – where rulers exit the political realm for the (private) economic realm to reconstitute their lost (public) authority. Increasingly, one sees 'rulers drawing authority from their abilities to control markets and their material rewards.'[67] The power exercised by state officials is, in large measure, the result of non-state affairs. Reno's Shadow State is as Englebert sees it (that it has been largely the enemy of Africans) and is also comprised of the logic of Hyden's economy of affection (e.g., the importance of personal connections over professional competence). Together, however, Reno argues these facts make recognizing entirely 'new manifestations of state power all the more imperative. Personal connection with elite privilege may protect citizens against a state that does not protect them in an institutional sense.'[68] This fact is not insignificant for an analysis of a state-centric human protection norm.

Thus, we see the power that comes from controlling markets – formal or informal. The Shadow State is one in which illicit markets – in drugs, guns, diamonds – is 'integrally linked to the exercise of political power.'[69] Hence in place of what Durkheim envisaged as an entity that would act essentially peacefully and morally, what has emerged even in Africa's most successful states is a moral polity of endemic corruption: commissions for illicit services, unlawful fees for public services, "string-pulling" and so on. [70] This has led Bayart, Ellis and Hibou to conclude that the state in Africa has fundamentally been criminalized.[71] Far from a morally responsible agent, the modern state in Africa is an 'an agent of deception' whose kleptocracy has now risen in many cases to such a level it merits the label "felonious state" – one that 'trades in human beings, drugs, nuclear material, and works of art; piracy and banditry' to mention but a portion of their list.[72] In the end, it is an entity whose central characteristic is 'the illegitimate use of the state's coercive resources or of resources of violent coercion which [may be] private and, hence, illegitimate.'[73] Penumbric politics, which in the worst cases involves warlord leaders or entrenched rebels enriching themselves by the illicit sale of minerals that fuel the fires of Africa's resource wars, and where Weber's monopoly on the use of force is manifest as terrorizing people into submission by drawing on the worst legitimating strategies of *Bula Matari* – amputating the hands and feet of men, women and children – is a far cry from the merely prebendal, neopatrimonial or clientelist states earlier theories of the African state have described. This is an entirely different species. As a moral polity it by definition operates as a moral agent, but in some, or even many, instances it is a moral agent in only the most perverse ways imaginable. This new form, this new moral polity, appears to be a selectively responsible moral agent. It is unavoidably so. For it has been so constituted as the *longue durée* reveals.

Discussion

Achile Mbembe laments that 'while we now feel we know nearly everything that African states . . . *are not*, we still know absolutely nothing about *what they actually are*.'[74] I do not offer here a complete theory for that which has taken the place of the State in Africa, the post-*Bula Matari*. I have, rather, offered a simple, but perhaps provocative, proposition. Africa may lack the very thing R2P requires for it to be operationalized successfully – states, as we typically understand them.

The R2P is a decidedly state-centric framework. The World Summit Outcome document reads:

> Each individual *State* has the responsibility to protect its populations. . . . We (the heads of state) accept that responsibility and will act in accordance with it. The international community should, as appropriate, encourage and help

States to exercise this responsibility. . . . [W]e are prepared to take collective action . . . should . . . *national authorities* manifestly fail to protect their populations.[75]

This state-centric norm turns fundamentally on a contingent sovereignty, which is predicated on the assumption that the state has a natural moral obligation to promote the welfare of the society associated with its recognized territory. This assumption reasonably follows from the logically prior assumption that state and society are organically linked; given the way that the latter's growing division of labor presumably gave rise to the former. In light of that functional explanation for the state's origin, it is reasonable to assume that the state normally enjoys the autonomy needed to effectively marshal its resources (including the forces of violence) in the service of the nation – to know, and to act effectively on, its *raison d'état*.

I have suggested, however, that such a state is not to be found in Africa. Chabal and Daloz similarly argue 'that there are good grounds for thinking that the weak character of the state in Africa may be more perennial than has hitherto been envisaged. It may well be, therefore, that the state in contemporary Africa will durably fail to conform to our own Western notions of political modernity.'[76] If we are correct, then a state-centric framework for human protection centered on a contingent sovereignty may complicate matters a good deal. If the state envisaged in R2P cannot be said to exist in contemporary Africa, if the classical model of the modern state that R2P assumes does not meaningfully capture the moral polity in Africa, then at least two initial problems are raised. First, having shown that one of the continent's most viable "states" can scarcely provide the most basic public goods expected of a state, and that it cannot do so because of the very way in which it is constituted, it seems logically unreasonable to expect it – and especially other less effectual states – to deliver on the considerably higher order responsibilities of the R2P. Second, this means that the contingent sovereignty of R2P can be said to have already relieved Africa of its juridical sovereignty.

To argue, as I have here, that the state in its classical formulation is not that which occupies Africa today is not to claim that Africa is a "train wreck". There is much going on in Africa that merits consideration outside the formal recognized state realm. This is especially true within the context of a human protection discourse. Growing attention, for example, is focusing on a resurgence of traditional authorities in Africa. Throughout this chapter I have spoken of the stark divergence between the state of the global political imaginary, the classical model of the sovereign state, and the realities of politics in contemporary Africa. The case of the *non-state* Somaliland is, perhaps, the paradigm case 'of the mismatch between internationally recognized sovereignty and what might be called "stateness", meaning *de facto* ability of a governing authority to exert control over its territory internally and protect it against external threats.'[77] The state centrism of R2P, however, binds international society to formal sovereign actors in a way that diverts our attention and efforts away from those actors and institutions that may well have the capacity and, therefore, the *responsibility,* to protect Africans from serious harm.

The problem of African statehood explored here does not imply that R2P is irrelevant to Africa's crises of human protection. But it does complicate efforts to operationalize its three pillars. The notion that the state bears primary responsibility for human protection seems on the surface self-evident, indeed a necessary starting point. But, underlying R2P's first and second pillars is a set of Westphalian assumptions that bear scrutiny. If the state has never been organically linked with society, whence, on an empirical level, its obligation to society? If, as is so often the case, the state lacks a meaningful monopoly on the use of violence, how reasonable is it to expect it to provide human protection on a national scale? Why should we necessarily operate as if the state is the most relevant human protection actor? Might it make at least as much sense to consider as agents in the prevention of and response to crimes associated with the R2P non-state actors, such as traditional authorities, civil society and community-based organizations? This is, in fact, consistent with the view of Welsh and Sharma, who conclude that

> the prevention of mass atrocity crimes (particularly through targeted measures) requires a willingness and capacity to deal with individuals – as perpetrators or victims – rather than sovereign states. This too challenges some of the core principles that have governed inter-state relations in the past, such as non-intervention and sovereign equality.[78]

If my view that states as they are conventionally understood are not entirely present in the African context, then indeed proponents of R2P will have to be prepared to challenge a good deal of conventional thinking about inter-state relations.

Notes

1 Brett O'Bannon, 'Receiving an "Empty Envelope": Governance reforms and the management of herder-farmer conflict in Senegal', *Canadian Journal of African Studies*, Vol. 40, No. 1, 2006, pp. 76–100.
2 Crawford Young, 'Zaire: Is there a state?' *Canadian Journal of African Studies,* Vol. 18, No. 1, 1984, pp. 80–82.
3 Young, 'Zaire: Is there a state?' p. 82.
4 Young, 'Zaire: Is there a state?' p. 80.
5 Young, 'Zaire: Is there a state?' p. 81.
6 Young, 'Zaire: Is there a state?' p. 82.
7 International Commission on Intervention and State Sovereignty (ICISS), *Report of the International Commission on Intervention and State Sovereignty: The Responsibility to Protect*, Ottawa: International Development Research Centre, 2001, p. viii [emphasis added].
8 ICISS, *Report of the International Commission on Intervention and State Sovereignty*, 2001, p. 11 [emphasis added].
9 United Nations, General Assembly, 'Resolution 60/1, World Summit Outcome document', UN doc., A/60/L.1, 2005, paragraphs 138 and 139 [emphasis added].
10 Mario Battati and Bernard Kouchner (eds) *Le Devoir d'Ingerence: Peut-on les laisser mourir?* Paris: Les Éditions Denoël, 1987.
11 Francis Mading Deng, Sadikiel Kimaro, Terrence Lyons, Donald Rothchild and William Zartman, *Sovereignty as Responsibility: Conflict management in Africa*, Washington DC: Brookings Institution Press, 1996.

12 Edward Luck, 'Implementing the Responsibility to Protect at the United Nations', Presentation of the Special Adviser to the United Nations Secretary-General at the Asia-Pacific Center for the Responsibility to Protect, University of Queensland, 3 August 2009.
13 Louis Montrose, 'Spenser and the Elizabethan political imaginary', *ELH*, Vol. 69, No. 4, 2002, p. 67.
14 Auguste Comte, *System of Positive Polity, Volume II,* trans. F. Harrison, London: Longman, Green and Co., 1875.
15 Emile Durkheim, *The Division of Labor in Society*, Glencoe, IL: The Free Press, 1947.
16 Georg Wilhelm Friedrich Hegel, *Elements of the Philosophy of Right,* trans. N. Nesbit, Cambridge: Cambridge University Press, 1991, § 259.
17 Max Weber, 'Politics as a Vocation', in H. Gerth and C. W. Mills (eds), *From Max Weber: Essays in Sociology*, New York: Oxford University Press, 1958, pp. 77–128.
18 Hegel, *Elements of the Philosophy of Right,* § 257.
19 Giddens, A. (ed.) (1986), *Durkheim on Politics & the State,* Stanford, Stanford University Press.
20 Weber, 'Politics as a Vocation', p. 78.
21 Richard Vernon, 'Auguste Comte and the Withering-away of the State', *Journal of the History of Ideas*, Vol. 45, No. 4, 1984, pp. 549–66.
22 Hegel, *Elements of the Philosophy of Right,* § 258.
23 Robert Alun Jones, *Emile Durkheim: An introduction to four major works*, Beverly Hills, CA: Sage, 1986, pp. 27–28.
24 Crawford Young, *The African Colonial State in Comparative Perspective*, New Haven: Yale University Press, 1994.
25 Young, *The African Colonial State in Comparative Perspective,* p. 73.
26 Young, *The African Colonial State in Comparative Perspective,* p. 2 [emphasis added].
27 Catherine Boone, *Merchant Capital and the Roots of the Roots of State Power in Senegal,* Cambridge: Cambridge University Press, 1992.
28 Boone, *Merchant Capital and the Roots of the Roots of State Power in Senegal,* p. 38.
29 Boone, *Merchant Capital and the Roots of the Roots of State Power in Senegal,* p. 38.
30 Boone, *Merchant Capital and the Roots of the Roots of State Power in Senegal,* p. 39.
31 Achille Mbembe, *On the Postcolony,* Berkeley: University of California Press, 2001, p. 42.
32 Weber, 'Politics as a Vocation', p. 82.
33 Göran Hydén, *African Politics in Comparative Perspective,* Cambridge: Cambridge University Press, 2006, p. 94.
34 Richard Joseph, *Democracy and Prebendal Politics in Nigeria: The rise and fall of the Second Republic*, Cambridge: Cambridge University Press, 1987, p. 8.
35 Patrick Chabal and Jean-Pascal Daloz, *Africa Works: Disorder as political instrument*, Bloomington: Indiana University Press, 1999.
36 Chinua Achebe, *A Man of the People*, New York: Anchor Books, Doubleday, 1989, pp. 2–3.
37 Hydén, *African Politics in Comparative Perspective.*
38 Bayart, 1989, cited in Mbembe, *On the Postcolony,* p. 106.
39 Robert Bates, *Markets and States in Tropical Africa: The political basis of agricultural policies*, Berkeley: University of California Press, 1981, p. 96.
40 Bates, *Markets and States in Tropical Africa,* p. 3.
41 Bates, *Markets and States in Tropical Africa,* p. 4.
42 Catherine Boone, *Political Topographies of the African State: Territorial authority and institutional choice,* Cambridge: Cambridge University Press, 2003.
43 Linda Beck, *Brokering Democracy in Africa: The rise of clientelist democracy in Senegal,* New York: Palgrave Macmillan, 2008.
44 Hydén, *African Politics in Comparative Perspective,* p. 72; also, Göran Hydén, *Beyond Ujamaa in Tanzania: Underdevelopment and an uncaptured peasantry*, Berkeley: University of. California Press, 1980.

45 Chabal and Deloz, *Africa Works*.
46 William Reno, *Warlord Politics and African States*, Boulder: Lynne Rienner Press, 1999, p. 19.
47 Weber, 'Politics as a Vocation', p. 78.
48 Donal Cruise O'Brien, 'Senegal', in J. Dunn (ed.) *West African States: Failure and promise*, Cambridge: Cambridge University Press, 1978, p. 187.
49 Catherine Boone, '"Empirical statehood" and reconfigurations of political order', in L. Villalón and P. Huxtable (eds) *The African State at a Critical Juncture: Between disintegration and reconfiguration*, Boulder: Lynne Rienner Press, 1998, p. 129.
50 Henri Soupa, 'Côte d'Ivoire: Guerre, medias et violence symbolique', in M. Galy, (ed.) *Guerres Nomades et Sociétés Ouest-africaines.* Paris: L'Harmattan, 2007, p. 145.
51 Soupa, 'Côte d'Ivoire', p. 145.
52 Reno, *Warlord Politics and African States*, p. 139.
53 Reno, *Warlord Politics and African States*, p. 139.
54 Reno, *Warlord Politics and African States*, p. 19.
55 Peter Ekeh 'Colonialism and the Two Publics in Africa: A theoretical statement', *Comparative Studies in Society and History*, Vol. 17, No. 1. 1975, p. 91.
56 Ekeh, 'Colonialism and the Two Publics in Africa', p. 92.
57 Ekeh, 'Colonialism and the Two Publics in Africa', p. 92.
58 Ekeh, 'Colonialism and the Two Publics in Africa', p. 92.
59 Jean-François Bayart, *The State in Africa: The politics of the belly, second edition*, Cambridge: Cambridge University Press, 2009, p. xii.
60 Ekeh, 'Colonialism and the Two Publics in Africa', pp. 92–3.
61 Ekeh, 'Colonialism and the Two Publics in Africa', p. 111 [emphasis added].
62 Central Intelligence Agency, 'Senegal', *World Factbook*, 2010, https://www.cia.gov/library/publications/the-world-factbook/geos/sg.html.
63 Giorgio Blundo and Jean-Pierre Olivier de Sardan, *Everyday Corruption and the State: Citizens & public officials in Africa*, London: Zed Books, 2006.
64 Blundo and Olivier de Sardan, *Everyday Corruption and the State*, p. 70.
65 Blundo and Olivier de Sardan, *Everyday Corruption and the State*, p. 70.
66 Pierre Englebert, *Africa: Unity, sovereignty & sorrow*, Boulder: Lynne Rienner Press, 2009, p. 1.
67 William Reno, *Corruption and State Politics in Sierra Leone*, Cambridge: Cambridge University Press, 1995, p. 3.
68 Reno, *Corruption and State Politics in Sierra Leone*, p. 19.
69 Reno, *Corruption and State Politics in Sierra Leone*, p. 3.
70 Blundo and Olivier de Sardan, *Everyday Corruption and the State*, pp. 72–80.
71 Jean-François Bayart, Stephen Ellis and Beatrice Hibou, *Criminalization of the State in Africa*, Bloomington: Indiana University Press, 1999.
72 Bayart, Ellis and Hibou, *Criminalization of the State in Africa*, p. 14.
73 Bayart, Ellis and Hibou, *Criminalization of the State in Africa*, p. 15.
74 Mbembe, *On the Postcolony*, p. 9.
75 United Nations, General Assembly, 'Resolution 60/1, World Summit Outcome document', , paragraphs 138 and 139 [emphasis added].
76 Chabal and Deloz, *Africa Works*, p. 4.
77 Alexis Arieff, 'De Facto Statehood? The strange case of Somaliland', *Yale Journal of International Affairs*, Vol. 3, No. 2, 2008, pp. 60–79.
78 Jennifer M. Welsh and Serna K. Sharma, 'Operationalizing the Responsibility to Protect', Policy Brief, Oxford: Oxford Institute for Ethics, Law and Armed Conflict, Oxford University, 2012.

5 The responsibility to protect in Congo[1]

The failure of grassroots prevention

Séverine Autesserre

Much has been written on the blue helmets' failure to protect the population in the Democratic Republic of Congo. For the past thirteen years, every time a massacre or an egregious series of rapes and killings took place close to a United Nations (UN) peacekeeping base – such as in Kisangani in 2002, Bukavu in 2004, Kiwanja and Dungu in 2008, Luvungi in 2010, and Beni in 2014 – Congolese and foreign journalists, civil society activists, human rights and humanitarian organizations, and international politicians would blame UN soldiers for failing to intervene. These criticisms were particularly harsh in late 2008, when the resumption of war in eastern Congo led to a spike in massacres virtually under the watch of peace-keepers tasked with protecting the population.

One of the many shortcomings with these criticisms is that they miss the central problem with protection efforts, in Congo and elsewhere. They put the emphasis on the failure to react instead of regretting the failure to *prevent* these atrocities.

The original proponents of the Responsibility to Protect doctrine convincingly demonstrated that prevention is a far better policy option than reaction. Prevention is less costly than reaction to crises, and it is much less intrusive than military intervention when the population is in immediate danger of physical violence. Furthermore, once a crisis has erupted, it is often too late and too difficult to adequately protect the population.[2]

Understanding the failure to prevent the recurrence of violence in Congo has potentially broad implications. An *Enough* report noted that 'there are myriad examples from recent history – Liberia, Sudan, Pakistan, and others – where the United States and its international partners have successfully helped to stabilize a situation, but have then reduced engagement only to see crises recur.'[3] In situations like Congo, where international involvement assisted the country in transitioning from war to peace and democracy (from 2003 to 2006), why did international actors fail to help prevent renewed large-scale violence?

Building on the argument I developed in *The Trouble With the Congo,*[4] this chapter argues that studying the dominant international peace-building culture helps explain this failure of prevention. Western and African diplomats, UN peace-keepers, and the staff of non-governmental organizations involved in conflict resolution – all of the actors that the Responsibility to Protect doctrine tasks with preventing the resumption of large-scale violence when the state is unwilling or unable to do so – share a set of ideologies, rules, rituals, assumptions, definitions, paradigms, and standard operating procedures. In Congo, this dominant culture shaped the intervention in a way that precluded preventive action at the grassroots, ultimately dooming the international efforts.

To develop this claim, I first show that prevention was the most important aspect of the original Responsibility to Protect doctrine and subsequent advocacy efforts, but that the implementation of the new norm has overlooked this dimension, in Congo and elsewhere. I then develop a case study of the 2008 war resumption in Congo in order to understand the reasons behind this neglect of prevention. I explain that preventive actions did take place in Congo, but not as part of specific protection efforts; rather, these actions were associated with the standard template and core work of interveners in any post-conflict environment, regardless of whether they are specifically tasked with protection. I argue that the prevention strategy failed to avert the resumption of large-scale violence because it was incomplete: it focused on preventing renewed national and regional wars but it ignored grassroots conflicts, which generated massive human rights violations and fueled the broader tensions. This strategy allowed a crisis localized in the province of North Kivu to escalate once again into a full-scale war.

To explain why prevention was focused on national and regional issues and not on local ones, I review the three essential conditions for effective prevention, as identified by the *Responsibility to Protect* Report: political will, early warning, and the preventive toolbox. I demonstrate that the dominant peace-building culture shaped how international actors understood their roles and the paths toward peace in such a way that these three conditions were present for the prevention of renewed national and regional fighting but absent for the prevention of local violence.

When not otherwise indicated, all material for the Congo case study comes from over 500 in-depth confidential interviews, more than two-and-a-half years of field observations in Congo's most violent provinces and Kinshasa between 2001 and 2014, and several additional years of participant observation research with international peace builders in other conflict zones.

Protection without prevention: A general trend

Prevention, the lost dimension

Prevention of crises or of crises' recurrence was the most important component of the original Responsibility to Protect doctrine. The idea of moving from a reactive approach to conflicts to a culture of prevention became influential in policy circles in the 1990s, notably within the UN and the World Bank and among frustrated diplomats.[5] In 1997, the Carnegie Commission on Preventing Deadly Conflict published a landmark study that clarified the three broad aims of preventive action – avoiding the emergence of war, the spread of ongoing conflicts, and the resumption of violence – and its three main principles: 'early reaction to signs of trouble,' 'a comprehensive, balanced approach to alleviate the pressures that trigger violent conflict,' and 'an extended effort to resolve the underlying root causes of violence.'[6]

(In line with the actual practice of prevention on the ground, most of the article focuses on the last two aims of preventive action.)

The International Commission on Intervention and State Sovereignty (ICISS), which introduced the Responsibility to Protect concept in its 2001 final report, emphasized the centrality of prevention – although it was the question of how to protect populations caught in the midst of war that had triggered its work.[7] The first point of the report's 'priorities' section stated that 'prevention is the single most important dimension of the responsibility to protect.'[8] All subsequent key policy documents pertaining to the new Responsibility to Protect concept reaffirmed the importance of prevention, although prevention was never given as central a role as it occupied in the ICISS report.[9] In 2005, a heads of state summit took place to discuss the ICISS's recommendations. After heated debate, the 150 heads of state present adopted a document stating that 'each individual State has the responsibility to protect its populations from genocide, war crimes, ethnic cleansing and crimes against humanity. This responsibility entails the prevention of such crimes, including their incitement, through appropriate and necessary means.'[10] The UN Security Council later endorsed this consensus through Resolution 1674 on the Protection of Civilians in Armed Conflict, which 'underlin[ed] the importance of taking measures aimed at conflict prevention and resolution,' and then again 'emphasiz[ed] the importance of preventing armed conflict and its recurrence.' To prevent conflicts, it stressed the role of non-military measures, including 'promoting economic growth, poverty eradication, sustainable development, national reconciliation, good governance, democracy, the rule of law, and respect for, and protection of, human rights.'[11] Finally, during the 2009 debates on protection at the UN General Assembly, states 'consistently' emphasized that 'prevention was the key component of the responsibility to protect.'[12]

Prevention was also a key focus of advocacy efforts surrounding the responsibility to protect.[13] Activists emphasized that protection should aim primarily at averting the eruption, spread, or resumption of violence, and that it should primarily be a non-military endeavor; military intervention should be used only as a last resort, when all other means (whether diplomatic, economic, or political) have failed.[14] However, the advocates faced an important hurdle: neither the ICISS commission nor the subsequent UN debates and documents provided clear guidance on how such prevention could actually be conducted.[15] Worse, the actual implementation of the Responsibility to Protect doctrine mostly ignored the prevention dimension, with the possible exception of international action in Libya in 2011.[16] In Darfur for instance, non-governmental organizations, UN peacekeepers, diplomats, civil society, and state actors largely focused on reaction rather than prevention.[17] The same was true for the international response to electoral violence in Kenya in 2007 and 2008 and to the September 2009 massacre in Guinea.[18]

As the rest of this chapter demonstrates, the Congo case also illustrates this trend, but with an important twist. After Congo (supposedly) completed its transition to peace and democracy in December 2006, there was preventive action to avoid a return to violence at the national and international levels, but there was no such action to prevent the spread of remaining local conflicts or the resumption of violence at the grassroots. In addition, the prevention initiatives that took place were not part of protection activities; instead, they belonged to the standard template for international response to ongoing wars. Although the goals of war prevention and protection of populations overlap, there are important distinctions. Prevention of war addresses conditions that may trigger national or international conflicts, but it does not attend to local tensions that do not threaten national or international peace, even if these local factors create serious population protection issues.

Protection in Congo: A military, reactive task

The UN peacekeeping mission in Congo, or MONUC, was one of the first UN missions to receive a civilian protection mandate, as early as February 2000.[19] In the following years, MONUC eventually evolved into 'the UN's largest and most robust operation for which civilian protection is a central purpose.'[20] However, all UN Security Council Resolutions interpreted protection in a very restrictive way: it was limited to 'the areas of deployment of [MONUC's] armed units' (which, given the low capability of the mission, left out most of the Congolese territory), and included only action 'within [MONUC's] capabilities.'[21] Most importantly, the Security Council's Resolutions always reduced protection to a mere reaction to '*imminent* threats physical violence' [my emphasis], rather than trying to prevent such threats in the first place. Even when the UN Security Council gave MONUC its most robust protection mandate, in Resolution 1856 (December 2008), reaction to crises remained the primary focus. Resolution 1856 'emphasized that protection of civilians [. . .] must be given priority in decisions about the use of available capacity and resources, over any of the other tasks described [in the Resolution],' but it only required MONUC to 'ensure the protection of civilians, including humanitarian personnel, under imminent threat of physical violence.'[22] The resolution itself seemed to have been spurred as a reaction to a massacre that had just taken place in Kiwanja, a few kilometers away from a UN peacekeeping base, and after which Congolese civilians and international leaders had blamed UN soldiers for failing to intervene. Preventing conflicts was never explicitly mentioned in any of these resolutions, although several sections, such as 'to contribute to the improvement of the security conditions in which humanitarian assistance is provided,' could be interpreted as allowing for preventive activities.

The understanding of what protection entailed was similarly restrictive on the ground. Up to 2004, MONUC did not act on its protection mandate. When I was conducting fieldwork in Kinshasa and in eastern Congo from 2001 to 2003, MONUC personnel never mentioned the protection idea during formal interviews or informal conversations. MONUC officials rather talked about their role as if they had only an observer mandate instead of a Chapter VII one.[23] UN actors started mentioning protection in mid-2003 during the Ituri crisis, when fighting between Hema and Lendu ethnic groups in the north-east of Congo triggered concerns among international actors of an impeding genocide. Discussions, however, remained focused on the protection of civilians in two large refugee camps located on grounds that MONUC controlled. A year later, the UN failure to prevent large-scale killings and rapes by various armed groups in the town of Bukavu provoked massive protests by Congolese civilians all over the country and outrage in many foreign capitals.[24] From then on, MONUC started acting on its protection mandate.

However, this never meant focusing on prevention. Rather, UN military and civilian peacekeepers interpreted the protection mandate as a military task and as a duty to fulfill once crises had erupted. Holt and Berkman's excellent study of civilian protection in Congo perfectly illustrates this point.[25] The report details how MONUC's military component struggled to carry out the protection mandate, and it rarely discusses the civilian part of the mission. It shows how protection in the field involved purely reactive, military measures:

> removal of threats against civilians by 'a cordon and search operation and/or disarmament of individuals threatening civilian population;' the establishment of 'buffer zones between combatants' and safe areas 'with adequate military protection;' utilization of an 'area domination' strategy through frequent patrols, overflights, and 'mobile temporary operations bases;' escorting humanitarian and human rights actors to areas; and evacuating populations out of danger zones.[26]

The word *prevention* only appears in the report when associated with 'harm to civilians under imminent threat' – meaning, once a conflict had already erupted into violence and escalated to a point that the population was in danger. Tellingly, the report never mentions the idea of preventing a crisis from erupting, as if MONUC had never considered it.

Interviews that I conducted in Congo between 2003 and 2014 similarly showed that MONUC (then MONUSCO[27]) staff's understanding of its protection mandate mostly involved a military reaction to crises. Questions on the protection mandate invariably oriented the conversation toward a discussion of the mission's military strategy to respond to imminent threats of violence. At that point, the interviewee would explain that the mandate established clear priorities: UN soldiers should protect first, UN staff and property; second, humanitarian personnel; and third and last, Congolese civilians. Several people then deplored that, given the logistic and security conditions in eastern Congo and the cumbersome standard operating procedures for UN military contingents, only few peacekeeping troops could be deployed to protect civilians once the first two priorities had been fulfilled. Very few interviewees mentioned the idea of prevention, or (until 2009) the role that MONUC's non-military personnel could play in preventing conflicts. Even MONUC's much-touted initiatives of creating 'Joint Protection Teams' showed such a restrictive understanding of the protection mandate. In February 2009, MONUC started organizing the deployment of these teams in response to the 'renewed mandate to protect civilians' stipulated in Resolution 1856. The terms of references for the teams as well as the details of the standard operating procedures that they were expected to follow show that although UN civilians would be part of the experience, these teams were primarily military affairs.[28] And both the terms of reference and the actual practice on the ground is evidence that these teams intervened only in a reactive fashion, once a massacre or a series of egregious human rights violations had transpired.

In addition to this military dimension, civilian staff of various UN agencies claimed to contribute to protection in accordance with their respective mandate, but protection was not their main focus until 2009. Protection became one of the mission's central concerns in 2009–2010, and civilian peacekeepers became more involved in this issue at that time, but, just like their military colleagues, they acted in a reactionary manner instead of working preventively. The child protection section, for instance, looked after individuals who had been enrolled in armed groups. The human rights section investigated cases of human rights violations, notably rapes, torture, and killings. The DDR and DDRRR section tried to demobilize combatants and, when relevant, to repatriate them.[29] In sum, all of these civilian interveners focused on reacting to the consequences of violence rather than preventing their occurrence.

Preventive actions on the ground therefore remained rare, and they were little more than side effects of programs unrelated to civilian protection. For example, MONUC deployed troops in Baraka to support the UN High Commissioner for Refugees' repatriation program from Tanzania to Congo. These troops were primarily there to protect UN staff and property but, as a MONUC staff member argued during an interview, the deployment could also be conceived as 'preventive protection' of the population and non-governmental organizations. Even the Joint Mission Analysis Cell, which was mandated to monitor conflicts that could escalate and threaten the mission's main goal, failed to seize this opportunity to act as a catalyst for prevention of renewed crises. Until late 2007, it focused not on preventing harm to civilians, but on preventing whatever could jeopardize MONUC's first priority, the organization of 'free and fair' elections. At the time of this writing in 2015, the unit continues to be under-resourced, and its influence within the mission has remained limited.

Outside of the UN mission, other international actors similarly conceptualized protection as a responsibility that peacekeeping military contingents should undertake in times of crisis, and not as a task requiring preventive action by non-military interveners. Aid workers requested UN soldiers to 'conduct joint assessments, provid[e] military protection to humanitarian convoys, physically tak[e] civilians out of danger, demin[e], and establish field hospitals.'[30] The 'protection cluster,' a group of international non-governmental organizations, UN peacekeeping staff, and UN agencies involved in issues related to protection from 2005 onward, similarly focused on military and mostly reactive issues, such as advocating for a judicial reform to eliminate impunity within the Congolese army and improving MONUC's military presence in unstable areas.[31] The international response to sexual violence provides an additional illustration of the focus on reaction. Sexual violence programs overwhelmingly focused on responding to abuses once they had occurred – for instance, providing medical treatment to women who had been raped – at the expense of the prevention of sexual abuse.[32]

In sum, in Congo as in other places where it was implemented, the protection doctrine acquired two characteristics that were in direct contradiction with the spirit of the *Responsibility to Protect* report and subsequent advocacy efforts. First, instead of focusing on prevention, protection focused on reaction to crises. Second, instead of being mostly a civilian enterprise, with military intervention as a last resort, it was primarily a military affair.[33] These two developments were intimately linked. Military actors are trained and equipped for reaction to crises. They are not trained and not equipped for the diplomatic, economic, and social measures that prevention requires.

It does not mean that there were no prevention efforts at all. Preventive action did take place, but not as part of protection activities. Rather, these actions were part of the template for international interventions in post-conflict environments. Most importantly, these efforts were incomplete. They focused on assuaging national and regional tensions in order to prevent conflict renewal at the macro level, and they overlooked the local causes of violence, thus dooming the international efforts.

Prevention without protection: Understanding war resumption in 2008

The resumption of war in eastern Congo in late 2008 provides a perfect case to study these dynamics. Prior to 2008, Congo had experienced fifteen years of sustained violence. Localized violence erupted in the Kivu provinces in 1993 and escalated when more than a million Rwandan refugees poured into eastern Congo after the 1994 Rwandan genocide. Eventually, the tensions caused two successive civil and international wars, the first from 1996 to 1997 and the second from 1998 to 2003. Militarily, these conflicts involved up to fourteen foreign armed groups, three main rebel movements, and countless fragmented militias. They caused an estimated three million casualties and destabilized most of Central and Southern Africa.[34]

In 2003, a settlement was reached at the national and regional levels. (In this chapter, *regional* refers to the level of the African Great Lakes Region: Burundi, Congo, Rwanda, and Uganda). Foreign troops officially withdrew from Congolese territory and normal diplomatic ties progressively resumed between former enemies. From June 2003 to December 2006, Congo went through a transition from war to peace and democracy. Its main achievements were the official reunification of the country, the formation of a unified government, and an attempt at integrating the different armed groups into a single national army. General presidential, legislative, and provincial elections officially marked the successful completion of the transition. In early 2007, Congo was officially at peace.[35]

However, violence persisted at a very high level in the eastern provinces both during and after the transition.[36] Then, in the second half of 2008, the conflict escalated again. From his stronghold in North Kivu, rebel leader Laurent Nkunda launched an offensive against government troops and announced his intention to seize power in Kinshasa. By December 2008, he had conquered large parts of the

North Kivu province and threatened the provincial capital of Goma. While instability was growing in the Kivus, the situation also sharply deteriorated in Oriental Province. Local militias multiplied, and Ugandan troops re-entered Congo in December 2008, officially to fight the Lord's Resistance Army, a Ugandan rebel movement partly based on Congolese territory. A flurry of diplomatic action by international actors, coupled with MONUC's strongest military operation to date and a major reshuffle of alliances between regional leaders, finally managed to remove the immediate threat on Goma and halt the renewed war. However, the spike in fighting had already caused hundreds of casualties and forced more than half a million people to relocate.

This resumption of large-scale violence in North Kivu in 2008 is a textbook case of international failure to prevent protection crises. From the official end of the war in 2003 to the resumption of large-scale conflict in 2008, the situation of the Congolese eastern provinces indeed met the criteria for international action stipulated by the Responsibility to Protect doctrine. 'Serious and irreparable harm' was 'occurring' or 'imminently likely to occur' 'to human beings' as a 'result of internal war, insurgency, repression [and] state failure.'[37] Violence was the result partly of 'deliberate state action,' partly of 'state's neglect or inability to act,' and partly of 'a failed state situation.'[38] In short, the Congolese state was unable or unwilling to fulfill its responsibility to protect its population – or, to use the criteria agreed on at the 2005 head of states meeting, the Congolese state was 'manifestly failing at' protecting its citizens. International support to Congolese actors trying to prevent a resumption of war was therefore deeply needed.

This international support could have taken 'many forms,' including

> development assistance and other efforts to help address the root cause of potential conflict; or efforts to provide support for local initiatives to advance good governance, human rights, or the rule of law; or good offices missions, mediation efforts and other efforts to promote dialogue or reconciliation.[39]

As the rest of this section shows, international actors did carry out such efforts, but they focused on only some of the root causes of violence – the national and regional tensions. They neglected other critical ones – the local, bottom-up conflicts. They therefore let significant tensions fester, to the point that grassroots antagonisms over land and power created significant protection problems and eventually reignited broader conflicts.

Incomplete efforts to prevent the recurrence of national and regional conflicts

For analytical clarity, we can divide the root causes of the renewed crisis in North Kivu into two categories: first, national and regional causes and second, local ones.[40] At the regional level, the Rwandan government regularly deplored that rebel Rwandan Hutu militias were still present in Congo and that they posed an important threat to Rwanda because they included some of those responsible for the 1994 Rwandan Genocide. According to many sources, Rwanda was actually more interested in pursuing two other goals in Congo. First, it wanted to continue the illegal exploitation of Congolese mineral resources, which remained an important source of revenue for Rwanda. Second, it needed to protect the Congolese population of Rwandan descent living in Congo, a minority that Congolese indigenous groups had consistently discriminated against since Congolese independence in 1960.

At the national level, the president and most former rebel leaders maintained parallel command structures over their soldiers in order to retain their territorial control and weaken their political enemies. Consequently, the army integration process was mostly a failure, and the government could barely extend its authority in the eastern provinces. At the time of this writing, there is still no functioning justice system and no reliable police force there. Soldiers regularly prey on the population, which means stealing and usually beating, raping, torturing, or killing those who refuse to comply. Lawlessness, impunity, and absence of state authority thus persist, creating a fertile ground for continued and renewed violence.

The tensions between most Congolese leaders and the representatives of Congolese with Rwandan ancestry were another important cause of violence after the war officially ended. During the electoral campaigns, almost all the national actors that did not belong to the Congolese population of Rwandan descent used propaganda against this minority as a way to rally supporters. This hate speech led to many abuses against Congolese with Rwandan ancestry. The 2006 elections only reinforced their marginalization, as they managed to send only a few representatives to the provincial and national assemblies. Fearing for their lives, status, and properties, Congolese of Rwandan descent became increasingly radicalized, which fueled Nkunda's rebellion and Rwandan involvement in Congo.

National economic agendas were also highly influential. Numerous national factions remained involved in the illegal exploitation of resources after the war officially ended. A large part of the continued fighting centered on the control of mining sites and export routes, both before and during the 2008 resumption of large-scale violence.

International actors did try to address these regional and national problems. Diplomats and UN officials organized numerous conferences to provide Congolese, Rwandan, Burundian, and Ugandan leaders with a forum where they could discuss their economic and security concerns. In times of crises, African and Western states put pressure on the Rwandan and Ugandan governments in order to prevent them from invading Congo again. Diplomats and UN officials also strove to convince Congolese warlords to integrate their soldiers into the army, while a few African and Western countries trained integrated army brigades. Finally, all donors devoted massive resources to organizing general elections, which they saw as the best way to end the violent struggle for power and to reconstruct a legitimate state authority.

It is true that international actors could have done more to prevent national and regional antagonisms from causing a renewal of large-scale violence. They could have further prioritized supporting the Congolese army so that it developed ways to integrate all of the armed groups. They could have devoted much more attention and resources to the reconstruction of the Congolese justice system, which is essential to ending impunity and thus deterring violence. They could have further pressured the Congolese and Rwandan governments so that they stopped fueling violence on the ground and addressed the problem posed by the Rwandan Hutu militias.

However, the international actors' main failure was not related to intervention at the macro levels. Incomplete as it was, it achieved significant results between 2003 and 2008. It largely assuaged many national and regional tensions, in turn leading to a decrease in manipulation of local armed groups by national and regional actors. By early 2008, a relative peace and stability had returned to most of Congolese territory. Many inhabitants of war-torn provinces saw their living conditions improve; displaced people started returning home and reconstructing their villages; and items of basic necessity (such as oil and salt) reappeared in most markets. If national and regional tensions had been the only root causes of violence, Congo would have continued on its paths toward stabilization, development, and democracy. However, regional and national agendas were not the only causes of violence. Grassroots tensions also significantly mattered, and as national and international peace builders failed to address them they festered, escalated, and eventually jeopardized the macro-level settlements. The main flaws of the international prevention efforts lie precisely in this neglect of bottom-up dynamics.

Neglect of the root causes of violence at the local level

While there were clear national and regional causes for the resumption of war in 2008, the conflict was also motivated by distinctively local causes. (In this chapter, *local* refers to the level of the individual, the family, the clan, the district, the community, and, sometimes, the ethnic group). In other words, war renewal in Congo was *not* purely or even mostly a consequence of national and regional tensions.[41]

Grassroots political issues were key. There was significant competition at the village or district level over who could be chiefs of villages, districts, or territories; who were the highest ranked individuals, families, or ethnic groups; and who could be appointed to local administrative positions. All of these local political antagonisms led to small-scale and large-scale violence many times during the war, the transition, and the post-electoral period.

These political tensions usually interacted with economically motivated hostilities because political power guaranteed access to land and economic resources, while access to resources ensured the availability of funds to buy arms and troops that help secure political power. The economic competition usually revolved around the two key sources of wealth in Congo: land and mineral resources. The illegal exploitation of mineral resources in Congo and its links to renewed fighting has been largely documented.[42] However, the stakes of land distribution are similarly intense: land provides the main means of survival to rural Congolese families, and it is the primary way of integrating in the local social structures. It is also a means of securing natural resources. As a result, for centuries the distribution of land was at the core of a lot of small and large-scale fighting.

Finally, there were important social motivations to be part of a militia and to continue to wage violence. Most importantly, the lack of social opportunities in post-war Congo meant that being a militiaman or, even better, a militia leader, was the best way for the un-educated and the disenfranchised to claim resources and a social status that the traditional order denied them.

These grassroots causes of tensions constantly interacted with national and regional dynamics. For example, micro-level economic, political, and social issues often motivated local alliances between Congolese soldiers or civilians and foreign rebel groups. Similarly, the standard narrative presented the tensions between 'indigenous' Congolese and the minority with Rwandan ancestry as a purely national or regional issue, but again, local conflicts over access to land and to traditional and administrative positions motivated large parts of this ethnic violence.[43]

This analysis of the interaction between the local, national, and regional dynamics helps explain why grassroots tensions contributed to war resumption in North Kivu. After the war officially ended in 2003, local Mai Mai militias continued to ally with Congolese president Kabila as well as with Rwandan Hutu rebels and to fight Congolese of Rwandan descent because doing so was the best way for them to consolidate their claims over land and local positions of authority. Similarly, Congolese with Rwandan ancestry refused any kind of settlement because they were afraid of revenge killings of their families and kin and because they worried that they might lose the local economic and political power that they acquired during the war. In 2008, as had happened in 1996 and 1998, the local conflict escalated slowly but surely. It caused large-scale violence that no national and regional actors could stop. It fueled the national and regional sources of tensions – notably the threat that Rwandan Hutu militias posed to Rwanda, the tensions between indigenous Congolese and Congolese with Rwandan ancestry, and the complex patterns of illegal exploitation of resources – and eventually jeopardized the macro-level settlements.

Throughout this escalation, there was barely any peace-building action to assuage local tensions – sustained initiatives for the resolution of the local antagonisms took place only reactively, *after* extensive renewed violence had taken place. Before the crisis erupted in large-scale fighting, diplomats and UN officials left it up to Congolese authorities, Congolese religious leaders, and non-governmental organizations to conduct bottom-up peace-building work. With only a few exceptions, Congolese authorities and religious leaders were unable or unwilling to conduct local conflict-resolution, and some were involved in fueling the violence outright. Congolese and international non-governmental organizations did implement local conflict-resolution projects, but their numbers were too few, and they faced too many challenges to make much of a difference. The following section identifies the reasons behind this neglect to prevent bottom-up conflicts from causing massive violations of human rights and eventually escalating into renewed national and regional wars.

Assessing the three essential conditions for effective prevention: The influence of the dominant peace-building culture

The *Responsibility to Protect* report identified three essential conditions for effective prevention: first, political will; second, 'knowledge of the fragility of the situation and the risks associated with it' – called 'early warning' – and third, 'understanding of the policy measures available that are capable of making a difference,' called the 'preventive toolbox.'[44] This section shows that these three conditions were present only for the prevention of national and regional conflicts but not for the prevention of local ones. This section also identifies the reasons behind this difference: a dominant peace-building culture shaped the international intervention strategy in a way that precluded local conflict prevention.[45]

Political will

Take the problem most often mentioned by Congolese and international actors – the lack of political will. Building on previous research on peacekeeping,[46] one could hypothesize that international interveners decided to ignore the prevention dimension because of vested economic, political, security, or institutional interests. Two issues may have been especially important. First, major powers, which would bear the bulk of the cost of any protection program, may have been reluctant to devote the financial, diplomatic, and military resources to make programs successful. Second, all or most states may have prioritized upholding the sovereignty norm at the expense of bottom-up peace-building efforts.

This section shows that the dominant peace-building culture constructed international interests in such a way that these two explanations applied to local conflict-resolution and not to macro-level intervention.

Reluctance to devote resources to protection. During interviews, policy makers and practitioners often complained that, due to insufficient international political will to address the Congolese conflict, peace builders on the ground lacked the troops, funding, and equipment necessary to conduct effective protection.[47] The few countries and international organizations working in Congo lacked sufficient national interest to get strongly involved (this was the case of the US, France, and the UK), or they lacked the capabilities to follow through on their ambitions (as happened with Belgium, South Africa, and the African Union).[48] As a result, the resources devoted to Congo were paltry compared to the needs and, according to my interviewees, this precluded international action at the grassroots to prevent war resumption.

This explanation for the lack of preventive action at the local level is problematic for two reasons. First, preventing crises usually requires fewer resources than reacting to them. Given that prevention is not and should not be a military activity, focusing on prevention resolves the problem of finding better and more military troops and equipment. Furthermore, Smith and Sullivan have shown that, in most cases, it is much more cost-effective to prevent crises than to react to them.[49] The

Carnegie Commission made a similar point in its study of seven major interventions in the 1990s. It demonstrated that international interveners could have saved $130 billion out of $200 billion spent if it had adopted a more effective preventive approach.[50] No Congo-specific study has yet been developed, but there is little reason to believe that this case would have been an exception.

The second and most important problem with this explanation is that it is incorrect to argue that there was no political will to address the Congolese crisis or to prevent war resumption. International interveners devoted significant resources to address the perceived causes of the problem. The peacekeeping mission deployed in Congo was and still is the largest and most expensive UN mission in the world. In 2003, the European Union sent the first ever European-led peacekeeping mission to Congo, and it stayed in the unstable Ituri district for three months. The International Criminal Court chose Congolese warlords as its historic first cases. Foreign donors contributed half the Congolese budget for most of the 2003–2007 period, and they devoted over $670 million to the organization of the 2006 elections. As detailed above, diplomats and high-ranking UN officials also actively tried to promote national and regional reconciliation.

In certain cases, these resources enabled peace builders on the ground to overcome logistical and security obstacles. A comparison between the organization of elections (in 2006 and 2011) and local conflict resolution efforts is particularly illuminating in this regard.[51] Regional and national leaders, including spoilers, could (and at times did) derail the electoral processes in the same way that they could (and sometimes did) disrupt bottom-up peace-building projects. The collapse of the state bureaucracy in many eastern provinces hampered any kind of project needing state support, be it election organization or local conflict resolution. The unceasing security problems affected the electoral process – by preventing freedom of campaigning, endangering candidates, and limiting access to unstable areas – to the same extent that they affected local peace-building initiatives – by imperiling local peace builders and similarly restricting access to unstable locales. The lack of roads and communication infrastructures limited travel in a way that was as problematic for election organization as for local peace building. International interveners had to surmount the overwhelming complexity of the politico-military situation both in the case of elections (to ensure the 'fairness' of the electoral process) and in the case of local peace building (to find solutions acceptable to all parties). The polarization of Congolese society meant that the population saw electoral agents with about the same level of suspicion as they regarded local peace builders.

However, international interveners devoted massive logistical, financial, and human resources to the organization of elections in 2006 and 2011. These resources helped make logistical and security obstacles manageable, so that international and Congolese actors could successfully organize presidential, legislative, and provincial elections. There was, however, no such prioritization for bottom-up peace building, which prevented peace builders from overcoming logistical and security obstacles to their increased involvement at the local level.

In sum, the material constraints resulting from the lack of political will were not absolute obstacles to the prevention of war resumption. They did not affect action at the macro level in the same measure that they affected action at the micro level. We therefore have to understand why international actors perceived contextual and material constraints as obstacles to preventive action at the grassroots but not to preventive action at the macro levels.

The answer to this question is that the dominant peace-building culture constructed national and regional reconciliation as a first priority and relegated local conflict-resolution as a negligible task. As I have argued elsewhere, diplomats and UN staff members are trained to work on super-structures, such as national and international negotiations, and they are socialized to focus on predefined tasks and performance guidelines that fail to consider local violence.[52] They therefore believed that their only legitimate role was to intervene at the macro levels. Influenced by the ideological environment of the post–Cold War era, they especially viewed the organization of elections as a favorite state and peace-building mechanism. They saw other state- and peace-building tasks as secondary priorities, and if they approached them, they did so in a top-down fashion. The dominant culture thus enabled foreign actors to pursue an intervention strategy that overlooked the need for local conflict resolution, despite the presence of significant political will to prevent war resumption.

Sovereignty and double standards. The same approach is useful to analyze the significance of the sovereignty norm.

Many policy makers and practitioners hold state sovereignty as the central obstacle to a full implementation of the responsibility to protect doctrine.[53] Likewise, in Congo, during interviews, international interveners often mentioned the sovereignty of the Congolese state as the main obstacle to their trying to prevent bottom-up violence. Diplomats and UN staffers argued that local conflicts were an internal matter and therefore, as in any sovereign country, national authorities were the most legitimate actors to address these internal issues. As a result, according to peacekeeping officials I interviewed, it was, 'not necessary, even legitimate' to deal with questions other than the national peace process.

However, as the *Responsibility to Protect* report emphasized, prevention is usually much less intrusive – and therefore much more respectful of state sovereignty – than direct military intervention in reaction to a crisis.[54] Furthermore, UN and diplomatic interveners have not always considered the Congolese sovereignty as an absolute constraint. Instead, they have disregarded the sovereignty norm whenever they deemed it necessary. For instance, they closely supervised the writing of the new constitution in 2005 and 2006, the organization of elections in 2006 (and, to a lesser extent, in 2011), and various legislative processes, which were all principally matters of national sovereignty.[55]

International actors did not interpret state sovereignty as inhibiting their involvement in electoral, legislative, and constitutional matters for one central reason. The dominant discourse on sovereignty has significantly evolved in the twentieth century, and humanitarian goals have progressively become legitimate reasons for ignoring state sovereignty, especially in Africa.[56] In the case of Congo, this evolving discursive construction enabled international actors to legitimize over-looking Congolese sovereignty in order to address what they saw as the cause of the humanitarian and security problems in the region – the lack of elected (and thus legitimate) leadership in the 2000s.[57] By contrast, because international actors did not acknowledge the critical role of local conflicts in causing humanitarian problems or in threatening international peace and security, they viewed sover-eignty as an insurmountable obstacle to their involvement in this 'domestic issue.'[58] This analysis leads us to the second condition for effective prevention, the 'knowl-edge of the fragility of the situation and the risks associated with it.'

Early warning

As was evident in my interviews, between the official end of the war in 2003 and war resumption in 2008, international actors were perfectly aware of the fragility of the national and regional settlements and the likelihood of war resumption at the macro levels. By contrast, as I have demonstrated elsewhere, their knowledge of how fragile the local situation was, and of the risks that escalating local conflicts posed to general peace, was limited if not non-existent.[59] This was true both for organizations whose responsibilities include early-warning on issues that impact protection of populations (such as the UN Department of Political Affairs) and for early-warning bodies not directly related to the responsibility to protect (such as the specialized units within the US or British governments). Some staff members based in the field, as well as a handful of researchers based in headquarters or capitals, had a much deeper knowledge of local situations and a much more accu-rate sense of how risky it was to ignore local conflicts, but their hierarchies often ignored their reports warning of impending crises. Similarly, researchers and advo-cates trying to raise awareness of the risks of war resumption should local conflicts continue to fester – such as the Congolese think tank Pole Institute and the Swedish non-governmental organization Life and Peace Institute – were heard only once the crisis had already escalated.[60]

Once again, we can explain this situation by analyzing the dominant peace-building culture. UN staff and diplomats are trained to analyze conflicts from a top-down perspective.[61] As a result, they identify national and regional tensions as the causes of the continued fighting and massacres in the eastern Congolese provinces. In addition, between 2003 and 2008, UN staff and diplomats defined the Congolese context as a 'post-conflict' environment; the various bouts of large-scale fighting thus became mere 'crises' rather than evidence that the war was about to resume. To explain away the violence that they could not relate to any national or regional antagonisms, international peace builders used several interrelated frameworks of analysis. In their view, local violence was private and criminal, and it was the consequence of the lack of state authority in Congo. More importantly, because the image of the Congolese 'inherent savagery' had persisted since the Belgian colonizers constructed it a century ago, foreign actors usually saw extensive local violence as a normal feature of life in a peaceful Congo.

The North Kivu crisis illustrates how this understanding of violence precluded international preventive action at the grassroots. From 2003 to 2008, because Congo was officially labeled a 'post-conflict' country (and, in 2007, a country at peace), sub-national actors such as the 'renegade leader' Laurent Nkunda could no longer be conceptualized as rebels or warring parties. As a result, international mediation between different combatants was not an option any more because at least one of the parties was considered illegitimate.

In the first months of 2004, for instance, when warning signs of an impending crisis were developing, the MONUC leadership categorized Nkunda as an illegal actor whom it forbade its staff members from meeting.[62] At that time, the Congolese actors participating in the transition were the only legitimate partners for diplomats and UN staff. The logic of exclusion continued until it was too late: Nkunda took over the eastern city of Bukavu (South Kivu) in May 2004, and MONUC officials were forced to negotiate with him. Then again, in 2006 to 2007, when it became obvious that Nkunda was building a quasi-independent state in the territory under his control in North Kivu, the top UN hierarchy similarly prevented its staff from meeting with the agitator. The setbacks of this strategy became evident in late 2007 and in 2008, when heavy fighting resumed between Nkunda and the Congolese army.

Intervention took place only when a renewal of extensive violence demonstrated the fragility of the local situation and the risks that local conflicts posed to the broader settlements. From August 2008 onward, as the specter of a renewed national and regional war loomed larger, MONUC redeployed ninety percent of its troops to the Kivus. In late November, the UN Security Council authorized the temporary deployment of additional troops to reinforce the peacekeeping missions' capacity, and in December, it authorized an extra 3,000 peace-keeping troops and strengthened their protection mandate. By that time, however, it was too late. The time for prevention had passed, the Congolese populations were once more 'in immediate danger of physical violence,' and international interveners were merely reacting to a major crisis.

The preventive toolbox

The 'understanding of the policy measures available that are capable of making a difference' was similarly present in the case of national and international action, but not in the case of support to grassroots movements.[63] Foreign ministries, international and regional organizations, and even non-governmental organizations have developed an extensive expertise and numerous standard operating procedures to facilitate national and regional dialogues and to organize elections. However, none of the international bureaucracies involved in peace building, such as the UN and the diplomatic missions, have developed any organizational capacity to address local conflicts. None have specialized units for grassroots peace building, ready-made analytical frameworks to understand decentralized conflicts, standard operating procedures to address bottom-up problems, or predefined indicators to measure the successful completion of the task. And UN staff and diplomats have no training for work at the local level. During my interviews, whenever I asked a diplomat or a UN peacekeeper if he had received training on local conflict resolution, he always replied in the negative.

More broadly, peace-building bureaucracies have no standard operating procedures for preventive protection of populations, apart from a few early-warning systems.[64] During interviews, field-based peace keepers regularly complained that the units mandated to protect civilians were not used to implementing that kind of mandate and therefore they had to invent everything as they went. Eventually, one of the routines that developed was to think of protection as a military and reactive task, as detailed above.

This does not mean that local conflict prevention was impossible. To the contrary, it would have been perfectly possible to implement prevention programs with existing resources so that local problems did not again jeopardize the national and regional peace (although such a change would have required a significant reconceptualization in the way peace builders think and operate).[65] Rather than focusing all their efforts on organizing elections right after the war ended, which negatively affected the prospects for peace without helping promote democracy, international peace builders could have used part of the resources to finance local conflict-resolution efforts. This would have provided much-needed funding to Congolese non-governmental organizations. They could have implemented local reconciliation projects, such as building a market, a school, or a health center shared by two communities in conflict in order to reestablish social and commercial links between them. They could also have helped reconstruct social mechanisms for the peaceful resolution of conflicts, such as local justice institutions. In each peacekeeping site, MONUC could have deployed, alongside the military, a civilian staff member tasked with monitoring local tensions and providing suggestions for resolution. He or she could have been allowed to draw on military, diplomatic, or development resources to promote local peace.

Conclusion

In many cases, the implementation of the Responsibility to Protect doctrine has overlooked its central tenet: preventing crises should take precedence over responding to them. This flawed reconceptualization of the doctrine is all the more puzzling because the obstacles usually mentioned to explain protection failure – the sovereignty norm and the presence of financial, logistic, and human resources constraints – are more problematic for reactive than preventive action.

This chapter has demonstrated that in Congo, the failure to prevent the resumption of large-scale violence was due to the international neglect of bottom-up tensions. Preventive action at the grassroots was overlooked, not because of the often-mentioned constraints posed by the sovereignty norm and the lack of financial and human resources, but because a dominant peace-building culture shaped the international understanding of the causes of violence and the paths toward peace in a way that precluded support to bottom-up conflict resolution.

This suggests new avenues for research on the Responsibility to Protect. Local conflicts are often critically important in sustaining violence in most unstable environments.[66] Furthermore, as I have argued elsewhere, the dominant international peace-building culture regularly precludes international action at the local level, thus hampering effective preventive action.[67] As a result, millions of people regularly face imminent threats of physical violence, which heighten the need for reactive, military, and intrusive protection interventions. Only a focus on lowering the barriers to international support of preventive grassroots action has a chance to end this vicious circle.

Notes

1 This chapter was originally accepted for publication in *International Peacekeeping* in Spring 2015 (it will appear in volume 23, issue 1).
2 International Commission on Intervention and State Sovereignty, *The Responsibility to Protect: Report of the International Commission on Intervention and State Sovereignty*, Ottawa: International Development Research Centre, 2001.
3 Gayle E. Smith, David Sullivan, and Andrew Sweet, *The Price of Prevention: Getting Ahead of Global Crises*, Washington, DC: The Center for American Progress and The Enough Project, 2008, p. 20.
4 Séverine Autesserre, *The Trouble with the Congo: Local Violence and the Failure of International Peacebuilding*, New York: Cambridge University Press, 2010.
5 Alex J. Bellamy, *Responsibility to Protect: The Global Effort to End Mass Atrocities*, Cambridge, UK: Polity, 2009, p. 103; and Smith, Sullivan and Sweet, *The Price of Prevention*, pp. 10–11.
6 Carnegie Commission on Preventing Deadly Conflict, *Preventing Deadly Conflict – Final Report*, New York: Carnegie Corporation of New York, 1997, pp. xviii–xix.
7 Aidan Hehir, *The Responsibility to Protect*, Basingstoke, UK: Palgrave Macmillan, 2012, Chapter 4; and Thomas Weiss, "RtoP Alive and Well after Libya," *Ethics & International Affairs,* vol. 25, no. 3, 2011, p. 288.
8 International Commission on Intervention and State Sovereignty, *The Responsibility to Protect.*
9 Alex J. Bellamy, "Conflict Prevention and the Responsibility to Protect," *Global Governance,* vol. 14, 2008.
10 UN General Assembly, *2005 World Summit Outcome*, New York: United Nations, 2005.
11 UN Security Council, *Resolution 1674*, New York: United Nations, 2006.
12 Hehir, *The Responsibility to Protect* , pp. 90–1.
13 Ibid., Chapter 4; and Weiss, "RtoP Alive and Well after Libya," pp. 287–8. For a dissenting view, see Bellamy, "Conflict Prevention and the Responsibility to Protect."
14 Hehir, *The Responsibility to Protect*, p. 90.
15 Bellamy, *Global Effort to End Mass Atrocities*, pp. 52–3 and Chapter 4; and Hehir, *The Responsibility to Protect*, Chapter 4.
16 Bellamy, *Global Effort to End Mass Atrocities*, p. 4. On action in Libya as a case of prevention: Alex Bellamy, *The Responsibility to Protect: A Defense*, Oxford, UK: Oxford University Press, 2015, pp. 9–10. For an opposite view: Roland Paris, "The "Responsibility to Protect" and the Structural Problems of Preventive Humanitarian Intervention," *International Peacekeeping,* vol. 21, no. 5, 2014, pp. 569–603.
17 David Lanz, *Saving Strangers in Darfur: International Norms Lost in Translation*, PhD dissertation, Basel University, 2015; and Jon Harald Sande Lie and Benjamin de Carvalho, *A Culture of Protection? Perceptions of the Protection of Civilians from Sudan*, Oslo: Norwegian Instutite for International Affairs (NUPI), 2008.

18 Global Centre for the Responsibility to Protect, *Policy Brief: The Responsibility to Protect and Kenya: Past Successes and Current Challenges* and *Policy Brief – The International Response to 28 September 2009 Massacre in Guinea and the Responsibility to Protect*, New York: The CUNY Graduate Center, 2010.
19 UN Security Council, "Resolution 1291," cited in Victoria K. Holt and Tobias C. Berkman, *The Impossible Mandate? Military Preparedness, the Responsibility to Protect and Modern Peace Operations*, Washington, DC: The Henry L. Stimson Center, 2006, p. 159.
20 Ibid., p. 155.
21 See, for example, UN Security Council Resolution 1493 (2003), para. 25; UN Security Council Resolution 1592 (2005), para. 7; UN Security Council Resolution 1649 (2005), para. 11; UN Security Council Resolution 1794 (2007), para. 5; and UN Security Council Resolution 1856 (2008), para. 3, 5, and 6.
22 UN Security Council Resolution 1856 (2008), para. 3 and 6.
23 Holt and Berkman, *The Impossible Mandate?*, p. 159, makes a similar observation.
24 See also Sarah Katz-Lavigne, *Partial Peacebuilding and the Failure of Civilian Protection in the Democratic Republic of Congo, 2003–2006*, London: London School of Economics, 2008, p. 7, citing Zeebroek 2008.
25 Holt and Berkman, *The Impossible Mandate?*, especially Chapter 8.
26 Ibid., p. 174.
27 In 2010, the UN mission in Congo (MONUC) became the UN Stabilization Mission in Congo (MONUSCO).
28 MONUC, *Joint Protection Teams: Standard Operating Procedures and Terms of Reference for Join Protection Teams*, 2008.
29 DDR stands for Disarmament, Demobilization, and Reintegration of Congolese combatants, and DDRRR for Disarmament, Demobilization, and Reintegration, Reintegration, and Resettlement of foreign armed groups.
30 Holt and Berkman, *The Impossible Mandate?*, p. 174.
31 Ibid., pp. 173–4.
32 Séverine Autesserre, "Dangerous Tales: Dominant Narratives on the Congo and Their Unintended Consequences," *African Affairs,* vol. 111, no. 443, 2012, pp. 16–17.
33 On the military focus of protection efforts beyond Congo, see Bellamy, *Global Effort to End Mass Atrocities*, Chapters 2 and 3.
34 The casualties figure comes from International Institute for Strategic Studies, *Armed Conflict Database,* London, UK, last accessed in December 2014. https://acd.iiss.org/
35 See Autesserre, *The Trouble with the Congo*, pp. 232–3, for evidence that Congo was considered at peace in 2007, and Chapter 2 for a detailed overview of the historical events presented in this paragraph.
36 Ibid.
37 Citations from International Commission on Intervention and State Sovereignty, *The Responsibility to Protect*, Synopsis, Basic Principle 1A.
38 Citations from ibid., Synopsis, Point 7.
39 Citations from ibid., para. 3.3.
40 This section is based on author's confidential interviews and field observations (2001–2014). For more details and references on the topics discussed in this section, see Autesserre, *The Trouble with the Congo*, Séverine Autesserre, "The Trouble with Congo: How Local Disputes Fuel Regional Violence," *Foreign Affairs,* vol. 87, no. 3, 2008, and Séverine Autesserre, *Peaceland: Conflict Resolution and the Everyday Politics of International Intervention*, New York: Cambridge University Press, 2014, pp. 132–47.
41 See Autesserre, *The Trouble with the Congo*, Chapter 4, and Autesserre, "The Trouble with Congo: How Local Disputes," for a detailed demonstration of the points summarized in this section.
42 For a critical discussion, see Autesserre, "The Trouble with Congo: How Local Disputes," pp. 210–13.

43 For detailed examples of the dynamics mentioned in this paragraph, see Autesserre, *The Trouble with the Congo*, Chapter 4.

44 International Commission on Intervention and State Sovereignty, *The Responsibility to Protect*, para. 3.9.

45 This section is based on author's confidential interviews and field observations (2001–2014). For more details and references on the topics discussed in this section, and for a full presentation of this international peace-building culture, see Autesserre, *The Trouble with the Congo* and Autesserre, *Peaceland*.

46 For instance: Adekeye Adebajo, *UN Peacekeeping in Africa: From the Suez Crisis to the Sudan Conflicts*, Boulder, CO: Lynne Rienner, 2011; Michael W. Doyle and Nicholas Sambanis, *Making War and Building Peace: United Nations Peace Operations*, Princeton, NJ: Princeton University Press, 2006; and Lise Morjé Howard, *UN Peacekeeping in Civil Wars*, New York: Cambridge University Press, 2008.

47 See also Holt and Berkman *The Impossible Mandate?*, p. 155.

48 Autesserre, *The Trouble with the Congo*, pp. 235–9; Gérard Prunier, *Africa's World War: Congo, the Rwandan Genocide, and the Making of a Continental Catastrophe*, Oxford: Oxford University Press, 2008; Jean-Claude Willame, *Les Faiseurs De Paix Au Congo. Gestion D'une Crise Internationale Dans Un État Sous Tutelle*, Brussels/Paris: Editions Complexes, 2007.

49 Smith, Sullivan and Sweet, *The Price of Prevention*.

50 Carnegie Commission on Preventing Deadly Conflict, *Preventing Deadly Conflict*.

51 An earlier version of this paragraph appeared in Autesserre, *The Trouble with the Congo*, p. 226. For more details on the claims developed in the rest of this section, see ibid., Chapters 2 to 5.

52 Ibid., Chapters 3 and 5, provide a detailed demonstration of the claims made in this paragraph.

53 Bellamy, *Global Effort to End Mass Atrocities*, Chapters 1–2 and p. 107; Hehir, *The Responsibility to Protect*, pp. 180–1; and John Janzekovic and Daniel Silander, *Responsibility to Protect and Prevent: Principles, Promises and Practicalities*, London: Anthem Press, 2013, pp. 1–2.

54 International Commission on Intervention and State Sovereignty, *The Responsibility to Protect*.

55 See Autesserre, *The Trouble with the Congo*, Chapters 3 and 5 for details and evidence.

56 Martha Finnemore, "Constructing Norms of Humanitarian Interventions," in *The Culture of National Security: Norms and Identity in World Politics*, ed. Peter J. Katzenstein, New York: Columbia University Press, 1996; and Kevin C. Dunn, *Imagining the Congo: The International Relations of Identity*, New York: Palgrave Macmillan, 2003.

57 Autesserre, *The Trouble with the Congo*, Chapter 3.

58 See ibid., Chapter 5, for additional details.

59 See ibid., Chapters 2 and 4, for details and evidence on the claims developed in this paragraph.

60 Author's confidential interviews, field observations, and personal experience, 2006 to 2010.

61 This paragraph summarizes Autesserre, *The Trouble with the Congo*, Chapters 2 and 4; and Autesserre, *Peaceland*, pp. 149–53.

62 This paragraph is based on author's confidential interviews with UN officials and outside observers, 2003–2012.

63 A previous version of this paragraph already appeared in Autesserre, *The Trouble with the Congo*.

64 See Bellamy, *Global Effort to End Mass Atrocities*, Chapter 5, for details on existing international tools for prevention.

65 A previous version of this paragraph appeared in Séverine Autesserre, "Hobbes and the Congo: Frames, Local Violence, and International Intervention," *International*

Organization, vol. 63, 2009. For more details on this potential strategy, see Autesserre, *The Trouble with the Congo,* Chapters 5 and 6.

66 Patricia Justino, Tilman Brück and Philip Verwimp, eds., *A Micro-Level Perspective on the Dynamics of Conflict, Violence, and Development,* Oxford: Oxford University Press, 2013; and Stathis N. Kalyvas, *The Logic of Violence in Civil War,* New York: Cambridge University Press, 2006.

67 Autesserre, *The Trouble with the Congo,* Chapter 6; and Autesserre, *Peaceland,* pp. 149–53.

6 United Nations action in Sri Lanka and the responsibility to protect

Alex J. Bellamy

Introduction

In November 2012, the UN Secretary General released the Report of the Secretary-General's Internal Review Panel on United Nations Action in Sri Lanka. The Panel, led by Assistant Secretary-General Charles Petrie, reviewed in detail the UN's response to the unfolding crisis in Sri Lanka in 2008–2009. It concluded that the organization had failed to respond adequately thus failed to fulfill its responsibilities to the civilian population. The UN's response to this report gave rise to the Secretary-General's 'Rights up Front' Action Plan, which promised to place human rights protection at the core of the organization's work and open up opportunities for thinking about the implementation of the Responsibility to Protect (RtoP) across the whole system. This chapter examines the report's key findings and evaluates its implications for the implementation of the RtoP principle. It proceeds in three parts. The first outlines the main findings of the Review Panel. The second reviews the Report's specific references to RtoP in more detail. The third identifies ways in which the implementation of RtoP might assist the UN in learning the lessons of Sri Lanka.

Main findings of the internal review panel

After consulting around 7,000 documents as well as videos and photographs relating to the UN's response to the unfolding crisis in Sri Lanka from mid-2008 to mid-2009, the Internal Review Panel concluded that the UN failed to respond adequately. Specifically, the Panel found that

> events in Sri Lanka mark a grave failure of the UN to adequately respond to early warnings and to the evolving situation during the final stages of the conflict and its aftermath, to the detriment of hundreds of thousands of civilians and in contradiction with the principles and responsibilities of the UN. (para. 80).[1]

It noted that 'when confronted by similar situations, the UN must be able to meet a much higher standard in fulfilling its protection and humanitarian responsibilities' (para. 88). The Panel judged that the UN was not prepared to take sufficient action to improve the protection of civilians caught up in the crisis and that UN officials made repeated tradeoffs between protection and human rights concerns, on the one hand, and the perceived need to secure humanitarian access and maintain a cordial relationship with the Sri Lankan government, on the other. These views echo those of the former UN spokesman in Sri Lanka Gordon Weiss, and Senior Fellow at the Global Centre for the Responsibility to Protect James Traub.[2]

The Internal Review Panel pointed to several factors in particular as contributing to the UN's failure to protect civilians in Sri Lanka.

Withdrawal of staff. In September 2008, the government of Sri Lanka advised the UN Country Team (UNCT) that it could no longer guarantee the safety of its staff in the Wanni region affected by conflict. Although most UN staff perceived the statement as part of a stratagem designed to encourage the withdrawal of international observers, the senior UN official in Sri Lanka – the Resident Coordinator (RC) Neil Buhne – decided to evacuate international and national staff. National staff were prevented from evacuating by the rebel Liberation Tigers of Tamil Eelam (LTTE). The decision to withdraw came in the context of prolonged efforts by the government to restrict the access of non-governmental organizations to the region, persistent intimidation of UN staff, and non-compliance with rules relating to the privileges and immunities of UN employees. The Panel concluded that 'the relocation of international staff out of the conflict zone made it much harder for the UN to deliver humanitarian assistance to the civilian population, to monitor the situation, and to "protect by presence"' (para. 16).

Failure to publicly identify government responsibility for civilian casualties. Data generated in early February 2009 by the UNCT showed that government forces caused the majority of civilian casualties. Yet, not only did the UNCT leadership fail to make this information public, it did not communicate this fact to the government itself until the late stages of the crisis. Only very rarely did the UN attribute responsibility for civilian casualties to the government in its public statements.

Failure to confront the government directly with the fact that it was not complying with its international legal obligations. Although it lobbied both parties to the conflict (government and the LTTE) with requests for assistance and cooperation, the UNCT did not confront the government directly with the fact that some of its actions, such as the denial of humanitarian access, were contrary to its international legal obligations (para. 47). Moreover, in the few instances where the UN raised concerns privately with the government, it did not elaborate on the government's legal obligations under international humanitarian and human rights law (para. 52).

Failure to properly inform the Secretariat and UN Member States about the situation in the Wanni and the number of civilian casualties. The UNCT generated data about the number of verified civilian casualties in the Wanni. However, on 12 March 2009, the UN's Chef de Cabinet, Vijay Nambiar, and the Under-Secretary-General (USG) of Humanitarian Affairs, Sir John Holmes, argued against their dissemination by the Office of the High Commissioner for Human Rights (OHCHR) on the mistaken grounds that the estimates could not be verified.

Failure to inform the Secretariat and UN Member States about potential violations of international human rights and humanitarian law. The UN did not sufficiently communicate the fact that civilian casualties were being caused by the actions of both government forces and the LTTE or that these actions might constitute war crimes or crimes against humanity entailing individual criminal responsibility. Some Member States, including non-permanent members of the Security Council, and some officials in the Executive Office of the Secretary-General (EOSG) complained that they were not adequately informed about the legal implications of the situation in the Wanni.

Sending of inconsistent messages that undermined demarches pointing to civilian casualties caused by government action. There was no unified communications strategy. When the OHCHR released estimated casualty figures, their credibility was undermined by the RC and the USG-Humanitarian Affairs in a public statement that held that the figures were taken from an 'internal working document' that 'cannot be fully, reliably and independently assessed.'

It is important to stress that UN officials were operating in an exceptionally difficult environment. Not only was the situation on the ground extremely complex and fluid, but the Sri Lankan government adopted a policy of confrontation and intimidation towards UN officials. This included the frequent revocation and denial of visas, refusal to accept political or human rights action by the UN, the use of public threats, and the physical abuse of UN staff members and their dependents. In the final stages of the crisis, UN installations were subjected to artillery bombardment and several dependents of UN staff were killed. Shortly afterwards, individuals associated with the Sri Lankan police abducted, tortured, and imprisoned two UN staff members. One UN staff member was imprisoned without charge for twelve months. The LTTE engaged in similar practices and prevented UN national staff and their dependents from evacuating from the affected regions. Actions by both parties were violations of international human rights and humanitarian law and of the rules governing UN privileges and immunities (para. 41).

The international political context was also unsupportive of UN action on Sri Lanka. As the Panel reports, 'throughout the final stages of the conflict, Member States did not hold a single formal meeting on Sri Lanka, whether at the Security Council, the Human Rights Council, or the General Assembly' (para. 33, also para. 68). Member States were reluctant to receive formal briefings on the situation in Sri Lanka, showed little interest in adopting measures to strengthen civilian protection, encourage the parties to do so or hold the parties accountable. Member States also failed to signal their support for UN officials on the ground who were subjected to harassment and intimidation. In short, UN Member States created a political context that pushed the UNCT and UN Headquarters (UNHQ) to make trade-offs to protect the UN's limited humanitarian access. With some justification, many UN officials believed that they would receive no political support if they confronted the Sri Lankan government on its poor record of compliance with its legal obligations. Understandably, given the context, many UN officials judged that there was little to be gained by speaking out and something to be lost – the UN's limited humanitarian access.

With these considerations in mind, the panel attributed the UN's failure to adequately protect the civilian population in the Wanni to three interrelated sets of problems:

1 *Cultural challenges:* Because the UN relied on the support of the Sri Lankan Government for humanitarian access and other essential assistance, it was reluctant to criticize the government for serious violations of international law. In that context, no part of the UNCT assumed responsibility for protection. The report found that

> there was a continued reluctance among UN Country Team institutions to stand up for the rights of the people they were mandated to assist. In Colombo, some senior staff did not perceive the prevention of killing of civilians as their responsibility.

(para. 76)

2 *In-country framework of action:* The structure of the UN's engagement with Sri Lanka was not appropriately configured to the organization's responsibilities, given the situation on the ground. Despite the adoption of a number of core protection standards, including international human rights law, international humanitarian law, and the Responsibility to Protect, which all UN entities are expected to implement, and despite the situation in Sri Lanka, the UNCT was primarily configured to support economic development. Although changes were made in response to the deteriorating situation, including the addition of a Humanitarian Coordinator (HC), the composition of personnel and structural posture of the Country Team remained unchanged. This left the UN with a model of UN action in the field that was clearly unsuitable for discharging the UN's human rights and humanitarian responsibilities during in a crisis situation (para. 78, iv).

3 *Systemic failure:* The UN system failed to respond adequately to early warning signals because (i) it lacked an adequate and shared sense of responsibility for human rights violations; (ii) of an incoherent internal UN crisis-management structure that failed to conceive and execute a strategy in response to early warnings; (iii) of an ineffective dispersal of capacity and responsibility at UNHQ due to overlapping human rights and humanitarian law mandates; (iv) of lack of sufficient training and experience among senior staff; (v) of inadequate political support from Member States; (vi) of a framework for Member State engagement with international human rights and humanitarian law protection that was outdated and unworkable, in part because it did not enable Member States to reach a sufficiently early and full political consensus on the situation and the UN response (para. 80).

From this, the Panel made six substantive recommendations (all from para. 87):

> First, *the Secretary General should renew a vision of the UN's most fundamental responsibilities regarding large-scale violations of international human rights and humanitarian law,* especially among senior staff. In other words, the UN's senior staff should be reminded that, above all else and

irrespective of specific mandates in individual countries, the UN is judged primarily on its ability to protect populations from serious abuses.

Second, *a human rights perspective should be embedded into UN strategies*. The report calls for measures to ensure that international human rights and humanitarian and criminal law perspectives are brought into overall UN analysis and strategies when needed and that the UN's capacity to secure support from Member States for advocacy and action should also be strengthened. The report identifies several ways of doing this, including: (1) ensuring that the Secretary-General's office has senior staff with backgrounds in human rights and humanitarian law; (2) awarding OHCHR an oversight role over all human rights and humanitarian law aspects of crisis response and consolidating staff working in this area within the OHCHR's New York office; (3) strengthening day-to-day collaboration between the Department of Political Affairs (DPA) and OHCHR; (4) establishing small teams of experts that could be deployed rapidly into crises affected areas.

Third, *management of system-wide crisis response should be strengthened*. The UN's response to crises involving large-scale risks to populations should be made more coherent. In particular: (1) one senior official should be given overall responsibility for overseeing crisis response (UN Senior Official); (2) there should be a single coordinating mechanism per crisis situation and this should provide meaningful information to the Policy Committee; (3) during crises involving the potential violation of international humanitarian and human rights law, the UN must be prepared to generate and publicly release the best available information; (4) field-level coordinators should have relevant expertise in crises involving violations of international human rights or humanitarian law and should report to a relevant headquarters entity (including the UN's Senior Official).

Fourth, *promote accountability and responsibility*. The UN should strengthen its internal mechanisms to ensure that it responds promptly and effectively to human rights crises. In particular, departments and agencies should conduct minimum human rights 'due diligence' checks and regularly request information from the OHCHR on serious human rights concerns. The UN should also review its actions in response to every crisis involving large-scale risks to civilian populations.

Fifth, *improve UN engagement with Member States and build political support*. The Secretary General and Secretariat must be able to provide credible information to Member States about an unfolding protection crisis and suggest courses of action. To facilitate this: (1) the Secretary General should invite interested Member States to attend briefings by the heads of the Department of Political Affairs (DPA), OHCHR, and the Office for the Coordination of Humanitarian Affairs (OCHA); (2) the Secretary General should make explicit use of his convening authority under Article 99; (3) the Secretary General should work with Member States to suggest new models for convening and beginning consideration of the potential responses to a crisis at an earlier stage; (4) the Secretary General should use RtoP as a 'convening' initiative to invite Member States to receive and consider relevant information; (5) the Secretariat should make use of digital media to inform Member States.

Sixth, *better address violations of privileges and immunities*. The Secretary General should invite Member States to consider adopting measures in situations where one Member State engages in sustained actions that violate the privileges and immunities of UN personnel. More work is needed to strengthen the support given to staff who are threatened, intimidated, and harassed.

The place of RtoP in the United Nations action in Sri Lanka

The Review Panel found that the Responsibility to Protect (RtoP) principle and the Special Adviser for the Prevention of Genocide (now the UN Office for Genocide Prevention and the Responsibility to Protect) played a relatively minor role in the proceedings. It also judged that, to the extent that it played any role at all, RtoP was an extraneous and distracting factor. It should be recalled, however, that the events recounted in the Report occurred at the same time as the completion and release of the Secretary General's first report on the *Implementation of the Responsibility to Protect*.[3] The UN General Assembly considered this report only after the main crisis phase in Sri Lanka had passed. In that context, it is not surprising that RtoP's potential contribution remained unclear.

The main practical engagement with the RtoP principle came in the context of initiatives undertaken by the Special Adviser for the Prevention of Genocide, Francis Deng. On 9 March, the Special Adviser raised concerns with the Sri Lankan Permanent Representative to the UN, advising that there were 'massive civilian casualties' but noting that he would raise his concerns only in bilateral meetings and not 'speak out' in public statements on the issue (Annex III, para. 85). Later, presumably once it became clear that this quiet approach had failed to change the government's behavior, the Special Adviser changed his position. He sent two notes to the Secretary General detailing the known international humanitarian law elements of the crisis and sought approval from the Executive Office of the Secretary General to issue a public statement. Approval was not granted.

More generally, with regard to RtoP, the Review Panel suggested that there was uncertainty about how the concept ought to be employed and disagreement about its intrinsic merits. It found that

> the Concept of a Responsibility to Protect was raised occasionally during the final stages of the conflict, but to no useful result. Differing perceptions among Member States and the Secretariat of the concept's meaning and use had become so contentious as to nullify its potential value. Indeed, making reference to the Responsibility to Protect was seen as more likely to weaken rather than strengthen UN action. The events in Sri Lanka highlight the urgent need for the UN to update its strategy for engagement with Member States in situations where civilian populations caught up in the midst of armed conflicts are not protected in accordance with international human rights and humanitarian law.
> (para. 74)

In addition to discussions about RtoP having 'no useful result,' the panel also identified 'frequently inconclusive discussions on the concept of the Responsibility to Protect' as one of the main extraneous factors that drew attention away from the grave situation confronting civilians in affected areas.

These findings are perhaps unsurprising given the nascent state of RtoP implementation at the time but they are troubling nonetheless and demonstrate the need for more attention to the paid to the practical implementation of RtoP within the UN system. The Report identified ways in which RtoP might be put to better use in future situations. Most notably, it suggested that RtoP could provide a framework for facilitating an early consensus among Member States on human rights protection – 'although many Member States still have serious concerns regarding some interpretations and implications of the Responsibility to Protect, in practice possibly the greatest contribution of this concept would be as a process to help facilitate the emergence among Member States of early political consensus on human rights protection' (para. 86). In this vein,

> the Secretary-General should use the Responsibility to Protect as a "convening" initiative to invite Member States to receive and consider information on the human rights aspects of a relevant crisis situation; and in this regard [the] Department of Political Affairs [DPA] and Office of the High Commissioner for Human Rights [OHCHR] should be jointly tasked with managing its use and fulfilling the Secretariat's own responsibilities under the concept.
>
> (para. 87, e4)

Learning the lessons of Sri Lanka in implementing RtoP

This section examines ways in which implementation of RtoP within the UN system might help strengthen the UN's capacity to respond to protection crises similar to the one in Sri Lanka in 2008–2009. It focuses on five thematic areas: early warning and assessment, use of the Secretary-General's convening authority invested in the Office on Genocide Prevention and the Responsibility to Protect, mainstreaming an atrocity prevention lens across the UN system, strengthening engagement and the provision of information to Member States, and improving the ongoing learning of lessons.

Early warning and assessment

The challenges

The Internal Review Panel repeatedly stressed that the UN system generated ample evidence and analysis to predict well in advance that a militarized crisis in the Wanni would pose serious dangers to the civilian population. There was also evidence to suggest that this risk included the danger of war crimes, ethnic cleansing and crimes against humanity. These signals were not translated into clear early warning assessments and were not systematically incorporated into policy planning. That was because 'the analysis and understanding of the conflict within the UN as a whole was inadequate' (para. 59).

Those with experience of Sri Lanka predicted that the restarting of armed hostilities between the government and the LTTE would trigger a protection crisis. For instance, after a visit to Sri Lanka in December 2007, the Special Representative of the Secretary General on the Human Rights of Internally Displaced Persons reported that

> important lessons applicable to future situations may be drawn from the experience of mass displacement in the East. . . . The campaign in the East saw repeated allegations on both sides that civilians were targeted, used as human shields, or prevented from fleeing hostilities . . . [and] allegations of deliberate co-location of military installations near civilian populations and indiscriminate shelling.
>
> (para. 7)

In January 2008, the DPA produced an 'Options Paper' in which it expressed concern that a revival in armed conflict would create 'anticipated massive new internal displacement' and the potential for a major humanitarian crisis (Annex III, para. 14).

The Internal Review Panel found that the UN's response to these early warnings was 'mixed' (para. 8). A range of initiatives were adopted to respond to these warnings: UN Special Rapporteurs and the OHCHR repeatedly advocated the establishment of a human rights mission, the Department of Political Affairs identified a strategy for responding to the situation (that included achieving a political solution, nominating a special envoy, establishing a human rights field presence, and ensuring accountability), and the UN agreed on a strategy of high-level visits to present concerns and recommendations. However, because key elements of this strategy (especially those relating to strengthening the UN's human rights presence and political engagement) were rejected by the Sri Lankan government, they were never implemented. From early 2009, according to the DPA, the leadership at UNHQ was aware of the risk that the fighting posed to the civilian population and 'adjusted' its Sri Lanka focus to 'avert[ing] a large scale loss of civilian life' by encouraging the parties to permit civilians to leave the area. However, with no mandate from the Security Council, UN officials judged that they could not play a more assertive.

One of the principal sources of this gap between the generation of early-warning data and its proper assessment and utilization was the fact the fact that no office in UNHQ was specifically mandated to perform this task. The UN's lead-agency on human rights (OHCHR) had no direct role in monitoring and assessing the situation (para. 63). The crisis predated the establishment of an early warning and assessment capacity within the Office on Genocide Prevention and RtoP. The nub of the problem was that before the crisis erupted there was no consolidated assessment of available information with a view to early warning and no atrocity-specific analysis informing the UN's program of action in Sri Lanka.

RtoP and potential responses

The Sri Lanka experience clearly demonstrates the capacity of the UN system to generate sufficient information to guide early warning of genocide, war crimes, ethnic cleansing and crimes against humanity. However, because no particular entity was charged with receiving this information, assessing it, and disseminating advice about its implications for the protection of populations from grave crimes, the information was not sufficiently utilized. Early-warning assessments could have been used to:

- Sensitize senior UN officials to expect a major protection crisis.
- Provide the analytical basis for measures such as reconfiguring the UNCT, providing support and advice to the RC, establishing a single coordinating group at UNHQ, and establishing a new framework of engagement focused on protection.
- Inform and engage interested Member States at an early stage in the crisis.
- Shape and inform diplomatic engagement with the parties to the conflict.
- Provide an analytical basis on which to develop policy options.

In addition, rigorous and systematic early warning and assessment adds to the credibility of information and increases the confidence of potential users. The Sri Lanka experience reaffirms evidence found elsewhere that officials are often reluctant to adopt assertive positions in relation to protection crises in part because they are uncertain about the validity of the information and advice they are presented with especially if it leads them into conflict with others. In the past, UN representatives in the field have worried that the use of early-warning indicators might jeopardize their relations with the local authorities.[4] However, an early-warning and assessment system housed in a designated office overcomes these problems in two ways: first, the development and use of a reliable predictive method that is recognized across the UN system gives analysts a sound basis on which to make their assessments and lends system-wide credibility to those assessments. Second, giving a particular office primary responsibility for early warning and assessment relieves officials with other mandates of the burden of having to decide whether to voice their concerns and insulates them from potential political blowback.

In the past few years there have been significant advances in the UN's capacity to provide early warning and assessment of situations that contain the risk of genocide, war crimes, ethnic cleansing, and crimes against humanity. These began with the appointment of a Special Adviser for the Prevention of Genocide and accelerated with the 2005 commitment to RtoP and the subsequent establishment of an Office on Genocide Prevention and the Responsibility to Protect with a mandate for early warning and assessment.

The Mandate of the Special Adviser for the Prevention of Genocide, appointed in 2004, included tasks directly related to early warning and assessment: (a) to collect existing information, in particular from within the UN system, relating to violations of human rights that could give rise, if nothing were done, to genocide; (b) to bring situations of concern to the Secretary General and, through him, to the Security Council; (c) to make recommendations to the Security Council, through the Secretary General, on actions to prevent or halt genocide; (d) to liaise with the UN system on activities for the prevention of genocide and to enhance the capacity of the UN system to analyze and manage relevant information.[5]

As part of their commitment to RtoP at the 2005 World Summit, Member States pledged to 'support the United Nations in establishing an early warning capability' covering the four crimes and violations relating to the concept: genocide, war crimes, ethnic cleansing and crimes against humanity (para. 139). In his 2010 report on *Early Warning, Assessment and the Responsibility to Protect,* the Secretary General observed that early warning was essential to facilitate the provision of assistance to states 'before conflicts break out,' to identify which states are 'under stress' and to guide timely and decisive collective action, when necessary, through Chapters VI, VII, and VIII of the UN Charter. He called for the incorporation of the work of his Special Adviser on the Responsibility to Protect into a new Joint Office for Genocide Prevention and RtoP that would, among other things, combine the existing early warning work of the Special Adviser for the Prevention of Genocide with an additional focus on the other three crimes covered by RtoP (war crimes, ethnic cleansing, and crimes against humanity). Through this office,

> the Special Advisers, based largely on information provided by, and in consultation with, other United Nations entities, conclude that a situation could result in genocide, war crimes, ethnic cleansing or crimes against humanity, [will] provide early warning to me and, through me, to the Security Council and other relevant intergovernmental organs.[6]

The expansion of the office's work was subsequently approved by the General Assembly's Fifth (Budget) Committee in December 2010. The Committee also affirmed the office's mandate for early warning, which stemmed from the original mandate of the Special Adviser for Genocide Prevention as well as from the World Summit Outcome Document, by approving a new P4 position to cover the early warning and assessment functions and provide support for the emergency convening functions described in the Secretary-General's report and discussed in more detail below.

Since then, the Office on Genocide Prevention and RtoP (OGPRtoP) has developed and refined an Analysis Framework for early warning and assessment,[7] monitored emerging situations, and issued statements of concern in the name of the Special Advisers about situations containing the risk of crimes and violations relating to RtoP – often reminding national authorities about their own protection responsibilities. The office has also begun to strengthen its ties with the rest of the UN system and to provide assistance to other departments where possible. In particular, it has established a network of focal points across the system and, in May 2012, assumed the responsibilities of co-chair of the United Nations Inter-Agency

Framework Team for Coordination on Preventive Action (Framework Team) for a one-year period. The Framework Team

> constitutes a forum that includes 22 UN departments and agencies. Its Expert Reference Group (ERG) works for the coordination of strategies and activities on conflict prevention, while incorporating the distinct perspectives provided by each Group member. Although it meets at UN headquarters, its members are closely connected to their field offices. The Framework Team supports RCs and UNCTs in developing integrated prevention strategies, and works to identify and deploy the technical resources required for their implementation. In May and June 2012, the Framework Team undertook consultations to identify priority situations for early engagement to promote measures for conflict and atrocity prevention, as well as measures to strengthen the effectiveness of this internal coordination mechanism.[8]

These existing mandates and evident progress towards strengthening the UN's capacity in this area means that there is no need to create new instruments or bureaucracies in response to the Internal Review Panel's findings on early warning and assessment. Instead, what is required is the augmentation of the UN's capacity to implement its existing mandates in this area. Because so much of the UN's work impacts on the prevention of genocide, war crimes, ethnic cleansing and crimes against humanity, the UN is already engaged in gathering information relevant to the assessment of future risk. The key goal is therefore not the generation of more information but rather the timely collation and assessment of existing knowledge and the timely dissemination of assessed information to decision-makers. Beginning in 2008, what is now the OGPRtoP has liaised with its counterparts in other UN departments to consider ways of fostering greater collaboration and information sharing. One particularly useful aspect of this collaboration was the development of an inventory of sources relevant to early warning and prevention. With the sharing and overlapping of prevention responsibilities, a parallel project was developed involving the collection of 'monitoring and information collection systems within the UN,' related to the prevention of genocide. Contacts with various departments were maintained in the office by an 'information management officer' to ensure that its resources were used effectively by gathering existing sources of information in the UN system relevant for the prevention of genocide.

In light of the Internal Review Panel's findings and recommendations, it seems clear that the OGPRtoP's early warning and assessment role needs to be given fresh impetus and emphasis. The 2014 publication of a new framework for analyzing risk was an important step forward in this regard. There are four key priorities in this regard:

First, *emphasize that early warning and assessment is one of the primary responsibilities of the Office on Genocide Prevention and the Responsibility to Protect.* The office ought to communicate the importance of early warning and assessment and the centrality of this to its mandate to both the UN system and the wider public. Without prejudice to their own monitoring and reporting activities,

UN bodies need to be aware that early warning and assessment in relation to the four RtoP crimes is the primary responsibility of the OGPRtoP and should support the office in the exercise of its mandate.

Second, *early warning and assessment ought to be identified as a key daily function of the office.* OGPRtoP should support the P4 responsible for early warning and assessment in his/her information-gathering activities and provide analytical support. Where appropriate and possible, the Special Advisers should be actively involved in setting priorities, guiding analysis and reviewing assessments.

Third, *strengthen working level relationships within the UN system to facilitate information sharing.* It is not sufficient that the UN system generates information relevant to the prevention of genocide, war crimes, ethnic cleansing and crimes against humanity. The Internal Review Panel makes it clear that relevant information and analysis must be shared be properly assessed. Because OGPRtoP has a mandate for early warning and assessment, it is imperative that UN bodies ensure that relevant information reaches the office both to inform its ongoing assessments and to alert it to new and emerging situations. The Framework Team provides a useful vehicle for developing and clarifying information sharing processes but it may also be useful for the Office to work bilaterally with relevant UN entities, especially the OHCHR, to establish processes for information sharing. The OGPRtoP should also continue to examine ways in which it might participate in other UN frameworks for early warning, assessment and the monitoring of ongoing situations.

Fourth, *develop protocols governing the character and scope of early warning assessments, the audience, and the mode of dissemination.* To be effective as a guide to decision making, not only does information acquisition and assessment need to be systematic, so too does dissemination. Assessments need to be provided in a clear and consistent format that is meaningful, reliable, accurate, and easy to use. They need to be directed towards officials; departments and/or inter-departmental mechanisms that expect to receive them and contain processes for acting upon them. Moreover, consideration needs to be given to whether it is the place of early warning assessments to recommend activation of the Secretary-General's convening authority (see below). Moreover, expectations need to be created about relative scales of threat and these ought to be reflected in the format and dissemination of warnings. There may be circumstances in which the threat is judged so extreme as to warrant direct communication to the Secretary General and recommendations that the matter be brought to the Security Council. Both of these conditions (direct communication with the Secretary General and advice relating to the Security Council) are explicitly mentioned in the OGPRtoP's early warning mandate and expectations should be framed accordingly. In many, if not most, cases, however, the threat may not be immediately imminent or severe. It is important nonetheless that relevant assessments are fed into the UN's normal processes for country engagement in such circumstances. In the case of Sri Lanka, for example, assessments would have made explicit what many UN officials thought implicitly – that any resumption of armed conflict would likely cause massive civilian suffering and, in all probability, the commission of war crimes and ethnic cleansing. This would have forced both the UNCT and UNHQ to consider these threats in existing and contingency planning and would sensitized senior officials to the latent risks. In that event, protection concerns would have been raised and discussed well before the onset of the crisis.

Convening

The challenges

One of the most critical problems identified by the Internal Review Panel was that 'it was unclear who had overall leadership or responsibility for the UN response to the escalating crisis' (para. 61). This created confusion with the UNHQ, UNCT, and among Member States resulted in the sending of mixed messages, diluted support for the RC, inhibited engagement with Member States, and contributed to the diffusion of responsibility such that no one saw the protection of vulnerable civilians as being their primary responsibility. In that context, the Report noted at least four major sets of problems with respect to the structure of the UN's engagement with Sri Lanka.

First, UNHQ 'leadership and coordination' utilized a number of different mechanisms that were not always well cohered. As a result, it was not clear who had overall leadership. UN development engagement was organized through the UN Development Assistance Framework (UNDAF, 2008–2012) and the Consolidated Humanitarian Appeals (CHAPS, 2008 and 2009). Overall coordination of the UN's analysis and political engagement was initially led by the DPA (Assistant Secretary-General [ASG] Political Affairs), but in 2008, the Secretary General gave this role to his own Chef de Cabinet. As the situation in Sri Lanka deteriorated and the UN's efforts came to focus on the provision of humanitarian relief, the USG-Humanitarian Affairs came to play a more prominent leadership role, and the Executive Committee on Humanitarian Affairs (ECHA) became more central as a vehicle for coordination. At the working level, UNHQ established an Inter-Agency Working Group on Sri Lanka (IAWG-SL) to coordinate responses (para. 9). The Chef de Cabinet did not attend IAWG-SL meetings. The Secretary-General's Policy Committee also considered the situation in Sri Lanka. Significantly, with the partial exception of the DPA and, during the final stages of the crisis, the Secretary General himself, none of these mechanisms were focused primarily on protection.

Second, the UN's Resident Coordinator (RC) in Sri Lanka was not provided with adequate advice and support by UNHQ. The RC was the senior UN official in Sri Lanka and, in keeping with emerging policies on 'delivering as one,' fulfilled several responsibilities: RC responsible for development assistance (reporting to the Secretary General through the Administrator of the UNDP), Humanitarian Coordinator (HC) responsible for coordinating humanitarian activities (with support from OCHA), and Designated Official with responsibility for staff safety and security. Country heads of the various UN entities reported to their own regional offices. The RC was therefore confronted with the challenge of having to juggle simultaneous mandates that sometimes imposed contradictory demands. The Internal Review Panel found that the RC was not provided with sufficiently clear guidance or support from UNHQ. As a result, critical decisions such as the withdrawal of staff were taken without advice from conflict, protection or RtoP experts at UNHQ. This problem was compounded by obvious divisions among the UN's most senior headquarters staff, which made it difficult for the RC to identify and act on priority issues – the foremost of which should have been the protection of civilians. In addition, both the DPA and OCHA avoided giving advice on the human rights dimensions of the crisis on the grounds that this was not their mandated responsibility.

Third, the composition and mandate of the UNCT in Sri Lanka and the UN's overall framework of action was configured primarily for managing development assistance and was not changed sufficiently to reflect the new circumstances and the UN's protection responsibilities. Relatively minimal changes were made to the structure and work of the UNCT to reflect the dramatically changed situation in Sri Lanka in late 2008. A Human Rights Adviser was appointed to support the RC and provide a link to the OHCHR and a Reconciliation and Development Adviser was appointed to provide a link to the DPA. A Gender Adviser was also appointed. The UNCT also established a Crisis Management Group (CMG), which initially focused on logistical and operational issues in the north but as the situation deteriorated was confronted with political, protection, and human rights questions (para. 11).

These modest changes were insufficient to configure the UNCT to address a situation characterized by violations of international humanitarian law and human rights law and where RtoP considerations and numerous Security Council Resolutions on the protection of civilians in armed conflict came into play. The UN system as a whole is charged with implementing and monitoring compliance with these standards. The Internal Review Panel recognized that, irrespective of individual country mandates, the UN is expected to follow up on these protection responsibilities and that the organization's performance is measured largely on its ability to exercise these responsibilities. However, the dramatic deterioration of conditions in the Wanni and repeated early warnings did not prompt a reconfiguration of the UNCT from a development-led to a protection-led entity. Indeed, the Report found that 'there was a widespread perception that the international human rights and humanitarian law aspects of protection were not a part of UNCT priorities' (Annex V, para. 8).

Fourth, the UN did not communicate with a single voice. During crisis situations, it is imperative that communication from the UN be unified and consistent. Inconsistencies undermine the credibility and hence the effectiveness of messages. In the case of Sri Lanka, public communication should have indicated the UN's best understanding of the situation, recognized government (as well as LTTE) responsibility for civilian casualties, located these responsibilities within the framework of international humanitarian and human rights law, and established a degree of accountability (Annex V, para. 6). In the event, communication was fragmented and divided. It conveyed only the message that UNHQ was divided and that the RC was relatively isolated. Senior UN staff reported that the Sri Lankan government was aware of the divisions within the UN (Annex III, para. 87).

RtoP and potential responses

The Internal Review Panel made a range of recommendations aimed at improving the coherence of the UN's response to crisis situations through two principal mechanisms: (1) measures to ensure that the UN system pursues a common strategy and (2) processes to facilitate the reconfiguration of UNCTs to take account of changed circumstances.

In relation to the second of these, the Panel pointed to the January 2012 Policy Committee decision on 'special circumstances' as a useful step in the right direction that could be further built on. This decision recognized that changes in the political context in which a UNCT operates might require the UN to do additional things. In some circumstances, development-led UNCTs may prove insufficient. The 'special circumstances' policy states that in these situations, the UN's framework for engagement should reflect the changed circumstances and that headquarters should provide additional support to RCs. This policy provides a framework for reconfiguring UNCTs as need dictates, but needs to be further developed and clarified.

The key problems in relation to the coherence of the UN's response to the crisis in Sri Lanka were unclear lines of leadership and multiple overlapping coordination mechanisms that lacked clear hierarchy. The Internal Review Panel recommended that new mechanisms be established to remedy this problem, focusing on the appointment of a Senior Official with ultimate responsibility for the UN's response to a crisis. Whether or not this specific recommendation is adopted, the UN already has a mechanism for coordinating responses to major crises involving the threat or commission of genocide, war crimes, ethnic cleansing and crimes against humanity – the convening authority invested in the OPGRtoP.

The idea of granting the OPGRtoP authority to convene UN departments to discuss and evaluate policy options and provide advice to the Secretary General in crisis situations involving the commission or imminent risk of genocide and mass atrocities was first raised in the Secretary-General's 2009 report on *Implementing the Responsibility to Protect*. There, he wrote:

> Information is a necessary but hardly sufficient condition for an effective collective response. How the available information is assessed matters a great deal in situations relating to the responsibility to protect, given the patterns of behaviour, action and intent involved in the four specified crimes and violations. Similarly, because the United Nations response could involve a mix of policy tools under Chapters VI, VII and/or VIII of the Charter, and because that mix should be reviewed and adjusted as events evolve on the ground, the decision-making process should be relatively broad-based, inclusive and

flexible at both the Secretariat and intergovernmental levels. To ensure system-wide coherence in policymaking within the Secretariat, as well as an early and flexible response tailored to the needs of each situation, an inter-agency and interdepartmental mechanism will be utilized to consider policy options to be presented to me and, through me, to relevant intergovernmental bodies.

(para. 5)

The Secretary-General returned to this theme the following year, providing more information about what he envisaged:

If the situation persists, and if national authorities are manifestly failing to protect their populations from these crimes, I will invoke new internal procedures to expedite and regularize the process by which the United Nations considers its response and its recommendations to the appropriate intergovernmental body or bodies. In such cases, I will ask the Special Advisers to convene an urgent meeting of key Under-Secretaries-General to identify a range of multilateral policy options, whether by the United Nations or by Chapter VIII regional arrangements, for preventing such mass crimes and for protecting populations. Such an emergency meeting will be prepared through a working level process convened by the Special Advisers, and the results, including the pros and cons of each option, will be reported promptly to me or, should I choose, to the Policy Committee. This is without prejudice to the role of the relevant United Nations entities, acting within their mandates, to bring any situation to my attention and, through me, to the Security Council and other relevant intergovernmental organs.[9]

The General Assembly's Fifth Committee recognized the convening authority of the OPGRtoP in December 2010 when it approved the appointment of a P4 with a job description that included provision of administrative support to it.

It is not difficult to see how the convening process described by the Secretary General might address some of the concerns raised by the Internal Review Panel. At the request of the Secretary General, and potentially in response to early warning advice, the Special Advisers on Genocide Prevention and RtoP would convene a meeting of Under-Secretaries General to provide policy advice to the Secretary General. Some clarifications may be required, however, in light of the findings of the Internal Review Panel. In particular:

• The convening mechanism should not be limited to a single meeting but should instead operate for the duration of the crisis or until another coordinating mechanism is established.
• The meetings should not only adopt views on the merits of individual policies but should aim to develop advice relating to a system-wide strategy for responding to the crisis at hand.
• Once the Secretary General has determined the strategy, the mechanism should maintain overall responsibility for overseeing its implementation and

- providing ongoing advice until such a time as an alternative framework is established or the Secretary General determines that improved conditions on the ground remove the need for a coordinating mechanism.
- It needs to be widely understood that, once convened, the mechanism acts as the principal coordinating body. Other mechanisms would be subordinate until or unless the Secretary General determines otherwise.
- The Senior Official role recommended by the Internal Review Panel could be accommodated into this system.

The convening authority has not yet been used. Reticence about using the mechanism is partly a product of continuing concerns within some parts of the UN about the system's merits and concerns about the capacity of the small OGPRtoP to manage such a large and potentially complex administrative undertaking. Because the convening authority has not yet been used, there remains uncertainty about how it would work, what it would do, and how it would relate to other coordinating mechanisms. These concerns notwithstanding, the Internal Review Panel identified a clear need for a single coordinating mechanism in crisis situations involving the commission of RtoP crimes. There are at least four reasons for thinking that the OPGRtoP's convening authority is particularly well suited to the task. First, the mandate and basic shape of the process are already in place and have been recognized by the General Assembly. Second, the OPGRtoP's mandate is primarily and explicitly concerned with the protection of populations from crimes and violations relating to RtoP, making it an appropriate convening actor and clearly signaling that the UN's primary purpose in such situations is to protect human life. Third, the OPGRtoP has a specific early warning and assessment mandate that is closely related to the convening authority mandate. Fourth, the OPGRtoP is a small office that does not have a field presence. It can therefore play the role of impartial convener somewhat more effectively than departments that are invested directly in the field. If OGPRtoP is to retain its convening authority, it is imperative that the UN makes use of it when needed.

To overcome concerns about the use of the convening authority, however, it is important to advance thinking on its operationalization. Next steps could include the following.

First, *in consultation with UN partners, the OGRtoP could develop draft terms of reference for the convening authority.* There remains considerable uncertainty about what is entailed in the OGRtoP's convening authority. These include questions about how it would be triggered, how it would relate to other coordinating mechanisms, mandates, the Policy Committee and the UNCT, how decisions would be taken about what advice to convey to the Secretary General, the proper content of strategies of engagement (including communications strategies), and questions about procedural matters relating to composition, term, and termination. To address these questions, the OGPRtoP could prepare draft terms of reference in close consultation with UN partners and the Secretary-General that address these and other concerns with a view to finding terms that are efficient, effective and command a consensus among stakeholders.

Second, the administrative challenges for the OGPRtoP associated with the convening authority might be overcome by sharing bureaucratic responsibilities with another, larger, UN office. The Internal Review Panel makes a strong case for giving the OHCHR office in New York a stronger role in crisis decision making. One potential avenue for achieving this goal and improving the OGPRtoP's administrative capacity would be for the two offices to share responsibilities by co-convening the coordinating mechanism.

More consultation is required within the system to develop a coordination process that is effective but that also commands trust among stakeholders. Consultation within the UN system could be directed to develop protocols to govern the convening authority. At the same time, the OGPRtoP ought to be prepared to advise that the Secretary General use the convening authority when crises emerge in countries that do not already have an appropriate coordinating framework. As mentioned earlier, the OGPRtoP could offer advice on situations where circumstances dictate use of the convening authority as part of its early warning assessments.

Mainstreaming an atrocity-prevention lens

The challenges

One of the problems highlighted by the Internal Review Panel was that the grave situation confronted by civilians in Sri Lanka was only one among a "mosaic of considerations" guiding UN staff (para. 77). At the time of the crisis, the UN's engagement with Sri Lanka was guided by the UNDAF and CHAP, neither of which included atrocity specific considerations. At UNHQ, neither the EOSG, DPA nor OCHA paid particular attention to the parties' compliance with international human rights and humanitarian law. The OHCHR was the only body to focus consistently on the human rights dimensions of the unfolding crisis. However, the OHCHR had a limited field presence (a single Human Rights Adviser who was not consulted on major decisions) and was not supported in its efforts by other parts of the system. As such, despite predictions from within the UN that the resumption of armed conflict in Sri Lanka would lead to war crimes, ethnic cleansing, and/or crimes against humanity, the UN's engagement there was not restructured to make the organization better able to fulfill its protection responsibilities. Moreover, the UN did not plan for contingencies including crisis escalation requiring a protection-focused response. In rapidly deteriorating situations, such as that confronted in the Wanni in late 2008, there is a critical need to focus on core priorities. When confronted by the actual or potential imminent commission of war crimes and crimes against humanity, the central organizing principle for UN engagement ought to be the protection of human life from these grave threats. The Internal Review Panel pointed out that humanitarian access, delivery of assistance, freedom of movement, and dissemination of casualty information were 'all fundamental to the protection of life' (para. 46).

RtoP and potential responses

Immediately after the 2005 World Summit, the Special Adviser on the Prevention of Genocide (then, Juan Mendez) initiated dialogue within the Secretariat's Executive Committee on Peace and Security (ECPS) on how to translate the agreement on RtoP into the working practices of the UN system.[10] The ECPS established an informal working group to 'identify and develop a repertoire of measures within the mandates or responsibilities of UN departments and agencies that would assist Member States fulfilling effectively their responsibility to protect.'[11] Chaired by the Office of the Special Adviser (OSAPG) and the OHCHR, the group developed a repertoire of measures – classified as diplomatic, humanitarian, and other peaceful means – that could be employed to support Member States to fulfill their protection responsibilities.[12] The working group also called on the ECPS to seek a common system-wide understanding of RtoP, undertake a detailed review of the availability or lack thereof or specific measures to prevent genocide, war crimes, ethnic cleansing and crimes against humanity, and for its members to continue discussion on operationalizing RtoP in the Policy Committee.[13]

The appointment of Edward Luck as the Secretary-General's Special Adviser on the Responsibility to Protect represented a clear step forward in this process. Luck recognized that the Special Adviser on RtoP would need to develop a close working relationship with the Special Adviser on Genocide Prevention and that the work of the two advisers would depend 'on close substantive and institutional relationships' with the OHCHR, DPA, OCHA, the Department of Peacekeeping Operations (DPKO) and the Office of Legal Affairs (OLA).[14] He judged that implementation of the second pillar of RtoP, which relates to supporting and encouraging states to fulfill their responsibility to protect, required the 'buy-in' of the UN Development Program (UNDP) and 'other development and peacebuilding actors,' including the Peacebuilding Support Office (PBSO) and the World Bank. Also 'critical to implementing RtoP would be other entities mandated to address parts of the broader human protection agenda,' including UNICEF (the UN Children's Fund), the UN High Commissioner for Refugees (UNHCR), and the Special Representatives of the Secretary-General for Children and Armed Conflict and Sexual Violence and Conflict.[15]

These ideas about the need for a system-wide approach to implementing RtoP were translated by the Secretary General into a call for the mainstreaming of RtoP's goals into the work of system. In his 2009 report on *Implementing the Responsibility to Protect*, the Secretary General wrote:

> The United Nations and its range of agencies, funds and programmes have in place critical resources, activities and field operations that are already making important contributions to the elimination of these man-made scourges. They could do that much more effectively if goals relating to the responsibility to protect, including the protection of refugees and the internally displaced, were mainstreamed among their priorities, whether in the areas of human rights, humanitarian affairs, peacekeeping, peacebuilding, political affairs or development. Each of these areas of United Nations activity have much to bring to

the common effort. The emphasis of the present report is therefore on forging a common strategy rather than on proposing costly new programmes or radically new approaches.[16]

One of the most important elements of 'RtoP mainstreaming' is the adoption of an 'atrocity prevention lens' by UN entities to inform and in some circumstances direct their work across the full-spectrum of prevention activities that they undertake. As the Secretary General explained:

> I would therefore ask the relevant line departments, programmes, agencies and inter-agency networks to incorporate considerations and perspectives relating to the responsibility to protect into their ongoing activities and reporting procedures to the extent that their mandates permit. This would have two major benefits. First, adding the perspective of the responsibility to protect to existing perspectives would help the United Nations to anticipate situations likely to involve the perpetration of such crimes and violations by enhancing its ability to identify precursors, recognize patterns, and share, assess and act on relevant information. The wrong questions produce the wrong answers. Second, such a unifying perspective would facilitate system-wide coherence by encouraging more regular dialogue, information-sharing and common analysis among disparate programmes and agencies.[17]

In other words, UN entities should have the capacity to: (1) understand the factors associated with heightened and imminent risk of genocide and mass atrocities; (2) the extent to which these factors are present in the countries in which they operate; and (3) the ways in which their activities impact on those factors. Where possible, this analysis should inform policy planning and programming by highlighting areas that might warrant additional attention, identifying potential unintended negative consequences of programming for which mitigation strategies might be needed, and potential contingencies. Some field missions already conduct this type of analysis (for example, UNMISS conducts relevant analysis as part of its civilian protection analysis) but the Internal Review Panel highlighted its centrality to all UNCTs. In short, therefore, UNCTs should conduct analysis focused specifically on the threat of genocide, war crimes, ethnic cleansing and crimes against humanity and this analysis should be allowed to guide planning and practice.

The 'atrocity prevention lens' might be likened to establishing a mass atrocity prevention seat at the policy-planning table. Assessments produced of the risks, challenges and opportunities, would introduce the mass atrocity prevention perspective to internal policy debates. This perspective could also contribute to longer-term planning by providing advice about the impact of programming on atrocity prevention and the identification of long-term preventive programs, as well as calling attention to areas where contingency planning may be necessary. As a 'seat at the table,' however, the atrocity prevention lens would be just one voice among many contributing to policy development and need not always be the determining voice. It is important though that RC/HCs are presented with atrocity-specific analysis and that this information is taken into account. The mainstreaming of an atrocity prevention lens would mean that protection crises could be identified earlier. This would, among other things, inform decisions about the transition of country programming to a protection focus and assist the transition. In extreme situations, the atrocity prevention lens could provide UNCTs with the capacity to identify imminent dangers and transfer the relevant information to UNHQ. This would help entities develop situational awareness and policy responses more rapidly as well as improving the flow of information and analysis from the field to UNHQ.

The adoption of an atrocity prevention lens might also contribute guidance in relation to decisions about the withdrawal of staff. The UN has developed a 'programme criticality' framework to guide judgments about which programs ought to be considered essential and therefore subjected to higher levels of risk. In situations such as that confronted in the Wanni, 'criticality' may need to include judgments about the likely commission of war crimes and crimes against humanity in the context of the UN's enduring responsibility to protect populations from these crimes.

Mainstreaming an atrocity prevention lens across the UN system presents innumerable challenges. Anecdotal evidence suggests that there is much work to be done to sensitize officials to the risks of genocide, war crimes, ethnic cleansing and crimes against humanity and the need to spotlight the risks in the advice they provide.[18] There is the additional danger that 'mainstreaming fatigue' and the fact that few, if any, new positions would be approved to do this new work could produce inertia, whereby the rhetoric of atrocity prevention mainstreaming is engaged but not the practice. To avoid these twin pitfalls, mainstreaming should begin by working through and building on existing activities and offices rather than by establishing wholly new processes. Initial steps may include the following.

First, *incorporating an atrocity prevention lens into existing early-warning analysis*. Some UN entities, missions or UNCTs already house early-warning mechanisms of one form or another. Where these exist, atrocity prevention mainstreaming might simply entail the inclusion of an atrocity perspective into those already existing mechanisms. To achieve this goal, entities, missions or UNCTs would need to ensure: (1) that relevant field staff are trained to detect and report the warning signs of genocide, war crimes, ethnic cleansing and crimes against humanity; (2) that reporting procedures specifically call for analysis relating to these issues; and (3) that headquarters have sufficient capacity to monitor information from the field and transfer it to the relevant offices at UNHQ (including OGPRtoP). The OGPRtoP could provide assistance and training to facilitate these capacities.

Second, *the OPGRtoP should continue to work through the Framework Team Expert Reference Group (ERG) to develop a system-wide approach to atrocity prevention, where useful and possible*. The ERG provides a vehicle for identifying countries where a system-wide approach to the prevention of genocide and mass atrocities might be useful and for developing a common approach or strategy. Naturally, this would need to take into consideration the needs of the country and the extent to which an integrated approach is preferable to a non-coordinated approach, as well as avoiding the duplication of work.[19] The ERG may also provide a vehicle to increase system-wide sensitivity to atrocity prevention more broadly. The OPGRtoP and ERG have already begun this work, but it is important that it be given support where needed.

Third, *the OPGRtoP should continue to engage the UN's Peace and Development Advisers (PDAs), offer them training and assistance, and encourage them to utilize an atrocity prevention lens*. The UN has deployed around thirty PDAs. These advisers assist RCs in developing generic strategies for conflict prevention and/or national reconciliation. They are therefore potentially important conduits through which to channel the atrocity prevention lens into the work of UNCTs. The OGPRtoP has been reaching out to PDAs to explain its mandate and work and include them in its information collection and early warning and assessment system. It has also worked with PDAs in developing appropriate responses to situations of concern.

Fourth, *senior officials should be trained to understand and, where appropriate, report*

- local sources of *risk;*
- local sources of *resilience;*
- the legal, moral and political *responsibilities* of the UN in relation to the protection of populations from genocide, war crimes, ethnic cleansing and crimes against humanity; and
- appropriate *responses* to evidence of risk or the commission of crimes or violations relating to RtoP.

One of the major findings of the Internal Review Panel was that few officials saw the protection of the civilian population in the Wanni as their primary responsibility. The Panel called on the Secretary General to 'renew a vision of the UN's most fundamental responsibilities regarding large-scale violations of international human rights and humanitarian law in crises' (para. 87, a). Among other things, it suggested that senior staff be given "refresher" briefings on the principles and values of the UN, with a focus on how this relates to their own work. Chief among those principles is the Responsibility to Protect. To support this goal, the OGPRtoP could consider offering briefings and training to UN officials (both UNHQ and UNCT) on the four themes described above. This would sensitize them to the relationship between conditions in-country and the risks of RtoP related crimes and violations, help them identify sources of resilience to support, reaffirm their legal, moral and political responsibilities and – just as importantly – provide them with support and guidance on what to do when situations emerge that might lead to the commission of one or more of these crimes.

Informing and engaging with Member States

The challenge

The provision of timely and accurate information about situations involving the potential commission of genocide, war crimes, ethnic cleansing, and crimes against humanity can encourage Member States to become actively seized and provide the basis for the development of response options. The Internal Review Panel found that the attitude of Member States towards the Sri Lankan government became more critical after 2008–9 in part because of detailed reports about events there (para. 70). Civil society groups also reported that information sharing is critically important for advocacy (Annex (III, para. 153).

Member States, including non-permanent members of the Security Council, and some UN officials, including members of the EOSG, complained that they received inadequate information about the situation in the Wanni. Although, as the crisis worsened, the situation on the ground increased the challenges associated with data acquisition and verification, this was not the primary source of the problem. Some Member States and UN officials reported that at the peak of the crisis they were receiving almost no information from the Secretariat and relied on reports from NGOs, such as Human Rights Watch. This problem was exacerbated by the fact that the UN's framework for political engagement, which revolved around the "Co-Chairs Group" established at the 2003 Tokyo Donors Conference, did not include critically important neighboring states, such as India (Annex III, para. 20). The UNCT generated credible and verifiable data about civilian casualties in Sri Lanka and a wealth of more anecdotal information about the situation on the ground but this was not properly assessed at UNHQ or communicated to Member States.

On the initiative of individual staff members, the UNCT in Sri Lanka established a Crisis Operations Group. The UNCOG developed a methodology for collecting and verifying information on civilian casualties. Based on world's best practice, this methodology required that each verified civilian casualty be confirmed by three independent sources. This method produced a highly conservative estimate of civilian casualties – now generally considered to be far lower than the actual number of civilian casualties. The information collected by UNCOG clearly highlighted the government's responsibility for civilian casualties. However, as noted earlier, this was not translated into clear communications to that effect because some UN officials were unwilling to accept this information as 'verified' and undermined the information when it was released to the public. Some UN staff observed disagreements even within UNCOG on the collection of data and its use (Annex V, para. 22). Not only did this weaken the information itself, it also undermined the UN's credibility on a range of related matters and fundamentally weakened the UN's capacity to use information to persuade the Sri Lankan government to change its course.

The deeper problem exposed by this issue was the absence of a systematic approach to the collation, analysis, and dissemination of relevant information. There was no system for monitoring civilian casualties. UNCOG was ad hoc and informal. Although UNCOG developed a rigorous methodology, this was not recognized as such across the system. Nor was the first hand evidence of government responsibility for civilian casualties obtained by the UNCT communicated sufficiently to other parts of the UN system. This was primarily because there was no chain of communication between the UNCT and an office within UNHQ charged with evaluating, assessing and disseminating such information.

This ad hoc approach to the provision of information reflected a broader absence of strategy with regard to engaging Member States either to seek general support for the UN's action in Sri Lanka or their support for specific measures. This in part reflected differences of opinion within the Secretariat and in part judgments about the positions of Member States and the likelihood of unity in the Security Council and Human Rights Council. Echoing one of the central findings of the so-called Brahimi Report on UN peacekeeping, the Internal Review Panel concluded that the Secretariat's engagements with Member States on Sri Lanka 'were heavily influenced by what it perceived Member States wanted to hear, rather than by what Member States needed to know if they were to respond'. Of course, this was partly attributable to the failure of Member States to give direction and purpose to the UN's engagement with Sri Lanka (para. 79).

In the final stages of the crisis, the Secretary General undertook personal sustained advocacy, which the Panel found had some positive effect in relation to the return of displaced persons and accountability in the aftermath of the crisis. The Panel argued that the Secretary-General's personal intervention had less of an impact at the height of the crisis because it was not supported by an adequate political strategy, was based on insufficient information, and had only the limited support of Member States (para. 73).

RtoP and potential responses

There is broad agreement that early and full consensus among Member States is critical to improving protection. While the UN Secretariat's capacity build consensus among Member States is obviously limited, it could do more to ensure that they are provided with information about events on the ground and their relation to the legal obligations of the parties (there is evidence that information about atrocity crimes increases the pressure on Member States to take action).[20] The Internal Review Panel also found that the Secretariat could introduce new avenues for engaging interested Member States.

In relation to *the provision of earlier and better information to Member States,* there is a clear imperative for the UN to collect and pass on information about the number and source of civilian casualties in any given situation involving armed conflict or one-sided violence and to provide information and analysis about potential violations of international human rights and humanitarian law. It is the primary responsibility of the OHCHR to provide such information as it relates to gross violations of human rights, though the OGPRtoP also has a mandate to collect information on human rights violations that might give rise to genocide. The collection and dissemination of basic information relating to civilian casualties could be made standard practice within the UN and a dual responsibility of OHCHR and OGPRtoP. Basic information might include:

* Civilian casualty estimates.
* Estimated casualties among specially protected groups (e.g., children).
* Sources of responsibility for civilian casualties.

- Analysis of the extent to which civilian casualties appear to be caused by violations of international humanitarian and human rights law and thus warrant further examination.

It is *imperative* that the UN system speaks as one in relation to the provision of this information. Public or private communications from within the UN that questions the validity of the UN's publicly released information damages the credibility of the Organization's entire approach to a crisis, undermines its diplomacy, and promotes uncertainty among Member States that results in ambivalence and delay. In addition to assigning primary responsibility for the dissemination of basic information to the OHCHR and OPGRtoP and ensuring that the system is aware of this responsibility, two steps would help to systematize the provision of information about civilian casualties.

First, *a standard methodology for civilian casualty estimates should be developed and disseminated.* This methodology should reflect world's best practice as, indeed, the UNCOG's method did in the case of Sri Lanka. That method recorded civilian casualties as 'verified' when they were confirmed by three independent sources. This produced a casualty estimate that proved to be very conservative (very significantly lower than post-war estimate) but which was also very reliable (in that counted casualties were 'real'). In this case, the fact that UNCOG was established in an ad hoc fashion and required to develop its own methodology allowed some officials to claim (wrongly) that the reported casualties were 'unverified' and the figures therefore unreliable. The development and articulation of a system-wide methodology for casualty estimating will give automatic credibility to estimates that employ the methodology and provide strict definitions, understood by the system as a whole, for the terms 'verified' and 'unverified' in this respect.

Second, *in crisis situations the UN should speak with one voice,* unless dictated otherwise by a coordinated communications strategy. As noted earlier, the Internal Review Panel recommended that the UN establish a single coordinating mechanism for responding to crises. It is imperative that coordination includes the UN's messaging to the parties, Member States and wider public. In crisis situations, final responsibility for messaging emanating from either UNHQ or the UNCT, including private messaging to the parties, should lie with the coordinating mechanism or Senior Official responsible for the UN's response. This is necessary to ensure that messaging is properly used as part of a broader strategy focused on human protection (it will be noted that the Panel found that the Secretary-General's personal efforts proved ineffective because they were not part of a strategy), is coherent (the Panel observed instances where UN officials undermined the UN's own statements), and is accurate (the Panel observed that some messaging described verified casualty estimates as 'unverified'). This process should recognize and respect individual mandates that include reporting, including the OHCHR/OGPRtoP mandate to report basic information about civilian casualties, attribution of responsibility, and international legal institutions.

The adoption of a communications strategy, deferral to the coordinating mechanism, respect for existing reporting mandates, and recognition of best practice methodology for casualty estimates will strengthen the UN's capacity to provide timely and accurate information to Member States by strengthening the credibility of its messages.

Generating, analyzing, and disseminating basic information about civilian casualties in a verifiable and systematic fashion would help provide vital information to concerned Member States and facilitate accurate media coverage of events. While this in itself might encourage some Member States to become more engaged, it may not be sufficient to generate political support for specific UN actions. While recognizing that the UN Secretariat has limited influence on decision making in the organization's political bodies, the Internal Review Panel recommended that it become more innovative in its engagement with Member States. Early and effective engagement is necessary in order to political build support for the UN. Irrespective of whether this is subsequently translated into timely and decisive political action, political support strengthens the position of UNHQ and UNCT, especially in relation to recalcitrant parties. One option, proposed by the Internal Review Panel, was the articulation of new models of engagement (such as limited low-impact civilian political and human rights missions) that impact less upon the sovereignty concerns of Member States.

The Internal Review Panel specifically called for the Secretary General to 'use RtoP as a "convening" initiative to invite Member States to receive and consider information on the human rights aspects of a relevant crisis situation' (para. 87, e4). This is appropriate since Member States have committed both to the prevention of the four crimes and violations relating to RtoP and to responding to them in a 'timely and decisive manner.' The commitment of Member States to work through the UN to achieve these goals creates a mandate for the UN to keep Member States informed about situations that relate to these crimes and to facilitate discussion about options for pursuing RtoP's goals. Where situations involve the likely commission of one or more of the four crimes and violations associated with RtoP, this is a function that could be discharged through the Secretary-General's 'Rights up Front' action plan. Finally, the Internal Review Panel suggested that new technology be embraced to facilitate the briefings directly from the field. This could prove an exceptionally useful avenue, especially if it allows Member States to pose questions directly to officials in the field and receive first hand information in an informal setting. The OGPRtoP could examine ways in which it might strengthen its network of UN officials in UNCTs in order to facilitate this kind of deeper engagement with Member States.

Learning lessons for the future

As the Secretary General has pointed out, there is no template for the prevention of genocide, war crimes, ethnic cleansing, and crimes against humanity that can be applied to all cases. As such, learning lessons from past experience is crucial for understanding how situations emerge and develop and how the UN system as a whole functions in crisis situations and might be improved. The Internal Review Panel recognized this and called for a 'limited internal review of UN action in every acute crisis that presents large-scale risks to the protection of civilians' (para. 87, d2).

RtoP and potential responses

Institutional learning is widely understood to be an important catalyst for improved effectiveness. One study of UN peacekeeping, for example, showed a link between a mission's capacity to learn and its operational effectiveness.[21] The UN needs to develop a way of understanding which combination of factors work best in different sorts of situations relating to the actual or imminent commission of the four crimes and violations associated with RtoP. This should be based on rigorous research, the sharing of past experience, the development of shared understandings of appropriate lessons, and consideration of ways in which lessons are learned in practice. Although each UN entity should undertake its own lessons learning where appropriate, the OGPRtoP is the most obvious entity to assume primary responsibility for leading lessons-learned exercises with respect to crises relating to genocide prevention and RtoP. Clearly, however, learning lessons is a politically sensitive undertaking so it might make sense for the UN to invite external research agencies, such as the International Peace Institute, to produce this work from which it could foster learning.

Conclusion

The Internal Review Panel's report on the UN's actions in Sri Lanka in 2008–2009 demonstrates the need for renewed commitment to the implementation of RtoP across the UN system. Between them, the further development of early-warning and assessment capabilities, refinement and use of existing convening authority, the adoption of an atrocity prevention lens, strengthening of information gathering and dissemination and ways of engaging with Member States, and the development of a more systematic approach to lessons learning, provide a basic framework for mainstreaming RtoP goals in the work of the UN system and for implementing a significant proportion of the Panel's recommendations. The objectives and pathways identified in this Occasional Paper should be viewed as a process, not an end state. RtoP goals are achieved, and working practices strengthened, through the act of doing these different sorts of activities. In that sense, giving meaning to the Internal Review Panel's recommendations by redoubling efforts to implement RtoP is about building habits of atrocity prevention and protection across the UN system so that the underlying risks, pathways to escalation and imminent dangers are identified and understood, consideration is given to what the UN system as a whole can do, responses are strategic, well-calibrated and focused on the core priority of protecting human life, and engagement with Member States is informative, engaging and designed to facilitate fulfillment of the responsibility to protect commitments made in 2005. Over time, these activities should become matters of habit and should develop organically into other areas. Should this happen, the prevention of genocide, war crimes, ethnic cleansing, and crimes against humanity could indeed become a 'living reality,' as proposed by Deputy-Secretary-General Jan Eliasson.

Notes

1 Except where otherwise noted, in-text references refer to the Report of the Secretary-General's Internal Review Panel, November 2012. http://www.un.org/News/dh/infocus/Sri_Lanka/The_Internal_Review_Panel_report_on_Sri_Lanka.pdf
2 Gordon Weiss, *The Cage: The Fight for Sri Lanka and the Last Days of the Tamil Tigers* (New York: Bellevue Literary Press, 2012) and James Traub, 'At Risk in Sri Lanka's War,' *Washington Post,* 22 April 2009.
3 *Implementing the Responsibility to Protect: Report of the United Nations Secretary-General,* A/63/677, UN doc, 12 January 2009.
4 James Sutterlin, 'Early Warning and Conflict Prevention: The Role of Conflict Prevention,' in Klaas van Walraven (ed.), *Early Warning and Conflict Prevention* (The Hague: Kluwer, 1998), p. 124.
5 S/2004/567, annex.
6 *Early Warning, Assessment and the Responsibility to Protect, Report of the Secretary-General,* A/64/864, 14 July 2010, para. 18.
7 See http://www.un.org/en/preventgenocide/adviser/pdf/osapg_analysis_framework.pdf [accessed 13 March 2014]
8 http://www.un.org/en/preventgenocide/adviser/engagement_partners.shtml [accessed 13 March 2014]
9 Ban Ki-moon, *Early Warning, Assessment and the Responsibility to Protect: Report of the Secretary-General,* para. 19.
10 Ekkehard Strauss, *The Emperor's New Clothes? The United Nations and the Implementation of the Responsibility to Protect* (Baden-Baden: Nomos, 2009). It will be recalled that para. 140 of the World Summit Outcomes Document had specifically pledged support for the Special Adviser.
11 Executive Committee on Peace and Security, *Report of the Working Group on the Responsibility to Protect,* Part I.
12 Strauss, *Emperor's New Clothes,* p. 61.
13 ECPS, *Report of the Working Group,* p. 13.
14 The OLA made a significant early contribution by helping to clarify the legal status of RtoP and other issues relating to its implementation. It remains actively engaged through the OGPRtoP UN system contact group and the proactive support of Under-Secretary-General Patricia O'Brien. See Patricia O'Brien, 'The Responsibility to Protect: Inception, Conceptualization, Operationalization and Implementation of a new Concept,' statement to the Association of the Bar of New York, Human Rights Committee, 7 February 2012.
15 Edward C. Luck, 'From Promise to Practice: Implementing the Responsibility to Protect,' in Jared Genser and Irwin Cotler (eds.), *The Responsibility to Protect: The Promise of Stopping Mass Atrocities in Our Time* (Oxford: Oxford University Press, 2012), p. 100.
16 Ban Ki-moon, *Implementing the Responsibility to Protect: Report of the Secretary-General,* 12 January 2009, A/63/677, para. 68.
17 Ban, *Implementing the Responsibility to Protect,* annex, para. 4.
18 Thanks to Ekkehard Strauss for this insight.
19 See Victoria Metcalfe, Alison Giffen, and Samir Elhawary, *UN Integration and Humanitarian Space: An Independent Study Commissioned by the UN Integration Steering Group* (Washington, DC: Stimson Center, December 2011).
20 One of the key findings in Alex J. Bellamy, *Massacres and Morality: Mass Killing in an Age of Civilian Immunity* (Oxford: Oxford University Press, 2012).
21 Lise Morje Howard, *UN Peacekeeping in Civil Wars* (Cambridge: Cambridge University Press, 2008).

7 The unintended consequences of UN peacekeeping in post-war South Sudan

Why everyone wants a uniform

Carol Berger

Introduction

Sudan ended a 21-year civil war in January 2005 with the signing of the Comprehensive Peace Agreement (CPA). According to the terms of that agreement, the government army, based in northern Sudan, and the Sudan People's Liberation Army (SLPA) were to be reorganized and their numbers reduced. Under a program of Disarmament, Demobilization and Reintegration, weapons were to be collected and combatants, particularly child soldiers, assisted in their return to civilian life.

The UN Mission in Sudan (UNMIS) was mandated by the UN Security Council to monitor and support the implementation of the CPA. UNMIS included up to 10,000 peacekeepers and additional civilian staff. While the UNMIS presence would suggest a demilitarisation of South Sudan, the reverse has occurred. The immediate post-war period was characterized by efforts to strengthen South Sudanese defences. I argue that the UN and other international agencies effectively reinforced the position of militaristic elements within the government of South Sudan and subverted initiatives to improve conditions for the civilian population. The international community's failure to recognise prevailing hierarchies within South Sudan led to deteriorating security conditions and the subordination of nonmilitary actors to military prerogatives in virtually all spheres of South Sudanese life.

This chapter arises from more than three years of fieldwork in South Sudan. My Doctor of Philosophy research was on the youth wing of the SPLA, which was formed in 1984 and given the name Gheish el Ahmr, or the Red Army. The veterans of that youth wing are now men in their late thirties to early forties. During the period of my research, year to year, I witnessed the ascendance of the military model in South Sudan. It is not surprising that the immediate post-war period was characterized by efforts to strengthen South Sudanese defences. What is perhaps surprising is the degree to which nonmilitary actors have been made subordinate to military prerogatives in virtually all spheres of South Sudanese life. The arrival of UN peacekeepers has, I argue, reinforced this militarization of life in South Sudan.

Begin

For the better part of an hour, the cattle passed along the Yirol to Rumbek road. Hundreds and hundreds of the long-horned cows were being brought to a makeshift cattle camp just north of Rumbek. The day earlier, more than a dozen men had died in fighting between two clans of Dinka living to the north.

South Sudan is awash with weapons. Four years after making peace with northern Sudan, insecurity has worsened for the civilian population. The entire region is in a period of heightened militarization. The cattle being moved into Rumbek on that fall day had been raided, taken by force. The herders were taking them to a place of safety – to the edges of the Rumbek airstrip, where several hundred international peacekeepers with the UNMIS were based. While the protection of looted cattle is not included in the UNMIS mandate, it was a somewhat predictable local understanding of the foreign troops who have come to keep the peace and monitor demobilization and disarmament in South Sudan.

But the livestock represented more than the continuation of cattle raiding between neighbouring Dinka clans. As the region attempts to emerge from more than two decades of civil war, corruption and the alleged taking of public funds by political appointees and senior military officials is frustrating both local and international initiatives. In some high-profile instances, currency has been converted into cows. Teachers and other civil servants have gone without salaries for months at a time. The payment of cash salaries to South Sudanese soldiers brought into sharper relief the Dinka culture's complex relationship with currency. Dinka world view and the centrality of cattle in the historical and cultural memory are in growing conflict with the emerging peacetime economy. Throughout Nilotic South Sudan, the post-war infusion of cash led to grossly inflated cattle prices, an upsurge in the taking of multiple wives and the use of governmental budgets for the building of large cattle herds.

I approach the subject from two vantage points. I first look at the performance implied by the use of uniforms. In the second part, I will show how these uniforms are reflective of the influence of militarization now present throughout South Sudan.

Over the course of the long and bitter war fought by the SPLA, the town of Rumbek was an important site for the symbolic notion of the New Sudan. The New Sudan, as envisaged by the SPLA leader, Colonel John Garang de Mabior, was not intent on separating the south from the north. Rather, the SPLA was challenging the centralized rule of Khartoum and, purportedly, offering a new deal for the marginalized peoples in all of Sudan, not only the south. Whether or not the rank and file supported this vision is for another discussion. As part of their attempts to engage with other disenfranchised groups within the borders of Sudan, the SPLA opened fronts in eastern Sudan, and was involved in the nascent armed uprising in Darfur, today the centre of the country's most grievous site of insecurity, displacement and death.

Rumbek, part of what was formerly known as Bahr el Ghazal region, was captured from government troops in 1997. It became the headquarters of the SPLA and the effective capital of guerrilla-held southern Sudan. Today, the town of

Rumbek is in the first stages of a multimillion-dollar reconstruction, or more correctly, construction. Other than a well-maintained airstrip, the town is little more than a large village. There are only a handful of roads, a crumbling market area and a colonial-era secondary school and hospital. The main form of transport is Chinese-made bicycle or by foot. People live in hastily erected *tukuls.* There is no running water or electricity, other than that provided by diesel-powered generators. More than 20,000 people live here.

Rumbek is an important site, both as the geographical centre of South Sudan and symbolically as the SPLA's historic seat of power. While Juba is the recognized capital of South Sudan, there are still those in the SPLA who would prefer that Rumbek be made the centre of government. This is due, in part, to the make-up of the SPLA. Until John Garang's death in July 2005, a particular section or kinship lineage of the south's largest single ethnic group, the Dinka, was advantaged within the SPLA. Garang was himself a Bor Dinka from the Upper Nile region.

Upon Garang's death and the appointment of President Salva Kiir, this advantage shifted to the Agar and Twic Dinka of Bahr el Ghazal region. I would note at this juncture that the entire notion of Dinka as a cultural group is convenient only in the most generalized way, the Dinka self-identifying according to section, clan and subclan, depending on the context. Within the senior ranks of the SPLA, however, these distinctions about section and clan are increasingly important given that the movement is highly regional in its command structure.

Social drama

Over the course of one week in November 2006, a series of events took place which was to have far-reaching consequences. The week marked an unusual opportunity to see the forces at work within the community I was to live in for the better part of a year. Social drama is a concept devised by the social theorist Victor Turner to study the dialectic of social transformation and continuity. It acknowledges the social process that occurs following a rupture in social relations. It is a time of crisis or transgression, a time when a society's relationships become more readily visible. In the example I am speaking of now, the social rupture was set off by the death of a motorcycle rider. As per Turner, the second act in this social drama – following the rupture of breach, was a crisis. And this is what happened.

On November 2006, a motorcycle was in an accident with a heavy truck on the road south of Rumbek. The dead man was an Agar Dinka, from the Amunum clan, which originates in the Rumbek area, while the driver of the truck was a Somali. Truck drivers have perhaps the most dangerous occupation in South Sudan. The few roads that exist are used by everyone from the massive Mad-Max style trucks that deliver food aid, to bicycle riders and men on foot moving large herds of cattle. Particularly, drivers who are South Sudanese usually have no training and accidents are common.

The driver of a vehicle involved in an accident, whether striking a pedestrian or another vehicle, must flee for his life or fall victim to revenge attacks. The previous year, a Ugandan driving a World Food Programme (WFP) truck struck and killed a pedestrian as he drove through Wau. The pedestrian was an SPLA officer who was crossing the road. The driver was taken out of the police station by vigilantes and shot fifteen times.

I would add here that the notion of revenge is not reserved only for those in vehicular accidents. Cattle rustling and killings between Dinka clans to the east of Rumbek have seen a spiralling toll as each side attempts to avenge a killing. Members of particular Dinka clans, though they may have had no personal involvement in a killing, are targeted by a victim's clan. The more prominent an individual, the more likely he will be targeted. It is for this reason that a Dinka physician working at the Rumbek hospital, one of only two, had his own bodyguard. His clan had been involved in the killing of an elderly chief. As an educated man, he is considered an equivalent target for revenge.

In the November accident, the driver was able to take refuge at the Rumbek police station. Within a short period of time, however, relatives of the dead man arrived at the police station and demanded that the driver be turned over to them. When the police refused to turn the Somali driver over, the bereaved relatives left but quickly returned with weapons. Shots were fired and a melee broke out which quickly spread into the town's market and public square. Several people were seriously injured and at least one man killed.

The injured people and the man killed by the blows of a *panga* were entirely unconnected to the accident but were considered outsiders, being non-Dinka from the neighbouring region of Equatoria. A curfew was imposed and the market closed. For the next several weeks, the SPLA carried out widespread arrests and beatings. Gatherings were forbidden and even elderly men who customarily gather in the shade of trees were whipped. Even the trees themselves did not escape unscathed: a particularly popular tree, known as the BBC tree, was set upon with axes and its branches felled to prevent people from sitting there.

From one day to the next, the relative calm of the town of Rumbek was shattered. And overnight, men and women who appeared to be civilians were revealed as being something else. The middle-aged woman who each afternoon took tea on a bench beside Liberation Square was in fact a commander in the SPLA, armed with a satellite phone and with vehicles at her disposal. The congenial man who laboured as a laundryman was a Red Army veteran of some standing. The tall and thin guard who had been described as a retired policeman was really an SPLA officer whose humble mud-walled enclosure was used to store his army uniform and AK-47. Hundreds of male students at the local secondary school were not, after all, demobilized soldiers but in fact were only on leave from the SPLA.

The donning of uniforms, the wearing of laminated pins showing the SPLA's flag and an individual's rank, became part of the display of authority within the fractious town of Rumbek. Even elderly men, long past active military service, wore green canvas hats bearing a Sudan People's Liberation Movement (SPLM) patch. The uniforms, or portions of them, indicated social relationships. It was also a way to communicate the motives of those wearing them.

At the same time, people who were recognizably not originally from Rumbek, or from the Dinka, either left town or hid inside their homes. Such is the identification of the ruling SPLM and SPLA with the predominant Dinka population in Bahr el Ghazal that those from non-Dinka groups appeared to not even engage with the wearing of clothing or accessories which would mark them as supporters. Equatorians from the region to the south closed their shops in the market. Kenyans avoided the roads and stayed within their compounds.

For the better part of the next three months, Rumbek was under the control of a contingent of SPLA led by a veteran of two civil wars. He has no formal education and is illiterate. With him at all times is a fellow SPLA officer, a middle-aged man who holds a degree in economics from the University of Khartoum. He acts as the brigadier general's translator, scribe and interpreter. Such was the commander's reputation and longevity that he operated independent of all centralized authority. He has twenty wives, several of whom are related to fellow commanders. Throughout the course of the civil war, senior members of the SPLA strengthened their positions within the SPLA itself by making strategic marriages. Military alliances were effectively ratified by marrying into the families of fellow commanders. He is related to both the president of South Sudan, Salva Kiir, and another former SPLA commander who is the governor of Lakes State.

His soldiers move throughout the region in pick-up trucks. A tattered red flag flies from the front bumper, and a heavy-machine gun is mounted in the rear box. No more than a dozen soldiers ride in the back of each truck, usually bearing not only AK-47s but also long switches and even whips which are used to beat people on the road. (I will return to Bol Akot later in this chapter.) During the weeks of arrests and beatings, the UNMIS peacekeepers withdrew from active patrols, contending that this was a purely local event. The common opinion was that the harsh crackdown on civilians by the military was an appropriate response.

Among my informants, men now approaching forty, many speak with affection about their first uniform – the adult-sized khakis that they donned as part of the Red Army. Of course, the uniforms were too large. In the SPLA's training camps inside Ethiopia young men who showed talent with a sewing needle were put to work customizing the uniforms so they would fit the twelve-year-olds destined to wear them. Two decades on, a future youth army may not have the same problem.

The most sought after gift for small boys at Christmas is the miniature uniform. In a sad irony, the uniforms worn by Dinka boys as they attended church services and paraded through the town were manufactured in the same country that is now northern Sudan's most important backer – China. The traders who brought them into the markets of South Sudan were Arab northerners, the south's enemy throughout the recently ended civil war. Throughout the Christmas season, such were the numbers of children in uniform that it was not uncommon to see three-star generals dissolving in tears as day-long reveries took their toll. Nor have young women been immune from the militarized fashions. The long skirts favoured by young Dinka women could be found in several different camouflage patterns.

Over the course of Britain's involvement in Sudan, the colonial administration was largely staffed by army officers. Shepperson (1960), writing on the military history of British Central Africa, described 'the narrowness of the line between the civilian and the military'. European culture was brought to the people of British Central Africa through its forces as much as its religious missions.

Terence Ranger, in his seminal article 'The Invention of Tradition in Colonial Africa', writes:

> The military neo-tradition, with its clearly visible demarcations of hierarchy and its obvious centrality to the workings of early colonialism, was the first powerful influence. Its impact reached a climax – particularly in eastern Africa – with the campaigns of the first world war.
>
> (2003, 227)

In the decades that followed, new military influences came into play. In the case of Sudan, the United States dominated imported notions of militarism until the late 1980s; in the Horn of Africa, during the same period, it was the Soviet Union and, to a less degree, Cuba and China. In the highlands of Eritrea, sandal-shod commanders of the Eritrean People's Liberation Front were prone to quoting from *The Art of War* by Sun Tzu, considered the world's oldest military treatise. In the mid-1980s joint military exercises between the US army and the Sudanese were occasions for displays of not only physical but technical prowess. Choreographed stunts were performed by the Americans. The aim was to awe their Sudanese counterparts. One exercise involved the night-time landing of heavy aircraft. The rear doors of the landing planes would open before the planes had coasted to a stop. Uniformed soldiers, their faces smeared with camouflage, would tumble acrobatically out of still-moving the planes, guns drawn, amid beams of coloured light and flashing strobes.

Where once the accents adopted by foreign-trained Sudanese soldiers would have been English, they were now American. South Africa has now begun to emerge as a source of military training for soldiers of the Sudan People's Liberation Army.

If for a moment we ignore the training of northern and South Sudanese armies by other nations, there are additional elements that are influencing the apparent acceptance of militarization as a social norm within South Sudan. In the late 1970s, Western oil companies began exploring in predominantly central and southern Sudan. Corporate practice, whether the company was French, American or Canadian, was to employ former military. In the early 1980s, the US Embassy's military attaché in Khartoum, a veteran of the Vietnam war and a career military man, took early retirement and moved several blocks across the Sudanese capital, where he re-entered civilian live as the head of security at Chevron Oil. The camp manager at Bentiu, the now famous site of Chevron's first major discovery in southern Sudan, was a retired British soldier.

In the immediate post-war years, the United Nations and even relatively small European-based NGOs appeared to favour hiring staff who had a military background. The UN Mission in Sudan was mandated by the UN Security Council to monitor and support the implementation of the Comprehensive Peace Agreement. UNMIS includes up to 10,000 peacekeepers and additional civilian staff. The result was a climate in which foreign observers hardly noticed that civilian South Sudanese salute their political leaders (the majority of them having been com-manders in the SPLA) nor seem to question why a Minister of Health would need to wear a sidearm in his office.

Ranger writes of the

> processes of neotraditional socialization. . . . European invented traditions offered Africans a series of clearly defined points of entry into the colonial world, though in almost all cases it was entry into the subordinate part of a man/master relationship. They began by socializing Africans into accep-tance of one or other readily available European neo-traditional modes of conduct – the historical literature is full of Africans proud of having mas-tered the business of being a member of a regiment.
>
> (2003, 227)

It could be added that Westerners now working in relief or UN positions in South Sudan are increasingly socialized in the same way. They follow strict security guidelines that prevent social or unmediated contact between themselves and South Sudanese. They sleep behind compound walls with perimeter fencing, in some cases, electrified and manned by security officers. Peacekeepers were discouraged from moving on foot through the town of Rumbek, as a security precaution. Oddly, there was no apparent concern about the same men taking evening runs in their shorts and T-shirts past the grass huts and tethered cattle of the rural Dinka.

Social drama II

But to return to our social drama in Rumbek in November 2006. Four days after the road death of the local Dinka man and the military crackdown on the town of Rumbek, another event occurred which brought the issue of authority and the symbols of that authority into even sharper relief. This transgression or crisis involved the uniformed peacekeepers and military observers based in Rumbek as part of the UN Mission in Sudan.

On November 10, as the people of Rumbek settled in for the night, the curfew already several hours old, a radio message was received at the UNMIS headquar-ters on the edge of the airstrip. A UN helicopter flying from the Congo was making an unscheduled landing for refuelling. As there is no control tower at the airstrip, let alone lights, UNMIS scrambled to receive the helicopter. Then came news that there were in fact two helicopters. While UN military observers moved Land Rov-ers into position to mark the landing strip with their headlights, the first of the two helicopters began to circle the town.

When the two Russian pilots stepped out of their craft some minutes later, they were greeted not only by UN personnel but the mobile SPLA force led by Briga-dier Bol Akot. Guns were drawn and the men were arrested on the spot. Of the two European UN military observers who had gone to meet the Russians, only one was wearing a uniform. Because of this, the senior UN observers decided that only the uniformed observer should accompany the SPLA and the Russians to the Rumbek prison. His concern was that without his UN uniform, the observer, a German national, might be more vulnerable to mistreatment. His fears were justified. An Ethiopian national, who did not wear a UN uniform, was also arrested and severely beaten.

Inside the prison itself, more than 100 SPLA soldiers had gathered to see the arrival of the arrested men. While the SPLA commander ordered his prisoners to kneel, the senior UN military observer, in a bid for self-preservation, saluted the commander. It was only then that he was released from the interrogation. The Russian pilots, wearing street clothes and flip flops, were not so fortunate. Both were taken to the cells and beaten throughout the night. They were released the next day and immediately flown out of the country.

Conclusion

In this chapter, I have attempted to describe the prevailing identification with all things military in a strategic area of South Sudan. Why would people wish to wear a uniform? I haven't mentioned that state salaries have in most instances not been paid. The most regular, and even this has been poorly managed, has been for members of the SPLA. But aside from salaries, the wearing of a uniform in South Sudan expresses power. And with power, an individual can acquire property, food, transport. It is relatively unchallenged.

When you drive past the primary school at the village of Akot, if you look closely, you will see the evidence of its occupation by the SPLA. Army boots hang from the lower boughs of trees. Foam mattresses spill from the windows. In the playing field you will see a circular enclosure of thorn branches. This is where the young men and even boys are held before and after their beatings.

Akot is where the SPLA holds its prisoners. It is eighteen kilometres to the east of Rumbek. As of early this year, UN human rights observers had failed to receive permission to visit the site. The Somali truck driver is believed to have been taken here, along with those injured in the rioting that followed the failed attempts to remove him from the police station to carry out revenge.

The man in charge of the Akot garrison and the makeshift political prison within the primary school is, of course, Brigadier General Bol Akot. I mentioned earlier that Akot, as with many of the commanders, has many wives. Some of these marriages were contracted to create kinship alliances that would strengthen already existing military relationships.

There is a worrying new development in the combination of militarism and kinship alliances. In a recent case, a soldier was arrested and held at the Akot prison. He was alleged to have killed another soldier. The case was never brought to court, nor were the police involved. The matter remained within SPLA hands. The decision was made that he should be executed. Perhaps with an eye to the future, the order was given that the soldiers who should carry out the execution should come from the same clan as the condemned man. You might ask, what importance does that have? The importance is that it threatens the social cohesiveness of that particular clan. The commander who ordered these particular individuals to carry out the killing is seeking to prevent a revenge killing for the taking of the man's life. In this way, the power of the uniform attempts to subvert pre-existing notions of justice.

I mentioned earlier that the UN and other international agencies, by their ignorance of prevailing hierarchies, are reinforcing the hold of particular strongmen. The brigadier general I have spoken of, the man who heads up a mobile force that operates with impunity and is answerable to no office of the SPLA, was last fall named to a new position: Head of Disarmament for Lakes State. This is the man who the UN Mission in Sudan liaises with on all matters to do with disarmament, demobilization and reintegration.

In the days before John Garang's death in a helicopter accident, the SPLA commander ordered his senior military men to surrender their commands and take up political positions. All but one of the men refused. It was after the heated meeting with his officers in Rumbek that Garang, apparently in frustration and anger, decided to take the fateful journey to see his old friend Yoweri Museveni in Uganda. To this day, his original commanders, those who survived the war, have largely retained their military positions. Some have been given political appointments but all continue to be seen as officers of the SPLA. Informants attest that demobilization will continue to be resisted. In addition to the loss of status, the removal from positions where they control transport, trade and revenues, there is the question of the uniform. Over the course of the war, the SPLA was riven with internecine strife. There were massacres of civilians and high death tolls among the youth recruits. As I was told, as soon as the uniform is removed, these men will once again be subject to cultural values surrounding revenge.

As a closing note, the SPLA now finds itself in the position of needing to re-appropriate the invented tradition of uniforms. Over the Christmas holidays, the brigadier of whom of spoken of throughout this chapter, introduced a morality code. In addition to a ban on women riding bicycles, the wearing of camouflage caps and all other garments that mimicked uniforms were banned.

References

Ranger, Terence, 'The Invention of Tradition in Colonial Africa', in Eric Hobsbawm and Terence Ranger (eds.), *The Invention of Tradition* (Cambridge, UK: Cambridge University Press, 2003), pp. 211–28.

Shepperson, G. (1960), "The Military History of British Central Africa: A Review Article," *Rhodes-Livingston Journal*, No. 26: 23–33.

8 Crying out for action

Do the dead say anything about the responsibility to protect?

John K. Roth

> Some truths are glimpsed only in the dark.
>
> Robert Pogue Harrison, *The Dominion of the Dead*, p. 159

The sixth chapter of *The Responsibility to Protect*, the 2001 report of the International Commission on Intervention and State Sovereignty (ICISS), refers to 'conscience-shocking situations crying out for action.'[1] The eighth chapter of the ICISS report comments briefly on moral appeals that might prevent, avert, and halt human suffering, aptly noting that 'getting a moral motive to bite means . . . being able to convey a sense of urgency and reality about the threat to human life in a particular situation' (para. 13).

According to the ICISS report, 'a large scale loss of life' (as defined at 4.19) cries out for humanitarian intervention. In such 'conscience shocking situations,' the outcries can arise from many quarters and in multiple ways, but do the dead themselves – those whose lives have been taken by 'deliberate state action, or state neglect or inability to act, or a failed state situation' or through 'large scale "ethnic cleansing"' (4.19) – contribute to them in ways that the living never can? The ICISS report observes that getting moral motives to bite is harder to do "at the crucial stage of prevention than it is after some actual horror has occurred' (8.13). With reference to one example of 'a large scale loss of life,' the Holocaust, this chapter explores how listening to what the dead have to 'say' might improve the odds that moral motives will bite in the ways we need for them to do.

Lest my intentions be misunderstood, two explanations are needed before proceeding further. First, when I speak of 'the dead,' doing so with specific reference to children, women, and men who have been murdered in 'mass atrocity crimes,' to use Gareth Evans's term, which will be explained below, my aim is not to lump individuals together in an anonymous, faceless, and ultimately disrespectful way. To the contrary, as I think of 'the dead,' and as I hope my discussion shows, the purpose and point are to underscore that individual persons have been murdered – often murdered en masse and as members of groups, but as individual persons nonetheless. If 'the dead' can be said to 'speak,' their 'word' comes from individuals who compel respect from us, the living, and also from their 'chorus,' individuals engaged and interacting with one another. In both forms, the voices of the dead reverberate in awesome ways if we allow them to do so. Listening, trying to hear what these voices – individual and collective – might say to us constitutes one of the most respectful actions we can take.

Second, this chapter calls attention to the Holocaust's dead, but the purpose and point are *not* to privilege that genocide over other mass atrocity crimes. My references to the Holocaust and to voices of the dead that may be heard from within that catastrophe have at least three dimensions. First, they call attention to the Holocaust, which can scarcely be avoided when 'mass atrocity crimes' are considered. But, second, the focus on the Holocaust evokes reflection on all mass atrocity crimes, before and after the Nazi genocide – each one in its particularity – and, third, that reflection may amplify respectful listening to the voices of the dead, so vastly and sadly expanded individually and collectively, as they reach a silent but deeply moving crescendo.

As noted above, Gareth Evans speaks about 'mass atrocity crimes.' Specifically, in the first chapter of his 2008 book, *The Responsibility to Protect*, he says that that the goal of 'the responsibility to protect' is to prevent or intervene against 'mass atrocities' or 'mass atrocity crimes,' categories that refer to 'genocide, war crimes, ethnic cleansing, and crimes against humanity.'[2] Evans's opening chapter includes an overview of the staggering extent of these atrocities in the twentieth and twenty-first centuries. Evans's enumeration makes no claim to be complete; in fact, it does not even rise to a bare minimum. Nevertheless, a summation of his numbers indicates that mass atrocities took at least 100 million lives during that period. What the real number should be is beyond calculation, but in their countless muteness the dead confront us nonetheless.

Those unjustly robbed of life by human decisions and human actions are the ones we need especially to see and to heed. But if we settle for calling these dead *victims* we misplace where key aspects of the emphasis needs to be placed. By speaking of victims, we rightly call attention to the victimizers, to the murderers. By speaking only of victims, however, we obscure the faces of the dead and the humanity of the murdered, those who, in George Steiner's words, have been 'done to death.'[3]

'Try to look,' wrote the Auschwitz survivor Charlotte Delbo, 'just try and see.'[4] She wanted people to see the defaced faces of the dead, to discern what those faces say about right and wrong, to take to heart how the humanity of the dead – even, indeed especially, in their silence – resounds the imperative against atrocity and murder.

Some of the interviews conducted in 1946 by the American psychologist David P. Boder are among the earliest with persons who survived the Holocaust. Using the wire recording technology that was state of the art at the time, Boder interviewed 'about seventy people, representing nearly all creeds and nationalities in the DP [displaced persons] installations in the American Zone.' He recorded 120 hours of testimony, which was translated, he said, 'to keep the material as near to the text of the original narratives as the most elementary rules of grammar would permit.'[5] Eight of these interviews were published by the University of Illinois Press in 1949. The last one contains the testimony given in Munich by a man named Jack Matzner on September 26, 1946.

Born in Wiesbaden, Germany, Matzner, 42 when the interview took place, was a Jew of Polish descent. Deported from Germany to Poland in 1938, he illegally returned to Germany for a time, and then he and his family were reunited in Antwerp, Belgium. On May 14, 1940, soon after the Germans occupied Belgium, Matzner went to France. Eventually arrested, he was deported to the East. The account he gave to Boder after surviving 'fifty-five months of concentration camps' included two episodes that were deeply embedded in his memory.[6]

First, Matzner recalled a work assignment in the Polish winter of 1941–1942. Assigned to dig holes for telegraph poles, several of the men froze to death. Matzner had to carry some of them from the work site back to Lager Fürstengrube, near Katowice. 'I shall never forget,' he told Boder,

> the impression that is made by the face of a man frozen to death. I got the impression that these people were laughing. You notice on the faces a kind of transition, as if at the beginning of the agony the people distort their faces, and for the onlooker it creates the impression that they are laughing. These dead men, dead from freezing – and this expression remains on their faces as if they were laughing.[7]

Second, in 1945, Matzner was inside Germany as a slave laborer for the Heinkel Aviation Industries. On one occasion, he was beaten and then imprisoned in a flooded cellar with 'about ninety or ninety-five people,' many of whom were already in water that was 'chest high.' Matzner's account to Boder continued as follows:

> Those who were lying there were already dead. And those who were standing had arranged the bodies of the dead in such a manner that they could stand or sit on them. Otherwise the ones who were still living would also have drowned. I did the same thing. I found myself a place at the wall. I dragged two bodies which were under the water and arranged them against the wall, and I sat on them. And so I remained in the water, counting from that morning, exactly two days and two nights.[8]

Boder interviewed Matzner, but perhaps with those frozen and drowned Jews from Matzner's account in mind – to say nothing of the millions who had been starved and beaten to death, shot, or gassed – he ended the introduction to his book with these words: 'The verbatim records presented in this book make uneasy reading. And yet,' he added, 'they are not the grimmest stories that could be told – I did not interview the dead.'[9] That last thought-provoking phrase – I did not interview the dead – became his book's title.

The frozen corpses that Matzner carried back to the *lager* did not laugh. The corpses on which he sat may have saved him from drowning, but they said nothing about their fate or his. Boder could not interview the dead because the dead do not speak. Nor, it might be added, should one even imagine interrogating the dead, for to do so would create a temptation that ought to be resisted. It is not the prerogative of the living to speak for the dead. With the Holocaust's murdered Jews foremost on his mind, the Auschwitz survivor underscored this point emphatically in his Nobel Peace Prize acceptance speech in Oslo, Norway, on December 10, 1986. 'No one may speak for the dead,' said Wiesel, 'no one may interpret their mutilated dreams and visions.'[10]

The living have no right to put words into mouths that death has silenced. The Holocaust, at least sensitive reflection upon it and other mass atrocities, seems to enjoin warnings and imperatives of that kind. Failure to heed them runs too many risks. To use Lawrence Langer's phrase, those risks include preempting the Holocaust by thinking that there is some meaning to find that transcends the mute abjection of corpses such as those that move grotesquely in the early postwar film footage from 'liberated' concentration camps, which shows lifeless, rotting bodies being bulldozed into mass graves, hundreds at a time.

Cautionary principles of the kind mentioned above are well worth remembering. Nevertheless, it may be no less important to think twice about them, for there are countervailing currents that deserve attention if ethical reflection about the Holocaust and other mass atrocities is to be at its best. Consider, then, at least two significant issues that warrant attention. First, to what extent is it true that the dead, including people murdered in the Holocaust and other mass atrocities, do not and cannot speak? Second, to what extent is it sound to say that no one should or even can speak for the dead, including those drowned or frozen, starved or hacked to death, shot or gassed during mass murder and genocide?

My response to the first of those questions – to what extent is it true that the dead, including people murdered in mass atrocities, do not and cannot speak? – is informed by a study that scarcely alludes to such catastrophes and yet has insights that are pertinent for reflection on them. I refer to Robert Pogue Harrison's 2003 book *The Dominion of the Dead*.

The point of departure for Harrison's eloquent and interdisciplinary study involves deep reflection on a fundamental and distinctive fact about human life: namely, that in one way or another we human beings bury our dead. This action takes place because human beings have memories; it also takes place for memory's sake. Absent memories, the dead would not even be forgotten, they would just be left to decay and disappear. Present memories, however, mean that we do not forget the dead, at least not entirely. In some ways, the dead even have dominion over us and rightly so, for we consciously dispose of their remains in ways that keep them – the dead and usually their remains – with us. That presence of an absence can affect people and policies profoundly.

Already, of course, the Holocaust and other mass atrocities may make one quarrel with Harrison's account. The German burning of Jewish bodies was the antithesis of an act of remembrance; it was intended to be part of the process that would obliterate Jewish life – and memory of it – root and branch. The remains of the Jewish dead were to be scattered in smoke and ash so as never to be retrieved. Even the vast number of mass graves from killing squadron actions in the East had to be exhumed and their remains burned, not only to cover the killers' tracks but also to ensure that erasure of Jewish presence was complete.

Nevertheless, not even the Nazi mind could free itself entirely from remembering the Jewish dead.

Trauma related to the murder of Jews and to the grisly work of corpse disposal often left its marks on the perpetrators, silent though they usually chose to be about it. Arguably even more important, if the Jewish dead were forgotten, the Nazis' frantic efforts to destroy Jewish bodies without a trace would have lacked the 'sense' that it made in the Third Reich's genocidal ideology. Nazism's many contradictions included a key fact: Its anti-Semitism entailed that Nazism had to remain preoccupied with the Jewish dead or its identity would have been lost. It can even be said that the Jewish dead, owing to the Nazis' obsession to make the world *judenrein*, had a kind of dominion over Nazi life. Dead Jews haunted the Nazi 'mindscape' as they do the psychological and geographical terrain of postwar Germany to this day. The same could be said about other scenes of mass atrocity, including African ones – Darfur, Congo, Zimbabwe – in the early twenty-first century.

As for those who resisted the Third Reich and the Holocaust – take Matzner and Boder as examples – remembering those who were utterly bereft of the rites of burial is central to what it means to speak of the Holocaust and other mass atrocities as massive and even unprecedented catastrophes.[11] Thus, even taking into account the overwhelming disrespect for the dead, to say nothing of the living, that characterized the Holocaust, the integrity of Harrison's governing claims still stands: The Holocaust's dead, and those of other mass atrocities, definitely remain with us, and to some extent that presence can and, I would say, should exercise a kind of dominion.

To be human, Harrison argues, 'is a way of being mortal and relating to the dead. To be human means above all to bury.'[12] Those propositions, which have their applicability in the Holocaust and the mass atrocities that preceded and succeeded it, make Harrison especially interested in how 'we follow in the footsteps of the dead' and what it can mean to speak about what he calls in the 'indwelling of the dead in the worlds of the living.'[13] Much of that 'indwelling' pertains to ways, literal and figurative, in which the dead can be said to speak. During his Nobel Peace Prize acceptance speech, Elie Wiesel may have had something akin to this insight in mind, for in addition to contending that no one may speak for the dead, he underscored how much he sensed their presence.

The dead do speak, including, and in some ways especially, the Holocaust-related dead. For instance, the voices of perpetrators such as Adolf Hitler and Joseph Goebbels can still be 'heard' in multiple ways through their writings or even through recordings of their voices. Much could be said about what the Nazi dead may have to say, but in this reflection I am concentrating on the Jews who were annihilated by Hitler and his followers. In their writings and in some cases through recordings of their voices, Anne Frank, Primo Levi, and non-Jews such as Charlotte Delbo can still be 'heard' in multiple ways as they testify about what happened during the event that is now called the Holocaust. Today, their voices are among those of the dead. Increasingly, the thousands of survivor testimonies from the Holocaust and other mass atrocities that have been collected in recent years also include the voices of the dead. Eventually, all of those testimonies will have to be heard in that way. For instance, the time is rapidly approaching when the term 'survivor of the Holocaust' will apply only to the dead. Meanwhile, among the living there are people who can still hear quite directly the voices of family members, friends, or acquaintances who experienced the Holocaust and other mass atrocities, some of them surviving and others not. While even the survivors may no longer be alive, their presence can be very real. Their remembered voices, their speaking, can be immensely moving and powerful.

Harrison does not miss the mark when he contends that 'the dead are not content to reside in our genes alone, for genes are not *worlds*, and the dead seek above all to share our worlds.'[14] Here it might be objected that Harrison enlivens the dead, that he gives them an existence that they do not and cannot have. But this objection does not hold, because human existence cannot be what it is apart from our dying, from our awareness that our lives, at least on this earth, do not last forever, and that our being here unavoidably, if not from desire, leaves its mark behind, faint and trace-like though that mark may be. What we leave behind when we die and after we are dead reveals – a corpse alone can do so – that the dead do seek to share the worlds of the living. To a considerable extent, moreover, that sharing works. No human identity is possible without the dead; they inform us profoundly. 'As human beings,' Harrison writes, 'we are born of the dead.'[15] In that sense, the dead have an afterlife. Although it does not depend on immortality or resurrection, the afterlife of the dead is nonetheless one that can and does speak.

There are voices, it has been said, that can be heard only in silence.[16] But can that really be the case if the Holocaust and other mass atrocities are the benchmark? Are that claim and Harrison's analysis credible when one considers, for example, the silence surrounding the corpses that Matzner lugged or sat upon, the remains bulldozed into pits at Bergen-Belsen, the thousands of Jewish bodies converted into ash and smoke as the *Sonderkommando* units did their gruesome work, day after day, at the Nazis' behest in Birkenau's gas chambers and crematoria? Contrary to the direction in which such questions seem to go, points made by Harrison, and about voices that can heard only in silence, are arguably even more deeply applicable, at least in some of their dimensions, in these cases that may involve persons who are nameless strangers to persons such as me or you.

Absent their presence and the silence surrounding it, there is no Holocaust, no Rwandan genocide, no genocidal crisis in Darfur, no sense of unfathomable and irremediable loss, no horror, no despair of the kind that honest encounter with those human-made disasters makes inescapable. Both in their individual particularity and in their collective enormity, the Holocaust's dead speak in the sense that their reality, their presence in the midst of silence, is what grounds our awareness of what the Holocaust was and is. It goes without saying that there is no 'justification' of the Holocaust or any other mass atrocity in this insight. The Holocaust's dead signify unredeemable disaster. What, in particular, the Holocaust's dead communicate, if anything, beyond that recognition is another matter, one to be taken up more fully in what follows. But that the Holocaust's dead, anonymous to us or intimately known, inform and communicate with the living can scarcely be denied without denying the Holocaust itself.

If the Holocaust's dead can and do speak in and through their silence, what do they say? To what extent, moreover, is even the raising of that question a temptation to speak for the dead – including those drowned or frozen to death, starved or beaten to death, shot or gassed during Holocaust – a temptation that ought to be resisted? Already it has been noted that there are writings and recordings to which one can turn to obtain some responses to these questions. The thoughts and voices of the once-living-but-now-dead live on, often with great authority. But Harrison's *Dominion of the Dead* proposes something intriguingly and profoundly paradoxical that goes beyond remains of that kind. The book does so because Harrison is suggesting, I believe, that the dead-in-their-muteness still speak.

Harrison contends that 'some truths are glimpsed only in the dark.' To discern them as fully as possible means turning to 'those who can see through the gloom.' These are the dead, he suggests, including the dead-in-their-muteness, who 'possess a nocturnal vision' that involves such seeing.[17] Again, objections come to the fore, especially when the dead from mass atrocities such as the Holocaust are at attention's center. Their eyes do not see; every flicker of life is long gone from them. Far from seeing through the gloom, the dead of the Holocaust constitute that darkness of oblivion. Apart from legal fictions, it is even problematic to say that the dead possess anything, least of all vision. Harrison's view, it seems, is not insightful because it is not true.

As with other aspects of Harrison's account, a second glance is important here too. In a sense of *owning* that is distinctively theirs, the dead, including the dead-in-their-muteness do *possess* something of the utmost significance. They do so because they *embody* a facticity that is *nocturnal*, if by such words one alludes to the darkness that death itself signifies. Without sharing the nocturnal vision that only the dead can give us, and in that sense they possess it, the living are blind – at least we are to what befalls us and may await us with regard to death's particularities, which are always real and often hideously so, as the Holocaust's dead and their brothers and sisters who are the victims of other mass atrocities make us see like no others.

Even granting Harrison this much, however, is it still not misleading, mystifying, to suggest, as he does, that the dead are 'those who can see through the gloom' and that 'in moments of extreme need' one ought to turn to them because 'some truths are glimpsed only in the dark'? Such analysis might be credible if one thinks of those writings and recordings that the once living have left behind. With the Holocaust in mind, turning to Primo Levi or Charlotte Delbo could make sense of Harrison's claims. I take him, however, to be holding a more radical position, one that points to something more fundamental about the reality, the afterlife, of the dead as dead.

The dead, including the dead of the Holocaust, we may say, are simply dead. But to say even that is far from being as simple as it may seem. A person's death is not his or hers exclusively or alone. It belongs to others as well, which becomes evident in the fact that there is a corpse to dispose of, or at least awareness that every human death involves a body, even if no one disposes of it. When one dies, and the Holocaust's dead are no exception to this fact, a person unavoidably gives his or her death to others, who do with it what they will. In Harrison's view, this means that the dead can

> speak from beyond the grave as long as we lend them the means of locution; they take up their abode in books, dreams, houses, portraits, legends, monuments, and graves as long as we keep open the places of their indwelling.[18]

To follow where Harrison's thought may lead, consider one of the minimalist dialogues that Elie Wiesel writes from time to time, specifically an imagined exchange between 'A Father and His Son.'[19] In the dialogue, the voices are nameless, but the reader hears individual voices nonetheless, including the possibility that the dialogue is a sharing of deep engagement between Wiesel and his father, Shlomo, as the son listens for the voice of his father and responds to it. In this dialogue, Wiesel does two things, which his collection of Holocaust-related dialogues does repeatedly. First, in Harrison's words, he lends the dead the means of locution; he keeps open the places of their indwelling. Wiesel allows them to speak, and in the dialogue between 'A Father and His Son,' the father, who is one of the Holocaust's dead, asks his living son, who is a Holocaust survivor, 'Who will speak for me?' Wiesel's dialogue answers. In doing so the second thing emerges. It consists of a two-fold putting of words in the mouth of the dead – first, by having the dead speak in the dialogue and then by emphasizing that the son is trying to speak for the dead father, trying to say what the dead one would say if he could but cannot. 'Who will speak for me?' says the dead father in Wiesel's Holocaust dialogue. 'We try,' comes the son's response. 'You must believe me. We try.' Such trying, the dialogue goes on to suggest, can make one weary, a testimony revealing that honest, credible speaking of and for the dead must concentrate both on the darkness that only the dead can make one see and on the reluctance to see that darkness insightfully, which blinds the living.

Do Wiesel's dialogue and his Nobel injunction against speaking for the dead contradict each other? Here it may be well to note that Wiesel has said that 'and yet . . . and yet' are among the most important words in his vocabulary.[20] In the dialectic of 'and yet . . . and yet,' the injunction should not be ignored; it must always be kept in play. Nevertheless, fidelity to the dead, bearing witness for them and for the living as well, may sometimes require breaking the injunction by speaking for the dead while always remembering that no one could fully recall or interpret for them what Wiesel rightly calls their mutilated dreams and visions. Meanwhile, the dead, even in their muteness, can speak through us. Indeed, if we do not allow them to speak through us, we betray one of the most penetrating ways in which the dead of the Holocaust deeply wanted to indwell our worlds. Again and again, the dying asked, as the father does in Wiesel's dialogue, to be remembered, to be spoken for – not just spoken *of* – as those whose lives were laid waste by atrocity.

Does being faithful to that last will and testament of theirs require putting words in their mouths so that they can speak? That is a good question, a right one, which should make us think long and hard. Yes, it does involve putting words into their mouths, but perhaps those words, if carefully considered and thoughtfully uttered, can be at least versions of what the dead would say if they could but cannot. If we keep open the Holocaust places – and all other atrocity-places – of their indwelling, the dead of Auschwitz and Treblinka, the frozen and drowned bodies that Jack Matzner saw, have much to say to us. To some extent, that saying may involve our imagination as well as our eloquence, but that saying also depends on the stark facticity of their deaths and what brought them about.

In our seeing them, in our discerning of what their presence-as-absence in our lives may mean, the sight of the dead may penetrate through the gloom of death and help us to see, in the dark, truths that are always ignored at our peril, not least because such ignorance tends to expand the abysmal count of those whose lives have been wasted by violence, brutality, genocide, and all the other practices of mass atrocity. It should go without saying that there is nothing triumphal or neces-sarily redemptive in these angles of vision. The sight/site of the dead, including the dead of the Holocaust and other mass atrocities, withholds, in Harrison's words, 'a presence at the same time as it renders present an absence. The disquieting character of its presence-at-hand comes precisely from the presence of a void where there once was a person.'[21] Yet, the truths that can be glimpsed and most profoundly heard only in the dark of that presence of a void may have much to teach.

To note but one possibility of that kind, Harrison stresses that a debt, an 'essen-tially insoluble' one, is owed to the dead.[22] This claim makes sense because no one is 'self-authored,' and we all 'follow in the footsteps of the dead.'[23] If that insight encompasses the Holocaust's dead, especially its victims, what is the debt that perhaps can be glimpsed fully only in the dark of the presence of a void? How could one start to respond to that debt and its obligations, keeping in mind that it is impossible to pay and meet them completely because the dead are dead?

Here, I believe, a combination of cautious restraint and bold statement must remain in respectful tension with one another. Restraint is needed because the bold responses that are right and good are also likely to sound like clichés if they are articulated. Silence followed by action that resists death's waste may be the wisest course. But silence, even when accompanied by action that resists death's waste, may be insufficient and irresponsible.

Perhaps one way to begin stating the truths that are glimpsed only in the dark, at least where the Holocaust and other mass atrocity crimes are concerned, is not-so-simply to say: Yes, we all are dying and will soon be dead, but no one's death should come *that way*. What *that way* was and means is partly knowable because we have testimony, memoirs, trial records, historical research that document the slaughter and horror. What *that way* was and means is also unutterable, for one cannot interview the dead. But because the latter realization persists, revealing as it does that, in David Boder's words, 'the grimmest stories' are not the ones that are told, responses in word and deed that can 'see through the gloom' may be found. Such seeing would not dispel the gloom of the Holocaust and other mass atrocities. Nothing can do so. But *seeing through* might suggest another combina-tion: namely, a linking of *seeing through* as enduring to the end, however bitter it may be, with a *seeing through* that entails doing as much as one/we can to find the ways that keep the gloom from overwhelming us. If the responsibility to protect is not one of those ways, nothing could be. It emanates from atrocity's dead, and fulfilling that responsibility, even if imperfectly, is arguably our best way to respect and hear them.

The Dominion of the Dead has such atrocity-related perspectives in mind when Harrison drew his book, and I draw my reflection, to a close by observing that the dead can be 'our guardians. We give them a future so that they may give us a past. We help them live on so that they may help us go forward.'[24] Or, as the responsibility to Protect requires, improving the odds that moral motives will bite in needed ways depends significantly on respecting and heeding the 'conscience shocking' calls for action crying out, as they alone can, from 'voices that can be heard only in silence.'

Notes

1 See *The Responsibility to Protect: Report of the International Commission on Intervention and State Sovereignty,* Ottawa: International Development Research Centre, 2001. Citations refer to the report's internal enumeration of sections and paragraphs.

2 Gareth Evans, *The Responsibility to Protect: Ending Mass Atrocity Crimes Once and for All,* Washington, DC: Brookings Institute Press, 2008, p. 11.

3 George Steiner, *Language and Silence: Essays on Language, Literature, and the Inhuman,* New York: Atheneum, 1967, p. 157. I am indebted to Paul C. Santilli for this reference. On the importance of encountering the face of the dead, especially the murdered dead, Santilli's thought influences mine. See especially Paul C. Santilli, 'Philosophy's Obligation to the Human Being in the Aftermath of Genocide,' in *Genocide and Human Rights: A Philosophical Guide*, ed. John K. Roth, New York: Palgrave Macmillan, 2005, pp. 220–32.

4 Charlotte Delbo, *Auschwitz and After*, trans. Rosette C. Lamont, New Haven, CT: Yale University Press, 1995, pp. 84–6.

5 David P. Boder, *I Did Not Interview the Dead,* Urbana, IL: University of Illinois Press, 1949, p. xiii.

6 Boder, *I Did Not Interview the Dead*, 1949, p. 200.

7 Boder, *I Did Not Interview the Dead*, 1949, p. 209.

8 Boder, *I Did Not Interview the Dead*, 1949, p. 217.

9 Boder, *I Did Not Interview the Dead*, 1949, p. xix.

10 See the speech as it is reprinted in Elie Wiesel, *Night*, trans. Marion Wiesel, New York: Hill and Wang, 1960, pp. 117–20, especially p. 118.

11 This point is augmented by contrast with the Nazi pomp and circumstance that could be found at Third Reich funerals such as the one that honored Reinhard Heydrich, one of the key masterminds of the Holocaust, after his death on June 4, 1942, following wounds inflicted by Czech resistance fighters who ambushed him near Prague on May 27 of that year. For helpful details on such matters, see Jay W. Baird, *To Die for Germany: Heroes in the Nazi Pantheon,* Bloomington, IN: Indiana University Press, 1992, especially pp. 213–18.

12 Robert Pogue Harrison, *The Dominion of the Dead,* Chicago: University of Chicago Press, 2003, p. xi.

13 Harrison, *The Dominion of the Dead,* 2003, pp. ix, x.

14 Harrison, *The Dominion of the Dead,* 2003, p. 84.

15 Harrison, *The Dominion of the Dead,* 2003, p. xi.

16 The Jewish philosopher Maimonides may be the source of this idea, but confirmation has eluded me. Meanwhile, I take the claim to mean more than that a listener must be

quiet to hear a voice and what it is saying. I take it to mean that the voices heard and what they are saying are inseparable from silence, are 'only in silence.' The paradox here is as inescapable as the insight it may contain.

17 Harrison, *The Dominion of the Dead*, 2003, pp. 158–59.
18 Harrison, *The Dominion of the Dead*, 2003, p. 153.
19 See Elie Wiesel, *A Jew Today*, trans. Marion Wiesel, New York: Random House, 1978, pp. 139–43, and especially p. 143.
20 See, for example, Wiesel's 1978 interview with John S. Friedman in *Elie Wiesel: Conversations*, ed. Robert Franciosi, Jackson: University Press of Mississippi, 2002, p. 96.
21 Harrison, *The Dominion of the Dead*, 2003, pp. 92–3.
22 Harrison, *The Dominion of the Dead*, 2003, p. 154.
23 Harrison, *The Dominion of the Dead*, 2003, p. ix.
24 Harrison, *The Dominion of the Dead*, 2003, p. 158.

Index

Lightning Source UK Ltd.
Milton Keynes UK
UKHW020803070321
379882UK00004B/1186